CONSCIOUS
MATRIX

CONSCIOUS
MATRIX

OUR PORTAL TO GOD

By Nancy J. Woolf

LIBERTY HILL PUBLISHING

Liberty Hill Publishing
2301 Lucien Way #415
Maitland, FL 32751
407.339.4217
www.libertyhillpublishing.com

© 2020 by Nancy J. Woolf

Paperback ISBN-13: 978-1-6305-0858-6
Hard Cover ISBN-13: 978-1-6305-0859-3
eBook ISBN-13: 978-1-6305-0860-9

TABLE OF CONTENTS

AUTHOR PREFACE

PEOPLE WRITE BOOKS for many reasons. I wrote this book to critically examine my belief in God. Like so many people, I struggle with my beliefs. I'm not one hundred percent certain of anything. But I'm driven, if not inspired, to dig deeper to try to understand. Part of my determination derives from a fundamental belief—a kind of optimism—that things in life are basically fair. And it follows that if I'm basically good, bad things won't happen to me.

But doubt inevitably creeps in. And this is true for many, if not all of us. We may feel doubt because we see bad things sometimes happen to good people. We may feel doubt because occasionally our behavior isn't as good as we'd like and we don't understand what got into us. But does believing in God require life to be perfect? When the questions are put on paper, the answers come more easily. While it's important to strive to be better, what's truly amazing is how the human mind is capable of imagining perfection. It's indeed a gift from God that our hearts and minds are able to resonate in a kind of grand harmony with the universe. Intuitively we sense we're connected, not only to others, but to the entire universe. This truth is born out literally in real-life outcomes, and metaphorically insofar as our best stories reveal the deepest, most subtle meanings of life.

Another source of doubt arises from the ancient battle between the heart and mind. Like most people, I sometimes struggle with the distance that exists between my emotions and intellect. Some people view belief in God as purely sentimental—incompatible with great intellectual achievement and progress. Indeed, many of the world's greatest scientists have denounced God as pure imagination. I believe God is our most evolved creation of imagination, and He's very real. Since nearly everything our mind perceives turns out to be matter, energy or organizing principle—God is as real as anything else we can perceive. Gloriously, the human mind has a special connection to God. It's not just our belief in God that makes Him real. It's the myriad roles God plays in our history and in our daily lives. We're intimately connected to God. He's wired into our thinking, enabling us to see moral principles in stories and in life.

Since our belief in God is our main connection to Him, understanding how the mind accomplishes consciousness is an important step to understanding God. In this book, I give step-by-step explanations, based on my years of inquiry and research, for how the brain accomplishes higher consciousness and how this relates to the existence of God.

My career in neuroscience started by tracing pathways that release a neurotransmitter called acetylcholine. These pathways are important to learning, memory, consciousness, and higher intellectual function. But a neurotransmitter like acetylcholine doesn't explain memory or intellectual function. This revelation led me to investigate a possible connection between acetylcholine and brain cell structure. I began to study the role structural proteins play in learning and memory—the basis of neural plasticity. It was nothing short of astonishing to discover how learning caused tubulins in particular brain cells to break down and reorganize into new neural structures.

By some magical coincidence, these tubulin proteins were designated as the site of consciousness by anesthesiologist Stuart Hameroff and mathematician Sir Roger Penrose. My finding that learning permanently alters the arrangement of tubulins was another piece in the puzzle. If we could combine the physics of consciousness with the biology of neural plasticity, it might explain how memory storage and conscious retrieval of our entire lifetime of experiences was possible.

I first met Stuart Hameroff in 2000 through a mutual friend who was struck by the coincidence. Stuart Hameroff has spent decades of his life orchestrating a diligent search for the scientific explanation of higher consciousness. He's written extensively on the topic, and he's organized illuminating annual conferences inspiring some of the greatest minds today to examine this important problem. After twenty-six years of meetings among the best minds in the world, some clear answers emerge. Quantum mind theory accounts for consciousness far better than traditional models that only consider neurons linking up with other neurons.

The work of Hameroff and Penrose is among the most prominent of quantum mind theories. Roger Penrose proved conscious thought couldn't be modeled by traditional mathematical algorithms. Instead, many features of mental computation are comparable to quantum computation. This is illustrated each time we decide among various options. Initially, we hold the many possible solutions in mind unconsciously. It's not until we make a decision to choose one option that the selected information surfaces to full consciousness. Hameroff and Penrose argue this moment of consciousness is due to the reduction of a complex quantum state to one solution, and it effectively pushes the restart button.

Accordingly, human consciousness arises from quantum entanglements spanning thousands of neurons. Hameroff gathered vast amounts of evidence for this entanglement occurring deep within pockets of the tubulin proteins. Stuart Hameroff and I worked together on a model for visual consciousness. Our model melded neural plasticity and quantum entanglement occurring in a specific brain architecture called the "conscious matrix." The conscious matrix serves to actually understand data input and to experience "raw meaning" in the first person. Ideas generated by the small details of visual input combine again and again until a cohesive unified image emerges.

Not only for vision, but for all thinking and belief, we combine ideas about the small details over and over until the grand explanatory "big picture" emerges. This highest principle we experience is for many people our concept of God. We commonly use language that describes God as a belief in a supreme or highest being. We talk about having faith in something we can't touch or see. But if you're like me, merely thinking of God as an organizing principle in our minds isn't satisfying. We sense we're connected to God and that He is real. That means something. Our perceptual apparatus is a finely-tuned instrument. In this sense, we're all scientists equipped with the most amazing interpretive device of all— the human mind.

The notion of quantum entanglement has enormous explanatory power for human connection. Entanglement means "never having to say goodbye." Any two electrons that are at one time coupled will forever share a relationship. If one electron changes its dipole moment, then the other electron, no matter how distant, will simultaneously flip.

If our minds are actually entangled, on a quantum level, with the mind of God—then suddenly our belief in something we can't see or touch makes sense. We experience God directly because He lives inside us. This perception is widespread among so many different people as to warrant serious scientific exploration. And the science has finally evolved to make this exploration possible.

While talking about entangled electrons is fine in technical science books, it leaves a lot to be desired when talking about general life issues. Fortunately, a recent discovery has made it easier to talk about quantum mind. Jack Tuszynski, a long-time collaborator of mine, along with his colleagues, showed how tubulin proteins could be conduits for transmitting weak electromagnetic energy. A real possibility exists for part of this ultra-weak energy to be light. Neurons are capable of generating bio-photons—faint light arising from living cells due to metabolism. When our brains receive their usual barrages of sensory input, we transduce that input into patterns of neural activity. But it's not the electrical activity that reaches consciousness. Electrical activity triggers cell metabolism and that releases small packets of light. So when people say: "he's enlightened" or "the light switched on in my head," they just might be scientifically accurate.

Throughout the various chapters of this book, I'll relate quantum mind theory to my personal experiences in life, my belief in God, and what God means. Quantum mind theory has the potential to explain the glorious phenomenal experience that all of mankind embarks on each and every day. Whether we're standing in awe at the site of a beautiful landscape, or being spiritually lifted to a higher place, the combination of neural plasticity and quantum mind theory explains how our mind connects with God and derives energy from the universe through the power of God. God is light. God is good. God transcends by connecting us internally, and to others, and to the overarching laws governing order in the universe.

So let me conclude by thanking all my colleagues over the years. My first and longest-lasting colleague was my late husband, Larry Butcher. Without Larry's unwavering support, and the patience and understanding of my two children, I'd have never been able to pursue my keen interest in neuroscience and to undertake research furthering our understanding of how the brain is wired. Secondly, had I never met

Stuart Hameroff I'd have never delved into the complex and deeply profound field of quantum mind theory. Last, but not least, my collaboration with Jack Tuszynski and Travis Craddock enlightened me to the fine scale mechanisms of higher consciousness. Thank you to these people along with many other collaborators over the years. And special thanks to my many friends for reading chapters of the book and giving me valuable feedback.

1

SCIENCE AND RELIGION ARISE FROM THE CONSCIOUS MATRIX

THERE'S NO WAY around the simple truth that human beings believe certain things intuitively. We're sentient beings capable of thinking great thoughts. Those thoughts can inspire actions, some of which can change the world. At times, we're nothing short of heroic action figures placed upon this earth. Our power comes from within. We're born with certain core understandings that enable us to develop intellectually, emotionally, and spiritually.

Both science and religion are belief systems that evolved within the human mind, yet they sometimes yield opposite conclusions. Exploring how the human mind attains its magical state of conscious awareness is a first step towards understanding our belief systems, what their purposes and meanings are to us. This book examines how ideas form in the conscious matrix—the part of the human brain that enables awareness and thinking. How the conscious matrix operates partly explains why there's conflict among our beliefs.

We're also our own worst enemy insofar as mankind repeatedly fails to see the perspective of others. Men and women still don't completely understand one another despite living together for nearly their entire lives. People of different cultures and religions are agape with horror at some practices of the other group. People of faith and atheists still can't comprehend one another's viewpoint. How is it that intelligent people can see the same picture and disagree about what it means?

1

People of faith far outnumber non-believers. Belief in God is prevalent across the globe. An estimated 86% of people claim to belong to one of over 4,300 religions, according to Adherents, an organization that keeps track.[1] This includes over 2 billion Christians, the largest group, which is concentrated heavily in the Americas and Europe. The second most prevalent religion is Islam with 1 to 1.5 billion adherents, followed by nearly one billion Hindus, half a billion Buddhists, half a billion people practicing traditional and folk religions, and 14 million of the Jewish faith. The sum total of believers overwhelmingly outstrips an estimated 1.2 billion people who are secular, agnostic, or atheist.

Fewer in number, out-spoken atheists have two main routes to influence others: a podium from which to speak and an attentive audience. Many of the world's most prominent and eminent scientists are atheists. Some have put their credentials and reputations on the line, and argued their areligious views emphatically and persuasively. A handful of scientists who profess atheism have written books on the topic. This is odd when you consider that few, if any, books are generally written about what we don't believe. We tend to read and write about what we do believe. One possible explanation is that whether believers or not, human beings are fascinated with God. A universal preoccupation makes it likely that our brains are wired to at least ponder the existence of God. We can't escape the underlying drive to think about the possibility of a higher-power.

A question to probe: What constitutes our conscious matrix? Understanding how human beings experience conscious thoughts and beliefs is critical to deciphering the disagreement between believers and non-believers in God.

All people possess a conscious matrix—defined as the sum total of quantum mind connections that arise deep inside neurons in the cerebral cortex, spanning the entire outer mantle of the human brain. Unlike traditional hook-ups between neurons using synapses, the conscious matrix is a quantum brain-wide system that relies on quantum entanglement between electrons, fueled by traveling photons, and suspended in space-time within a ubiquitous field.[2] More details on the conscious matrix will follow in this and subsequent chapters.

But why are human beings conscious in the first place? This enigmatic state needs an explanation. Consciousness appears to have a biological function. A conscious awareness of self and our surroundings enables decision-making, planning, and responding in a non-automatic way. Psychologist Brian Earl proposed that consciousness is a *flexible response mechanism.*[3] Human consciousness enables us to use virtually everything we know, bring it all to the table, and then make a decision. Our biological brain is smarter than any computer, and it beats artificial intelligence hands down. Much of the human brain's advantage is due to its great flexibility to handle new and unfamiliar situations.

> ***A possibility to ponder:*** *Scientific elites express their curiosity about God as pure skepticism. Their preoccupation with God is roughly equivalent to that of believers. Humanity needs both believers and skeptics to advance. Science and religion are the "yin and yang" of our belief systems.*

Why do so many of the intellectual elite reject belief in God? Wikipedia lists over 250 noted scientists who've gone on record claiming to be atheists, agnostic, or non-religious.[4] The list reads like a who's who of science. Close to 100 Nobel Prize winners identify themselves as non-religious. Even Alfred Nobel, the inventor of dynamite and originator of the prize in his name, was an atheist.

Among the list of avowed atheist scientists, some are people I've known or met. The first name to catch my attention is Paul Boyer, who won the Nobel Prize in 1997 for discovering how living cells make chemical energy. Paul Boyer was my college professor for biochemistry classes at UCLA. I remember him as a kind and gentle man who was accessible to students. During one of his office hours, I asked him why my answer on a test question wasn't marked correct. I pointed out there were alternative interpretations of his test question, and I saw the question differently than he did. But he said: "No Nancy, that wasn't the answer I was looking for and it's your job as the student to know what I want in an answer."

At that moment, it became abundantly clear how absolute right or wrong didn't matter as much as learning how your professor thought. University teaching is a passing down of "currently accepted" knowledge. It's taught that any scientific truth might be altered or expanded at some point in the future. Nonetheless, the critical thing for students is to know the consensus opinion: what's agreed upon by the majority of the most highly esteemed experts. If we used that measure on the atheism question, it's likely the elite scientists would win out. But they're not winning. And this book is about why they're not winning.

The second name to catch my attention is Sir Francis Crick, the co-discoverer of the structure of deoxyribonucleic acid (DNA), the material basis of our genes. Crick and Watson won the Nobel Prize in 1962, and are often touted as the most brilliant of Nobel Prize winners. Some took exception to that rumor, particularly those who felt Rosalind Franklin was inappropriately left out of the prize. After all, her data (the x-ray diffraction images) enabled Watson and Crick to deduce the structure of DNA. Crick always claimed they would've solved it sooner or later, with or without her data, but we'll never know. Crick could've been correct; understanding what the data meant is what's important. Watson and Crick were on the right track already, inches away from total understanding.

I never met Crick personally, but I frequently saw him at *The Society for Neuroscience* meetings. I remember one such meeting in San Diego where he wore a beautiful dark red dinner jacket. He was dining at the next table over to mine, and I remember thinking: "How could he have just said that no one intelligent believes in God?"

Crick had just given a presentation to a large audience of thousands of meeting participants. In his talk, he went one step further than merely professing his atheism. Crick actually mocked people who believe in God. He particularly teased a colleague of his, Sir John Eccles, another brilliant scientist who won a Nobel Prize in 1963 for discovering how nerve cells communicate. I met Eccles briefly at a meeting in Prague; he was a pleasant unassuming man, a perfect complement to the bombastic Crick. Eccles was a devout Catholic and remained so despite Crick's efforts to embarrass him into saying the notion of God was ridiculous. Crick thought this was hilarious. If elite intellectuals could bully others, Crick was certainly a prime example. But if Crick were truly comfortable in his a-religious beliefs, why did he need to mock others? I suspected this meant something.

Further down the list are Stephen Hawking and Sir Roger Penrose. Hawking and Penrose wowed the world by explaining how the universe

4

might have once started. The "big-bang" theory derives in a large part from their work on black holes. Stephen Hawking was an outspoken man up until his death, which came many years after doctors predicted. Hawking was erudite in a way in which his criticisms could be brutal and sharp. And there was no exception to this rule when it came to professing his atheism. Sir Roger Penrose, also a non-religious person, possesses a nearly polar opposite personality to that of Hawking. Always the consummate gentleman and scholar, Penrose expresses all his views with great humility and respect for differing opinions. The two oddly distinct personalities demonstrate how atheism is an idea shared by much of the intellectual elite. It's not reflective of a particular personality type or disposition. Both the arrogant and the humble are swayed by their commitments to reductionism and rational thought, which seems to exclude any belief in God. Many atheists are quite sincere in their lack of belief.

The atheist list also includes numerous physicists—many touted as the world's brightest stars, all genius-level thinkers to be sure. Albert Einstein stated many positions on God, but largely espoused an agnostic or non-religious view. Einstein won the Nobel Prize in 1921 for discovering the photoelectric effect, a critical step towards quantum mechanical theory. Richard Feynman, an avowed atheist, won the Nobel Prize in 1965 for his developments in quantum electrodynamics. Feynman led the way to further developments in quantum computing. Years later, David Deutsch formulated the first quantum algorithm (which is exponentially faster than typical algorithms), and he designed a potential "quantum Turing machine," a computer that could run his quantum algorithm. Brilliant indeed, but why did all these men reject the notion of God?

I find it odd that the path-finders to quantum mind theory didn't see how quantum mechanics would provide a means to prove God is real. Quantum mind theory is perhaps the only science that enables an all-knowing, all-loving, and all-powerful God to exist in the minds of men and women, while simultaneously connecting us to the universe. No other science supports the commonly held view of God as well as does quantum mechanics.[5] The dichotomy between believers and non-believers is furthermore an interesting paradox. Only quantum mechanical theory addresses paradox in a meaningful way. Contradictions and paradoxes may seem troubling, but they give our belief systems their necessary depth. Nothing worthwhile comes without a struggle.

But rather than inspiring a belief in God, serious study of technology seems to drive many people away from God. Key scientists at the forefront of study in artificial intelligence provide more examples. Marvin Minsky, one of the earliest proponents of artificial intelligence, is an atheist on record. Minsky invented the confocal microscope and a universal Turing machine. But perhaps his most notable achievement was the artificial neural network model. Like neural network models today, Minsky's model was based on the human brain, which contains roughly 100 billion neurons, linked with other neurons through trillions of synapses. The Turing-machine computer can mimic some of those brain linkages and simulate the brain's computations, at least in a mechanistic non-conscious manner. But will these artificial neural networks ever become conscious?

Ray Kurzweil, another atheist on record, advanced the idea that computers would acquire consciousness at the precise moment these machines passed the "speed and capacity" threshold of human intelligence. Kurzweil wrote three books on the topic: *The Age of Intelligent Machines*, *The Age of Spiritual Machines*, and *The Singularity is Near*.[6] Kurzweil's hypothetical point-in-time when computers acquire consciousness is called the "singularity."

But the main problem with Kurzweil's speculation is that human consciousness is an experience, not a computation. A machine can be faster, more capable, and more efficient at cranking out solutions to pre-programmed algorithms, but human intelligence handles real-life situations better. Human intelligence comes alive in our conscious matrix, allowing for a wide range of flexible responses. Our conscious matrix has inborn understanding and intuition. Computers aren't alive or sentient; they're mechanical and lack certain human qualities. Can a computer ever be built to express emotions or feel awareness? Recent simulations on computers and "smart robots" produce the façade of emotion, but it's not clear if a machine will ever be conscious in the way people are conscious.

Besides having a capacity for flexible responses, why is it even important to have consciousness? According to some, we experience God through our consciousness and it's our personal connection to a higher-being. Isn't it odd that Kurzweil calls his special union between man and machine the singularity? Isn't he borrowing a concept from God-believing folks who speak of the unity between men and women with God?

It's not just the artificial intelligence crowd who reject belief in God. Despite everyday proofs that believing in God promotes physical, emotional, and spiritual health—the most notable among biologists are also among the avowed atheists. Charles Darwin wrote the game-changing book, *On the Origin of Species,* in 1859.[7] In his seminal book, Darwin developed the theory of evolution. But does the idea that "man evolved from lower animal species" go against religious teachings of creation or "intelligent design"? This is hotly debated, with some scientists claiming science and religion aren't really in conflict concerning creation.[8] What I find striking is how this apparent conflict between believers and skeptics resembles the inner conflict many of us face when our faith is challenged. History teaches us that resolution of conflict is nearly always possible, although some battles are fierce.

A select few biologists are outright hostile in their rejection of God. Richard Dawkins was so inspired by the work of Darwin that he chose the study of animal behavior as his career. In 2008, Dawkins wrote the *God Delusion*, a harsh volume berating belief in God. Dawkins called religious ideas "out-of-date" and "petty."[9] Despite his harsh criticism of religion in general, Dawkins had faint praise for his own Anglican religion, expressing gratitude for not being taught "creationist lunacy." But the mere fact that there's a diversity of religions ultimately shook his faith. Rejecting religion for that reason is kind of surprising. Being a devoted fan of Darwin, Dawkins was well aware of the diversity of species in the animal kingdom. Apparently, Dawkins could wrap his mind around many animal types, but not around many perspectives of God.

Dawkins was taken to task by theologian John Lennox and a "God Delusion Debate" was held in Alabama by the Fixed Point Foundation.[10] The upshot of the debate was that people are polarized on religion and science. Those who believe tend to believe strongly. Those who don't believe are equally energized. Do the takers of the two extreme positions need one another? Of course, they do. They need each other to keep the controversy alive and to fine-tune their ideas.

Peter Atkins, a British chemist and author, goes even farther and is perhaps the most outspoken critic of religion among scientists. Atkins wrote several books on atheism and also appeared in a couple of documentaries.[11] Atkins could be counted upon to provide particularly caustic responses such as religion is "a fantasy," "empty," and "evil." Unfortunately, there's little beyond passionate disdain in his arguments. What all non-religious scientists seem to bank on is that believers in God openly admit they have faith in what can't be proven. Those like Atkins take this to mean belief in God is false because it's commonly accepted the existence of God can't be proved or disproved.

I'm taking a huge step by claiming we can prove God exists using the scientific method. It goes without saying we'll not all agree, at least not today, nor any time this year. But sometime in the future, God's existence can and will be proven, and then His presence will be commonly accepted. It's not impossible. Proving God exists is merely a case of successive approximations, as I'll explain throughout this book.

An idea to examine. Let's approach whether God exists as a scientific problem and see how it plays out.

We can apply the scientific method to the existence of God. As shown in the figure on the adjacent page, our initial observation is that billions of people believe in God. According to the flow chart, whether God is real or illusory depends on whether neural network models of mind explain consciousness, or if we need quantum mind theories to explain human consciousness.

Several quantum mind theories have been proposed, but only one has a significant following. The most developed and highly cited is the quantum mind theory pioneered by anesthesiologist Stuart Hameroff and mathematician Roger Penrose.[12] Hameroff contributed the idea that brain cell filaments called microtubules compute consciousness. Roger Penrose contributed his ideas on reduction of quantum superposition and quantum gravity. Together, Hameroff and Penrose formulated a plausible and falsifiable model. Many scientists, I among them, continue to work on the Hameroff-Penrose quantum mind theory.

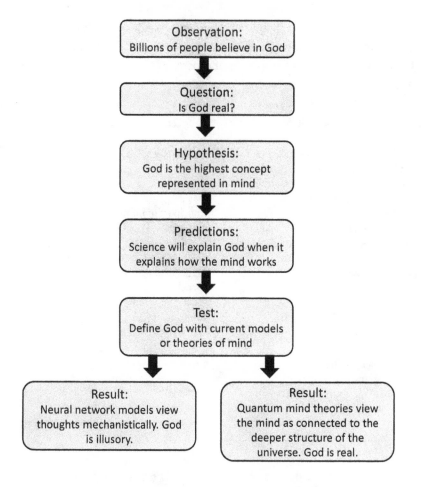

The research and theoretical work I've done is on the physical matrix, the anatomy of the quantum mind. This "conscious matrix" is the mind within our brains. The conscious matrix is capable of far more than what neural networks can do. In our book *Nanoneuroscience,* and in other publications, I've described the anatomy of a massive nanowire-network within neurons that forms the physical architecture that houses higher consciousness.[13] Networks of filaments fill the interiors of individual neurons of the human cerebral cortex, such that each individual neuron has the computing power of a simpler brain, like that of a sea slug.

Neurons come in a variety of sizes and computational power varies in proportion. The large pyramidal neurons—found in the cerebral cortex and hippocampus—are enriched with filaments. And it's these cells that selectively participate in human consciousness. Quantum mind theorists, I among them, argue that consciousness emerges from the filament meshwork—composed of mostly of tubulin proteins arranged as microtubules.

Neural Network Model	Quantum Mind Theory
Neurons—billions of nerve cells that transmit data using chemical signals (neurotransmitters) and electrochemical activity (graded potentials and action potentials).	**Microtubules**—long filaments made of tubulin protein that function within neurons to guide transport, growth, plasticity, and quantum computation (transport of photons).
Synapses—trillions of contacts between neurons where neurotransmitters are released and then bind to exert an effect.	**Entanglement**—a persistent state of coherence forged between neighboring sub-anatomic particles (electrons in tubulins, photons). Once entangled, particles maintain coherence when separated, even at great distances.
Cerebral cortex—outer mantle of the brain where most conscious processing occurs. The cortex has occipital (visual), temporal (auditory), parietal (touch and motor), and frontal (motor and planning) areas.	**Superposition**—particles have spin, speed of travel, and position. The sum total of these parameters are unknowable because measurement causes reduction. Before reduction occurs, particles can be in combination states—both up and down spin, for example.
Hierarchical organization—the cerebral cortex is arranged in ascending levels. Primary areas receive sensory information and send that on to higher association areas.	**Reduction**—collapse of the superposition.

Recent discoveries suggest Hameroff's proposal of consciousness occurring in these filaments is correct. Jack Tuszynski and Travis Craddock, physicists and quantum mind researchers, have shown how microtubules inside neurons are capable of transporting electrons and photons of light.[14] This observation strongly supports quantum mind theory. Photons are governed by quantum mechanical physical laws rather than by the laws of classical physics. Neurons, synapses, and other nervous system structures are simply too large and noisy to carry out quantum computations. Contrary to that noisy environment, electrons buried inside protein pockets can entangle. And occasional photons traveling inside the open centers or along the outside of long filaments can spread that quantum entanglement. Quantum computation can achieve enough momentum to reach conscious awareness only because the architecture of the conscious matrix contains a meshwork of filaments possessing precisely-positioned protein pockets. These pockets evolved or were "intelligently designed" to endow the conscious matrix with a profound ability to "connect the dots." These are dots of understanding and awareness, not data points of information.

More new science supports the conscious matrix model. Scientists recently rediscovered that the brain generates its own light. All living cells produce very low levels of light, about one photon per neuron per minute.[15] This ultra-weak photon emission is triggered by metabolic activity level. This emitted light spans the human visible spectrum and additionally includes some portion of infrared and ultraviolet band lengths. Newly generated photons can spread quantum entanglements along filaments, as would be expected to occur when neurons are highly active.

The whole story fits together like hand-in-glove. Human consciousness is better explained by quantum entanglement, superposition, and reduction, than by any other model or theory. No neural network model, neither real nor artificial, is computationally powerful enough to handle consciousness. Our conscious matrix literally takes everything that's ever happened to us into account every time we think the smallest thought. And thoughts are experiences, not data. Synaptic linkages aren't connecting anything beyond one data point of information shared between two neurons. Only quantum mind theory deals with real mental connection and explains how the human mind might entangle with the universe.

And it's precisely when our thoughts connect to a higher-power that we discover and come to understand universal truths. Moreover, it's consistent with scripture that light is foundational to everything else. As stated in the Bible, Genesis 1:1-3 (KJV), "*In the beginning God created the heavens and the earth and the earth was without form, and void, and darkness was upon the face of the deep. And the Spirit of God moved upon the face of the waters, and God said, let there be light; and there was light.*"

Another thought to ponder. Visual consciousness is a good way to illustrate how the conscious matrix builds an inner image of the outside reality.

Do we need anything beyond neural linkages through synapses to explain consciousness? Yes, we do indeed need something more sophisticated to account even for simple visual perception, like seeing the computer screen in front of you or a page of printed matter. Even the simplest of sights involve conscious integration of many details, viewed in the context of space and time.

Countless visual illusions or "tricks" prove we don't necessarily perceive exactly what's present in our fields of vision. Instead, we manipulate simple images to fit our ideas about how things are supposed to look.[16] Our brains revise visual images in various ways to produce consistency. One example is *color constancy*. Light reflected off that bright yellow jacket of yours may actually be sending "dull gray" visual input to your eyes because you're walking outside at dusk. Your brain will compare the wavelength of light reflected off your jacket with light reflected off everything else and compute "bright yellow" by comparison. Color constancy works until dusk turns to night, then all visual input goes gray. But color constancy is only one of many adjustments made. Other perceptual tricks include *filling in*, which enables us to identify familiar objects that are partially obstructed from view, and *figure-ground* comparison, which enables us to ignore huge areas designated as background.

But things get tricky when scientists try to explain how visual imagery reaches consciousness. In one neural network model, the front of the brain looks at ongoing activity at the back of the brain.[17] But this explanation has cracks and flaws. For one, it's highly unlikely that neurons in the frontal cortex have conscious ability, whereas those in the back of the brain don't. One chunk of cortex is as good as the next: all have the same circuits, and all are thought to operate by the same cortical mechanisms. As far as the human mind is concerned, perceiving a visual scene has more to do with thinking about what's in plain view and interpreting what it all means. For these reasons, among others, many scientists have turned to quantum mind theories of consciousness to explain vision.

In 2001, I wrote a paper with Stuart Hameroff on visual consciousness.[18] In that paper, we described a means whereby information about the visual scene—its various shapes, colors, and movements within the scene—would be melded together by quantum entanglements and superposition. These entanglements and superposition occur among electrons in protein pockets of the long filaments called microtubules. When a sufficient threshold of entanglement is reached (or a clocking mechanism runs out of time), a grand reduction of the quantum wave-form occurs. This reduction, which describes the final state of entangled particles, emerges as visual consciousness.

In that 2001 paper, we proposed that entanglements build up in 40 Hz cycles, culminating in a grand quantum state reduction every 300–500 msec. That's about the time it takes to collect a single thought, and most people generate two or three thoughts per second. We argued that only quantum phenomena can account for visual consciousness because vision is much more than the sum of neural processing. Our brain's synaptic linkages merely map what appears in the visual field, extracting very specific information at each level. Each level of cortical mapping is like a video monitor with a dedicated function. We have a brain area to analyze color, another for shape, one for movement, and so forth. But all this information condenses into a single idea, and only the idea reaches consciousness. We get the picture, so to speak, as it all comes together. The sum-total view is what psychologists called the "gestalt."

The gestalt provides context for our conscious matrix. Looking out at the world, we may barely see parts of our own body, like the tip of our nose, our hands, or our feet—but that tells us we're in the scene. Our conscious matrix adds information about our internal state—whether we're hot, cold, or hungry. Next, we'll make some deci-sions about various shapes, colors, and figure-ground relationships. If we're sitting outdoors taking in a beautiful landscape, we'll see land as shades of textured green hues. We'll see the water as a deep blue smooth surface. And we'll see the sky as a large expanse of light blue and white puffs. If there are any objects in the scene—like houses, boats, or cars—we'll distinguish them as well. Millions upon millions of neurons in the various sensory systems will analyze these inputs at several levels of cerebral cortex arranged in a hierarchy. That's a lot of information!

To get an idea of how much information is analyzed, consider these numbers: Visual input arising from any scene reaches the primary visual cortex, which contains some 280 million neurons. We can quadruple that number to include higher visual areas of cortex. Scientists have found that only one to ten percent of visual system neurons are active when we pay attention to an interesting visual scene—that amounts to roughly 10–100 million neurons. But each large neuron contains thousands of microtubules, averaging 1 µm in length. That translates into as many as one billion tubulin proteins. We know that small numbers of photons are emitted throughout visual cortex when processing a visual scene. Given the estimated 1 photon per minute per neuron, one can calculate that thousands of photons dart across brain filaments per second to bring about conscious experience of a visual scene. In a fraction of a second, a massive amount of data analyzed is reduced to flashes of light in our mind. In that very instant, our mind experiences one beautiful scenic view, not billions of data points. We pull all that information together and package it into a single emotional reaction: our complete and utter awe of nature.

Thousands of photons emitted per second is a substantial amount of light, particularly when one considers that the human visual system is sensitive to a single photon of light presented in complete darkness. The brain, as it rests protected inside of the skull, lies in complete darkness. Light doesn't enter the brain through the eyes; light is transduced first by chemical means and relayed to the brain using electrochemical impulses. The light we see in our "mind's eye" is light generated by the neurons, the ultra-weak photon emission triggered by increased neural activity. Actual visual experience is a self-constructed illusion in our conscious matrix. Nonetheless, our impression that we're observing the real world that surrounds us is pretty close to the truth. It's something like the magician who makes the lady disappear and then reappear. It might not be the same lady, but they look very similar.

We hold many beliefs about things being real. We believe that what we see with our own eyes is real, even though it's more like a reality-triggered illusion. We believe the stars in the sky that we'll never touch are real. And we believe subatomic particles are real, even though those particles are invisible to the naked eye and to every microscope yet invented. How are any of those beliefs any different from our belief that God is real? In much the same way that the brain recreates the scene and produces visual consciousness, the human mind "sees" or "experiences" God. To believers, our God, which our mind experiences, is real.

God is every bit as real as the outside world we think we see. God is certainly as real as the unobservable physical nature of matter, which is presented as fact, but is actually theory.

> **Another thought to ponder:** *If spontaneous emissions of light from neurons are responsible for visual consciousness, then visual experiences should be possible in the absence of any light shone onto the eyes.*

Several examples support the conclusion that what we experience as vision in our minds can occur in the absence of outside light reaching the eyes. For one, we experience vivid visual imagery without any light entering the eyes every night when we dream. What we see in our dreams can be quite meaningful, yet there's no real stimulus present to provoke these nightly "hallucinations."[19] People blind from birth see only vague visual images in their dreams. But those who are blinded later in life report vivid visual images still occur while dreaming, even though these images fade over the years.[20] When we dream, the brain acts as if light was reaching our eyes. Electrical activity appears in all the same places of the cerebral cortex as with daytime vision.[21] Most scientists attribute dreams to spontaneous eruptions of electrical activity, so that part isn't surprising.[22] But what's amazing is how dream-state visual images seem so real. It certainly fits with our daytime visual consciousness being generated by photon emissions inside the brain. During the day, incoming light certainly triggers patterns of activity. But conscious realization of those images likely occurs because of ultra-weak photon emissions arising from brain tissue.[23]

Illusory visual images are also produced with certain mind-altering hallucinogens. Lysergic acid diethylamide (LSD) is an example. In one study, normal subjects were given LSD and asked to keep their eyes closed while they experienced hallucinations. These subjects showed brain activity similar to what's normal for vision occurring with eyes open.[24] How can the brain self-generate visual experiences without any light hitting the retina? Spontaneous photon emissions by the brain and eye might again be responsible for visual consciousness triggered from within.[25]

There's also evidence that light shone on the eyes doesn't always produce vision, indicating consciousness is a prerequisite. Anesthesia produces a loss of consciousness. When people are put under the influence of general anesthesia they're insensitive to light and don't experience conscious vision, even when light is directly shone into their eyes. Anesthesia interrupts the ability of microtubules to function and also causes a loss of consciousness.[26] And since microtubules serve as the waveguides enabling electrons and photons to entangle with one another to form coherent systems,[27] that might explain why we have no vision if the conscious matrix isn't working. Vision is an illusion created by our conscious matrix.

Given all we know, the scientific basis of visual perception is similar to our brain making a movie that we experience in our conscious matrix. The movie is a creation, based on real input, but it's heavily modified to produce consistent images we can easily understand. Our conscious matrix edits images, making them compatible with past experience and future expectations. Although vision is a total creation of mind, it nonetheless accurately captures something real: the outside world. All the landscapes and objects surrounding us are widely accepted to be the real world. Even the distant stars we can only see in a telescope are considered real. Reality is never provable beyond all doubt. Reality is what we consistently experience. Reality is what triggers a sense of awe in all of us.

> **Another possibility to ponder**: *When contemplating God, there should arise heightened brain activity above levels typical of ordinary conscious experience.*

Our belief in God elevates our state of mind. How does that happen? A research group at UCLA studied overall brain activity of believers and non-believers while stating their belief or disbelief in God.[28] The brain area consistently active when subjects express their belief in God lies in a specific part of the frontal cortex. Interestingly, the same brain area shows increased activity when non-believers express their disbelief in God. This part, called the ventromedial prefrontal cortex, is concerned with self-representation, emotion, and resolving conflict. The results of this study suggest both belief in and denial of God's existence is pre-wired into our brain. Our belief and connection to God is part of how we view ourselves. Our beliefs about who we are serve as a foundation to all our other beliefs. Thus, it would seem at our innermost core, it's just God and ourselves living harmoniously in our conscious matrix.

There's widespread belief that God is something real, but this alone isn't definitive proof. Another way to prove God actually exists is to show how our belief in God is useful in our everyday lives. The more we look, the more proof we find of how believing in God boosts our self-esteem, our emotional well-being, and aids in our survival. Our belief in God is always present and He gives our lives purpose, meaning, and satisfaction. In chapters to come, we'll examine the many ways God is useful. But first, let's consider what it means to the conscious matrix to be real.

One last idea to examine: *We must distinguish between proof for "having faith in God" versus proof for "the existence of God."*

Let's address this critical question: Is our "belief in God" provable scientifically? It's testable and falsifiable, so yes. It's obvious that many people believe in God, and opinion surveys prove that to be true. Even one person's authentic opinion is proof enough that belief in God exists, because we're the sole expert of our own opinions and thoughts. No one can tell us what to think, and only we are privy to our innermost thoughts.

But it's another quantum leap from proving belief in God exists to proving God exists. Is it enough if we prove we have a direct connection with God? And what would such a connection look like in our conscious matrix? Would the mere fact that the human brain is capable of deducing all the physical laws of the universe prove human beings are connected directly to God? Given all the amazing scientific discoveries over the ages, it would seem our best minds are capable of understanding nearly anything and everything, at least eventually. We know today how the cerebral cortex is hierarchically organized, and that organizational scheme provides clues about how we perceive God as a higher order concept.

But God is more than just a concept. He is as real as our experience reflects reality. Not just scientists, but ordinary people too, have great knowledge and insight without even seeking it. People noticed how gravity plants our feet firmly on the ground long before Isaac Newton developed the theory of gravity. So we have some kind of proof God exists insofar as we connect, get inspired, and discover the secrets of the universe.

Let's look at this connection from another angle. We believe in God intuitively and many of us profess to have an inborn moral compass. The behavioral sciences may have mapped many of the neural linkages through which we choose one behavior over another. But most of us, without having to study behaviorism, will choose behaviors that result in reward and avoid punishment. Most of us avoid mistakes based on con-templating past mistakes and this necessitates having a conscious aware-ness and a conscious memory of past events. In many cases, human beings exhibit wisdom beyond their ability to explain how we go about making good choices for ourselves. Sometimes ordinary common sense far exceeds the imaginations of scientists who seek to model our rea-soning ability. We must be connected to a higher-being; we simply know way too much for it to be otherwise.

Atheists can't make the unchallenged claim that believers don't seek or have proof of God. We can set up a hypothesis, test it, interpret the results, and formulate a theory about God. We already have a good understanding of the human mind, and its connection to the mind of God, from our personal experiences. And like scientists do, we're always updating information, changing our educated opinions, and rewriting our theories. But God is more than a theory; God is an experience. And we either feel His presence or we don't. There are no wrong opinions, just different points of view. As stated in Hebrews 11:1 (KJV), "*Now faith is the substance of things hoped for, the evidence of things not seen.*"

Quantum mind theory suggests we should continuously question our belief in God. We can handle all the paradoxes, contradictions, and dichotomous thinking with pleasure—knowing full well that's how the human mind works. We can listen and openly explore other perspectives or ways of experiencing God, even disbelief. We don't ever have to cut ourselves off from our traditions—particularly if they give us comfort, joy, understanding, meaning, and enlightenment. We can look at the "other side" of any controversy and perhaps see something we missed.

It's scientifically plausible that our brains evolved to experience God and our connection to Him because He is real. Only by examining the myriad purposes of God will we ever come to understand ourselves, to know God, and contemplate the universe. Even atheists believe in something; they staunchly believe in their disbelief. All of the ideas presented in this book are testable and falsifiable. A scientific description of God is only as good as its last revision. We must continuously question the validity of our ideas and seek verification. Throughout the chapters of this book, we'll revisit quantum mind concepts in various contexts to explain how ideas about God vary across the ages and across cultures. Ideas expressed about God are never simple, but with few exceptions, they provide extremely useful guideposts.

CHAPTER 1: NOTES AND REFERENCES

1. Juan S. What are the most widely practiced religions of the world? The Register, Oct., 2006. https://www.theregister.co.uk/2006/10/06/the_odd_body_religion/

2. Woolf NJ. Dendritic encoding: an alternative to temporal synaptic coding of conscious experience. Conscious Cogn. 1999, 8(4):447-54.

    Hameroff S. Quantum walks in brain microtubules—a biomolecular basis for quantum cognition? Top Cogn Sci. 2014, 6(1):91-7.

3. Earl B. The biological function of consciousness. Front Psychol. 2014, 5:697.

4. List of atheists in science and technology. Wikipedia, https://en.wikipedia.org/wiki/List_of_atheists_in_science_and_technology

5. Wegter-McNelly K. The Entangled God: Divine Relationality and Quantum Physics. Routledge, 2011.

    Zetting D. A Quantum Case for God. Quantum Creation Ministries, 2016.

    Selbie J. The Physics of God: Unifying Quantum Physics, Consciousness, M-Theory, Heaven, Neuroscience and Transcendence. Career Press, 2018.

6. Kurzweil R.The Age of Intelligent Machines. MIT Press, 1990.

    Kurzweil R.The Age of Spiritual Machines. Viking, 1999.

    Kurzweil R. The Singularity is Near. Penguin Books, 2010.

7. Darwin C. On the Origin of Species, 1859.

8. Meadows L, Doster E, Jackson DF. Managing the conflict between evolution and religion. The Am. Biol. Teacher, 62(2), 2000.

    Pappas S. Creationism vs. Evolution: 6 Big Battles, Live Science, February 2014. https://www.livescience.com/43126-creationism-vs-evolution-6-big-battles.html

9. Dawkins R. The God Delusion, 2006.

10. Richard Dawkins versus John Lennox: The God Delusion Debate. 2015. http://www.protorah.com/wp-content/uploads/2015/01/The-God-Delusion-Debate-Full-Transcript.pdf

11. Atkins PW, The Creation. WH Freeman, 1981.

    Atkins P. On Being: A Scientist's Exploration of the Great Questions of Existence. Oxford Press, 2011.

12. Hameroff SR, Penrose R. Orchestrated reduction of quantum coherence in brain microtubules: a model for consciousness. SR Hameroff, AW Kaszniak, AC Scott (Eds.), Toward a science of consciousness; the first Tucson discussions and debates, MIT Press, Cambridge (1996), pp. 507-540.

    Hameroff SR, Penrose R. Conscious events as orchestrated space–time selections J Conscious Stud, 1996, 3(1): 36-53

    Hameroff S, Penrose R. Consciousness in the universe: a review of the 'Orch OR' theory. Phys Life Rev. 2014, 11(1):39-78.

Penrose R. The Emporer's New Mind. Oxford University Press, 1989.

Penrose R. Shadows of the Mind. Oxford University Press, 1996.

13. Woolf NJ, Priel A, Tuszynski JA. Nanoneuroscience: Structural and Functional Roles of the Neuronal Cytoskeleton in Health and Disease, Elsevier, 2009.

    Woolf NJ. A structural basis for memory storage in mammals. Prog Neurobiol. 1998, 55(1):59-77.

    Woolf NJ. Global and serial neurons form a hierarchically arranged interface proposed to underlie memory and cognition. Neuroscience. 1996, 74(3):625-51.

14. Hagan S, Hameroff SR, Tuszyński JA. Quantum computation in brain microtubules: decoherence and biological feasibility. Phys Rev E Stat Nonlin Soft Matter Phys. 2002, 65(6 Pt 1):061901.

    Jibu M, Hagan S, Hameroff SR, Pribram KH, Yasue K. Quantum optical coherence in cytoskeletal microtubules: implications for brain function. Biosystems. 1994;32(3):195-209.

    Craddock TJ, Friesen D, Mane J, Hameroff S, Tuszynski JA. The feasibility of coherent energy transfer in microtubules. J R Soc Interface. 2014, 11(100):20140677.

15. Salari V, Scholkmann F, Bokkon I, Shahbazi F, Tuszynski J. The physical mechanism for retinal discrete dark noise: Thermal activation or cellular ultraweak photon emission? PLoS One. 2016, 11(3):e0148336.

    Salari V, Valian H, Bassereh H, Bókkon I, Barkhordari A. Ultraweak photon emission in the brain. J Integr Neurosci. 2015, 14(3):419-29.

    Isojima Y, Isoshima T, Nagai K, Kikuchi K, Nakagawa H. Ultraweak biochemiluminescence detected from rat hippocampal slices. Neuroreport. 1995, 6(4):658-60.

16. Witzel C, Gegenfurtner KR. Color Perception: Objects, Constancy, and Categories. Annu Rev Vis Sci. 2018, 4:475-499.

    Lilienfeld S, Lynn SJ, Namy L & Woolf NJ. Psychology: From Inquiry to Understanding. Pearson, 2011.

17. Crick F, Koch C. The problem of consciousness. Sci Am. 1992, 267(3):152-9.

    Boly M, Massimini M, Tsuchiya N, Postle BR, Koch C, Tononi G. Are the neural correlates of consciousness in the front or in the back of the cerebral cortex? Clinical and Neuroimaging Evidence. J Neurosci. 2017, 37(40):9603-9613.

18. Woolf NJ, Hameroff SR. A quantum approach to visual consciousness. Trends Cogn Sci. 2001, 5(11):472-478.

19. Meaidi A, Jennum P, Ptito M, Kupers R. The sensory construction of dreams and nightmare frequency in congenitally blind and late blind individuals. Sleep Med. 2014, 15(5):586-95.

20. Bértolo H, Paiva T, Pessoa L, Mestre T, Marques R, Santos R. Visual dream content, graphical representation and EEG alpha activity in congenitally blind subjects. Brain Res Cogn Brain Res. 2003, 15(3):277-84.

    Horikawa T, Tamaki M, Miyawaki Y, Kamitani Y. Neural decoding of visual imagery during sleep. Science. 2013, 340(6132):639-42.

21. Jakobson AJ, Fitzgerald PB, Conduit R. Induction of visual dream reports after transcranial direct current stimulation (tDCs) during Stage 2 sleep. J Sleep Res. 2012, 21(4):369-79.

22. Hobson JA, Hong CC, Friston KJ. Virtual reality and consciousness inference in dreaming. Front Psychol. 2014, 5:1133.

23. Kataoka Y, Cui Y, Yamagata A, Niigaki M, Hirohata T, Oishi N, Watanabe Y. Activity-dependent neural tissue oxidation emits intrinsic ultraweak photons. Biochem Biophys Res Commun. 2001, 285(4):1007-11.

Kobayashi M, Takeda M, Sato T, Yamazaki Y, Kaneko K, Ito K, Kato H, Inaba H. In vivo imaging of spontaneous ultraweak photon emission from a rat's brain correlated with cerebral energy metabolism and oxidative stress. Neurosci Res. 1999, 34(2):103-13.

24. Roseman L, Sereno MI, Leech R, Kaelen M, Orban C, McGonigle J, Feilding A, Nutt DJ, Carhart-Harris RL. LSD alters eyes-closed functional connectivity withinthe early visual cortex in a retinotopic fashion. Hum Brain Mapp. 2016, 37(8):3031-40.

25. Kapócs G, Scholkmann F, Salari V, Császár N, Szőke H, Bókkon I. Possible role of biochemiluminescent photons for lysergic acid diethylamide (LSD)-induced phosphenes and visual hallucinations. Rev Neurosci. 201, 28(1):77-86.

26. Craddock TJA, Kurian P, Preto J, Sahu K, Hameroff SR, Klobukowski M, Tuszynski JA. Anesthetic Alterations of Collective Terahertz Oscillations in Tubulin Correlate with Clinical Potency: Implications for Anesthetic Action and Post-Operative Cognitive Dysfunction. Sci Rep. 2017, 7(1):9877.

27. Kurian P, Obisesan TO, Craddock TJA. Oxidative species-induced excitonic transport in tubulin aromatic networks: Potential implications for neurodegenerative disease. J Photochem Photobiol B. 2017, 175:109-124.

Barzanjeh S, Salari V, Tuszynski JA, Cifra M, Simon C. Optomechanical proposal for monitoring microtubule mechanical vibrations. Phys Rev E. 2017, 96(1-1):012404.

28. Harris S, Kaplan JT, Curiel A, Bookheimer SY, Iacoboni M, Cohen MS. The neural correlates of religious and nonreligious belief. PLoS One. 2009, 4(10):e0007272.

2

MYRIAD BELIEFS ABOUT GOD: ALL ROADS LEAD TO HIM

THE CONSCIOUS MATRIX has been our portal to God throughout the ages. Although modern ideas about God differ from earlier beliefs, some common themes stand the test of time. The single most recurring idea is that God reigns as a supreme higher-being: all-knowing, all-loving, and all-powerful. Even the ancient Greeks and Romans, who worshiped many gods, marked one of their gods as king above the other gods. As king of gods, he sat on the highest throne governing other gods, as well as ruling over all the people.

Our perception of God is seen through the lens of our conscious matrix. As discussed in Chapter 1, the human brain has a hierarchical organization, which is especially true for the outer mantle, the cerebral cortex. Neurons pass along information to successively higher regions of cerebral cortex. Each cortical level rearranges that input, enabling the conscious matrix to flash abstract concept after abstract concept, materializing like still photos from the constant stream of incoming sensory data. Information streams typically go from the back or sides of the brain to the front. Quantum mind theory postulates that the entanglements formed briefly in parts of our conscious matrix further entangle with entanglements in other parts, resulting in one grand reduction two or three times each second.

But ultimately, our conscious matrix likely entangles with energies flowing through the universe. Quantum entanglements and superposition are governed by physical laws of nature. The human brain seems to be "tuned in" to the laws of nature and to the properties of the universe. For believers, that's because our mind connects with the mind of God. God knows the laws of the universe, and perhaps He invented them. And, if any part of the conscious matrix connects to God, we'd expect it to be the part embedded in neurons at the top of our brain's cortical hierarchy. After all, what else could possibly be entangled with our highest levels of abstract thinking?

Perhaps the underlying reason our minds are hierarchically wired in a particular way is to make sense out of our "experience of God." That's why we think of God when we contemplate top-tier concepts such as rules of moral behavior. In a sense, God is the next highest step, outstripping the confines of our cortical hierarchy, reaching beyond our physical being, and traveling faster than the speed of light to reach the stars and beyond. Don't laugh at this suggestion. I don't mean this as a poetic metaphor.

Take a minute to absorb how much our conscious matrix can comprehend and transcend. We can "entangle mentally" with farthest stars in an instant in our minds. *Proxima Centauri* is our nearest star. It takes photons of light over four years to travel from there to earth. Yes, the photons hitting the photoreceptor cells in our eyes are at least four years old. But that's not what tickles our conscious matrix. Newly emitted photons in visual areas entangle with the abstract concept of "as-far-away-in-the-sky-as-the-eyes-can-see." We literally entangle with that distant star mentally; it's meaning to us is "an unimaginably distant object." It's truly amazing how our conscious matrix can transcend the speed of light. But that's only because it's not the light coming from the star, it's the light created in our minds, that connects us mentality to the nearest and the farthest star we can see. It's a conceptualization of the stars we experience. The experience transcends space and time. That's likely the same manner in which we connect to God. And perhaps that's how human beings have always connected to God throughout the millennia of recorded history. But let's examine what we know about ancient and modern religions and then reconsider the physical nature of that connection.

> **A question to probe:** *Why were the Ancient Greeks and Romans polytheists?*

Ancient Greeks and Romans believed in multiple gods and goddesses.[1] As polytheistic peoples, these ancients worshipped twelve major gods and even more minor deities. There were many gods, nearly one for everything or purpose in their lives. Each god served a particular function, but most importantly, these gods helped the ancients answer many questions about the unknown. Who are we? What's our place in the world? Where do we go when we die? When were we created? And, why do we have experiences? All these questions pertain to the human soul—a seemingly non-material spirit—and our interaction with others and with a higher life-force. These are early realizations of the conscious matrix.

The Greeks and Romans passed on many stories about their gods, starting as early as the eighteenth century BC. These stories served as both their religion and their mythology. The gods lived, loved, and engaged in conflicts—creating dramas that were colorful and complicated. All the gods were immortal by definition, but most also had characteristics of regular men and women. Continuously interacting with one another, the gods had offspring together, who were also gods. Some gods fought and started wars, while others busied themselves with the chores of everyday life. Occasionally the gods conceived children with mortals, blurring the line between their separate destinies. Understanding the blur between being mortal and immortal is only possible in quantum systems. Without knowing anything about biology, the brain, or physics, the ancients were aware of this dichotomy between the sacred and the earthly. The ancients' ability to perceive anomalous dichotomies doesn't prove quantum mind theory, but it's certainly consistent with it.

Mortal versus immortal: the ancients struggled with this concept. They could see with their own eyes that men and women die. People, whom they knew and loved, all died sooner or later. The ancients must have noticed the way the life-spirit immediately leaves the body upon death, and that must have bewildered them. But just like ourselves today, it's nearly impossible to imagine that our stream of consciousness will end someday. Since we have no memory of our stream of consciousness ever beginning, we feel as if we've always been here and always will be. Are our minds deceiving us with some cruel trick? Or is the human brain exquisitely sensitive to the absolute truth that our souls are immortal but our bodies are mortal? The most exotic and enigmatic part of us, conceivably the most amazing thing in the entire world, is the human soul. Our human soul is the purest core experience of the conscious matrix. Does our soul transcend the body and live forever? Can we set up disprovable hypotheses worthy of being called scientific inquiry on the topic of immortality?

The skeptical view is that man created the idea of God and that death is the end of us. So why weren't the ancients all skeptics? We have to imagine what ancient people thought while observing nature. Perhaps it was the sheer beauty of nature that inspired them to ponder gods and goddesses. The Greeks and Romans must have been in awe of their magnificent landscapes. They had long days to ponder the sky, the land, and the sea. Looking up at the vast skies, Greeks and Romans paid homage to Zeus and Jupiter, gods of the heavens. Looking out to the sea they praised Poseidon and Neptune, gods of the sea. And looking at the ground and wondering what lies beneath it, they recognized Hades and Pluto as gods of the underworld and the dead. Then at night, they must have gazed upon the stars and contemplated the vastness of the universe. Gods must live in the heavens at the ends of the universe; the ancients must have thought it so.

But as I've already mentioned, the Greek and Roman gods had social rankings. Zeus and Jupiter were the kings above other gods, and they governed the heavens, sky, and thunder. Why is heaven a better place to be than earth? For one, the sky is filled with light during the day. The ground is dark by comparison. And if one digs into the ground, shadows cast deep within the pit make the underlying earth appear even darker. Early on, people undoubtedly made distinctions between opposites, and they must have coupled some concepts together, such as: up equals light, down equals dark.

One can easily argue that how our brains are wired drove the ancients to create a hierarchy among their gods. The way neurons are linked imposes a hierarchical organization of our thoughts.[2] An upward direction is a concrete example of "higher," yet we create from that an abstract concept "higher," which means something better in value. The opposite of higher is lower, from which an opposite concept can be derived, lesser in value. Intuitively, people equate light with goodness. As the Bible says in Daniel 12:3, *"Those who are wise will shine bright as the sky, and those who turn many to righteousness will shine like stars forever."*

Moving from a concrete example to an abstract concept occurs in our nervous system when neurons send information to successively higher areas. Our conscious matrix takes several looks at what information the cerebral cortex is processing to construct successively more abstract and all-encompassing ideas in an ascending order. Not only our thoughts, but our behavior is affected. Our body language reflects our abstract thinking. A posture that includes the head tilted downwards is exhibited when people feel sad.[3] The number of hierarchical levels is also important. Non-human primates, like monkeys and chimpanzees, are less intelligent than humans because they have a few less levels in their cortical hierarchies. Nearly everything else about the primate brain is organized the same as ours.

Why do so many people believe in God or an all-powerful being or force? One possibility is an authentic life-force in the universe triggered the human brain to evolve the capacity to experience awe. Our earliest ancestors might well have experienced a rudimentary connection to their gods, to the universe, and to the fundamental laws governing unity. Atheists and seculars will favor the conclusion that the brain is wired to detect the "theory of everything," a grand theory that reconciles seemingly contradictory and incompatible theories.[4] Persons practicing any of the modern religions today might say the brain is wired to ultimately experience their version of the "one true God."

In addition to contemplating the heavens and the earth, the ancients experienced emotions much the same as we do today. Specific gods represented select emotions. Aphrodite and Venus, the goddesses of love and beauty, were favorites. There were additional gods and goddesses for hunting, homemaking, harvesting, waging war, and drinking wine. The stories about the gods made them equivalent to our current day celebrities. And perhaps that was the downfall of ancient religions. Their gods exhibited too many humanlike frailties. People are innately driven to worship gods that truly rise above the common person, something to look up and aspire to emulate. The downfalls of multiple gods being

29

less than perfect likely contributed to the conversion to monotheism, the belief in one true God. Our brain's hierarchical organization is always seeking to grasp a better idea of what's supreme and ethereal.

At the same time the Greeks were worshiping their many gods and practicing their culture, the Greek philosophers were developing their ideas about the mind and the human soul. Plato, one of the great classical Greek philosophers of the 4th/3rd century BC, took the dualist position. Plato believed the soul was immaterial, whereas the body was material: in other words, mind and body are dual in nature.[5] Aristotle disagreed, believing instead that the human soul was made of matter.[6] Unfortunately, Aristotle made the error of localizing the human soul to the heart, or more accurately, he suggested the heart as the best possibility.

Aristotle was wrong, but not totally off the mark. In all fairness to Aristotle, his views of the human soul were extensive and thoughtful. Aristotle viewed the soul as equivalent to a generalized life force, in good alignment with modern ideas and the views expressed here. We know today how the heart sends messages through nerves to the brain. The brain determines our emotional state based on how fast the heart is beating, internal measures of blood pressure, blood chemistry, and whether the G.I. tract is active or at rest. Experiencing emotion is how our conscious awareness takes into account our internal state. But how the brain does this is a bit tricky.

An intense emotional state is equivalent to heightened arousal of the sympathetic nervous system.[7] Levels of arousal gauge the intensity of a specific emotion but don't determine its identity. Emotions have valence; emotional states can be pleasurable or aversive depending on whether they're triggered by positive or negative events. If a man sees a bear and autonomic arousal gets triggered, he experiences fear. If the man instead sees a beautiful woman, and the same autonomic arousal gets triggered, he might experience attraction or even love.

Besides Plato and Aristotle, many other ancient Greeks expressed increasingly provocative ideas about the human soul. Epicurus (341-270 BC) was born of Greek parents, but lived outside of Greece in the lands nearby. Epicurus was prescient in that he hypothesized the soul was made of atoms.[8] This Greek philosopher reasoned like a modern-day scientist might and concluded: since the soul is made of atoms, when the body dies, the soul dies too. But in his day, Epicurus had no knowledge that, at the quantum level, energy and mass are interchangeable. Nor did Epicurus know life is something special that energizes matter.

Even to this day, not our scientists, philosophers, nor theologians definitively know the secret of life. All we know is that the living cell supports ongoing chemical reactions collectively called metabolism. Metabolism continuously nourishes the cell with new materials that keep the cell alive and healthy. That metabolism gives off an occasional photon.[9] We don't know exactly why. We could call it the "light of life." That light is hypothesized to fuel entanglement of electrons in the conscious matrix—that's the theme and basic premise of this book.

But why did the ancient Greeks and Romans believe in many gods, instead of one? It seems they recognized the multiple roles served by their gods, but hadn't developed the idea yet that it would be closer to the truth if they melded all those good traits into one deity. Quantum mechanical theory has the power to do that through entanglement and superposition. Perhaps the ancient Greeks and Romans had not yet discovered the full power of their conscious matrix, but others who followed in time would discover this miracle of mind.

> **An idea to examine:** *Modern religions moved away from polytheist religions because multiple Gods were too much like ordinary people; they had too many weaknesses.*

Religions practiced today evolved from the ancients' polytheism and mythology, yet most adherents to one of the many religions today believe in a single deity. The ancients worshiped multiple gods, each of which had a specific function. In contrast, our modern religions grant multiple purposes to one God, the "one true God." Judaism was the first major religion to develop the monotheistic view well enough to cause it to spread to other religions.[10]

The story in Exodus of the Bible is about how the Jewish people made a covenant with God. In exchange for their loyalty, the Jewish believe they are God's chosen people, a concept that's widely believed even today. Most contemporary religions of the world are also monotheistic. Some non-Christians have called into question whether Christianity is monotheistic because Christians believe in the Trinity. Christians believe themselves to be monotheistic and defend their belief against this criticism. The next three chapters of this book will discuss how our conscious matrix entangles three perspectives of God into the Trinity: The Father, the Son, and the Holy Spirit.

The Holy Trinity as a Quantum Entanglement

God, the Father

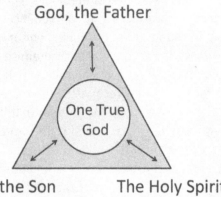

One True God

Jesus, the Son   The Holy Spirit

Christian scholars explain that the Trinity melds together three perspectives of one true God: The Holy Father, the Son (Jesus Christ), and the Holy Spirit.[11] For Christians, this amalgam blends three ways to connect with God into one idea. The Holy Father is our primary vision of God; it's whom we address in prayer. We're taught that we are molded in His likeness. The Holy Father has personhood, but we don't know what he looks like. The son, Jesus Christ, is fully visible as a living man, a real person in the flesh. We see the human side of God in Jesus Christ, making it easier to relate to our unseen God. Jesus also teaches us which human characteristics are best to emulate. And Jesus' death gives us the promise of everlasting life or immortality. The Holy Spirit is the experience of God being present, or perhaps more precisely, the experience of God's soul. One might feel the Holy Spirit in the room; it's pure experience without much imagery. The Trinity is analogous to three ideas of the same thing held in the conscious matrix as a quantum entanglement.

Judaism and Christianity aren't unique in our monotheistic views. Islamists, Hindu, and Buddhists believe or lean towards monotheism as well.[12] Islamic philosophers of the twelfth century AD translated the works of Aristotle and this had an important influence on the development of Islamic philosophy and religion, perhaps as much as did the prophet Abraham. As a result of these influences, Muslims are monotheistic in their views. Hinduism has roots far back in history, making its monotheistic threads independent of Judaism or Christianity. Hinduism permits a wide variety of views on God, including the belief in one supreme-being. Buddhists aren't totally monotheistic either. Nonetheless, Buddhist beliefs resemble monotheism in their belief of one supreme state, Nirvana, and the omnipotent rule of fairness, Karma.

Why do so many religions find monotheism attractive? Oneness or unity is appealing in that it resolves conflicts in the mind. When we can't decide, when two or more answers sound kind of right, we can simply fuse the ideas together into one. Solution found. Quantum mind theory accomplishes this with entanglement and superposition. In an evolved conscious matrix, both Plato and Aristotle can be right. Dualism is partly true: thoughts are invisible and might consist of pure energy without mass. But materialism is partly true as well: thoughts are stored in our brain and that bodily organ is made of material substance having mass.

The reason both ideas are partly true is because energy and mass are interconvertible. That's the reality. Our thoughts about this conundrum parallel the physical paradox in form. Quantum entanglements arising in our conscious matrix can piece together fragmented ideas into one whole. Many ideas that appear to contradict one another really don't. That's why we have prepositions such as *however*, *but*, *except*, and *unless*. Lots of things in life are true, except when they're not. Complex realities are handled by the conscious matrix because it functions to combine many perspectives into one gestalt. The Christian notion of the Trinity is a perfect example of melding many ideas into one.

Is it really necessary that the conscious matrix operates like this? My guess is yes. Our higher intelligence absolutely depends on the conscious matrix being able to blend ideas into one. The psychological function of blending ideas into one is what gives us the ability to inhibit blind alleys of thinking. Consciousness is associated with the reduction of many possibilities into one outcome. Once a path is chosen, it becomes possible to move on to deal with new problems. The ability to compartmentalize complex sequences of thoughts—to put them in a box, and move on—is the greatest advantage of consciousness. Otherwise, one's thinking gets caught up in endless loops. Quantum mind theory gives us a valid reason for monotheism; it saves time not to go down many fruitless paths. Human beings possess an innate drive to find the highest principle whether it's the "theory of everything" or "one true God."

> ***An idea to examine:*** *Monotheism is the logical religion of mankind because each quantum superposition in the brain is destined to reduce into successively larger ideas.*

To examine, and potentially falsify this hypothesis, we need to break it down into a succession of steps. It's more manageable to elucidate how lower-order ideas emerge. That was outlined for visual conscious-ness in Chapter 1. Quantum states that represent lower-order ideas combine and reduction occurs again and again, up until one grand idea finally emerges. This series ends in a grand reduction when the largest idea is reached. In the minds of billions of believers, God is that "highest idea." The highest idea represents the uniquely human experience and awe at the grand unification within our own soul, shared with the souls of other human beings, with all of nature, and with the soul of God.

The development of religion moving from polytheistic to monothe-istic religions is consistent with an upward mobility of quantum states when experiencing "one true God." Our conscious matrix seeks oneness and unity because that's how it operates. The universal trend towards monotheism illustrates a long-standing desire among human beings to settle upon a unified idea that holds up. We seek and our conscious matrix finds explanations for nearly everything about anything, including things about our personal world up to understanding the entire universe. And God answers, just like the Bible says in Jeremiah 33:3 (NIV). *"Call to me and I will answer you and tell you great and unsearchable things you do not know."*

> ***A possibility to ponder***: *The human soul is a nested group of entan-glements arising from electrons in the pockets of brain proteins and photons communicating their quantum states. These groups of entanglements are arranged in a hierarchy.*

In accordance with the hypotheses outlined so far, the conscious matrix consists of nested entanglements that are furthermore entan-gled with fundamental principles of the universe. We're the observer in the grand scheme of our existence. We're the center of our personal universe. The conscious matrix gives life or light to the individual mind; it collects our thoughts about ourselves into one unity.

Accordingly, is the conscious matrix the same thing as the human soul? Yes and no. Our conscious matrix highlights lots of earth-bound things in life, bringing them to our conscious awareness. The four walls around us, the trash that needs to be taken out—all the mundane, ordinary things in life that hardly inspire us; nonetheless, these ordinary things reach conscious awareness. The human soul is a special case of heightened conscious awareness. So for the purposes of describing the possible physical basis of the human soul, we can start with what would also be the physical basis of the conscious matrix.

A subatomic basis of the soul is partially consistent with what Epicurus believed, except that we now know much more about atoms and subatomic particles. Rather than the soul being made of whole atoms, the hypothesis presented in this book and elsewhere is that subatomic particles, namely electrons in the pockets of brain proteins and photons, comprise the human soul. It's the way the conscious matrix, a physical architecture in the brain, organizes this energy that brings about sufficient levels of entanglement and sufficient light darting about to highlight those clouds of entangled electrons. A single photon isn't energized enough to be perceived, but thousands of electrons entangled and then highlighted by the light are conceivably perceptible. There may well be another threshold, above absolute detection, where conscious awareness isn't merely activated, it's maximally activated. That's a moment of inspiration and typifies what we mean when we talk about the human soul. All of these are testable ideas if we take small successive steps.

The human soul is a network of peak conscious moments in life. We gain access to recall any of them when we're inspired again. That's because memory is context-specific, meaning that similar states of mind trigger memories of events that occurred while experiencing a similar state of mind or emotional lens.[13]

I remember the first time I became aware of my essential self. I was about five or six years old and riding one of those coin-operated horses in the grocery store while my mother shopped. Sitting there, I said to myself, "I am me...I am me." It was an "aha moment," a greatly energized feeling of awe, and it overwhelmed me. Looking back it reminds me of the famous quote by Rene Descartes: "Cogito, ego sum" which translates roughly into "I think, therefore I am."[14] So struck by the high-energy feeling associated with the "aha moment," it forever caused me to intuit that our raw consciousness is the brain creating some kind of new energy.

Ultra-weak photon emissions that highlight webs of entangled electrons in the conscious matrix, that's certainly a plausible candidate for being the spark of conscious awareness, or what Stuart Hameroff calls "bing."[15] And since there are no competing hypotheses that account for this phenomenon, quantum mind theory that posits entangled energy as a physical basis for the "human soul" is the best possible answer to date. And there are already reams of circumstantial evidence to support this theory.

The minds of men and women are an undeniable source of energy. Look at the great works of art, architecture, literature, and culture: What fueled all that? Nothing has been written, built, or otherwise constructed without first having been created in the mind of some artist, architect, or writer. But not created in the mind of man alone, as many of these artists attribute their creative works to divine inspiration. I agree. Moreover, we may be able to start exploring a scientific explanation for divine inspiration. We might be able to realistically describe the energy of the human mind and soul in scientific terms.

The current hypothesis presented here importantly includes the notion of entanglement. This physical phenomenon was unknown at the time of Epicurus, but interestingly he had the insight to look towards the small scale when explaining many phenomena that can't be seen with the naked eye. One thing interesting about the human brain is it has no nerves of its own, no pain fibers. Is the brain, at least in theory, capable of directly experiencing entanglement or traveling photons? And if you reflexively answer no, then my follow-up question is why not?

The mechanistic theory is that "brain experience" or consciousness is merely neurons firing off action potentials, at least according to the late Francis Crick.[16] Crick's idea has been proven largely false, or at least inadequate. Action potentials aren't conscious events as many occur in the complete absence of consciousness. Activity in the dendrites— where quantum entanglements occur in protein pockets—is more highly correlated with levels of consciousness and awareness.[17] And after we disentangle the brain's electrical responses to sensory inputs, most of the brain's electrical activity isn't correlated with consciousness.[18]

In further support of the present idea, a baseline consciousness or "human soul" is observable in the newborn or infant. Rather than being a "blank slate" with nothing stored upon it, activity recordings taken from the newborn's brain show all parts of cerebral cortex are active and able to participate in basic consciousness. The newborn human infant has one unified consciousness that melds all information about self and surroundings into one giant sense of awareness—with no reference to space or time. Some scientists argue from this example that the soul exists outside of space-time, and therefore is best explained by quantum mind theory.[19]

Although newborns have consciousness, they lack the ability to be reflective.[20] This is because newborns lack prior experience to reflect upon, and also because they're busy putting together all they hear, see, touch, taste, and smell into cohesive wholes. The way consciousness develops in the human infant shows how consciousness starts out as one unified whole. Then simple concepts form. Next, abstract concepts follow: our sense of self separates us from our perception of the environment. And finally we formulate concepts to explain what it all means. We start with one big idea, take it apart to examine all perspectives, and then put it back together again.

> **A thought to ponder:** The human soul is immortal. It achieves immortality through its connections with others and its connections with God.

The soul is present at birth, but when does it end, if it does end? Many of us have a sense that our souls are eternal. It may be an illusion, but an equally valid point of view is that we sense our soul's immortality because we "experience" a universal truth we don't yet understand. We simply can't talk about the human soul without discussing why so many believe in an afterlife. What happens after we die? We can't imagine the world without ourselves. Our perception of the world is that it certainly does continue after other people die, so it must continue after we die. But the world only exists as we perceive it in our minds, so our consciousness must persist—at least in some form, by some yet-to-be-discovered mechanism. Or so we believe.

While it could be that an afterlife is merely an illusion, billions of people believe there's more. And our brains have evolved over thousands of years to attain a good grasp of what's fundamentally real, and what's useful to our existence. Many people who have died and been resuscitated describe seeing a very bright light. Could this light be photons sending a final readout of the quantum entanglements to some distant receiver? This speculation might be testable at some future time, but not yet. And what would this accomplish, if anything?

If our consciousness consists of entanglements that transcend space and time, then maybe the notion of an afterlife isn't impossible at all. There are many examples of how the human spirit transcends death in the ordinary sense. People who live public lives or write books influence others. That influence will continue after they die. But not all people are highly influential or write books. Some people are mothers; and others are fathers. Some are teachers; others are doctors. An individual can outlive death by persisting in hearts and minds of others. That persistence of our soul past death can be triggered by our public deeds or by contributing to perceived archetypes.

Carl Jung described the "collective unconscious" consisting of universal archetypes.[21] This is where the persona transcends the individual and fuses into a unified prototype. For example, the universal depiction of "mother" is a collection of common features: loving, caring, and nurturing. So each woman who is a mother contributes a little to the collective unconscious idea of "mother." Quantum mind theory has tools to handle such a hypothetical concept. Through quantum entanglements of our own thoughts and actions with those of others we become part of a larger collective that enters consciousness through our unconscious preconceptions.

We can also interpret our eternal life as the connection we make to God. To the extent that our consciousness is based on quantum entanglements, especially our highest conscious connection to God, it's conceivable our souls are connected with the universe and will be connected with the universe for all eternity. As outlined in chapter 1, this hypothesis, or extended hypothesis, is falsifiable. Hence it's not out of the realm of scientific plausibility. I'll also discuss the possibility of a scientific explanation for an afterlife in Chapters 5 and 12. Our conscious matrix, or pieces of it, may exist in a larger physical matrix that includes billions of conscious matrices spanning all space and time. We simply don't know, but we have new science we can build upon. We can now speculate as to what might be possible. We can make educated and intelligent guesses.

> ***One last point to consider:*** *Every time we experience a conscious moment that existing quantum entanglement is destroyed. New entanglements that incorporate new information are formed de novo, replacing the old.*

We can make educated guesses about what the conscious matrix can do based on what we know about quantum communication, an exciting new field making real progress.[22] Secrecy is the advantage gained from using quantum encryption in communication. Any information sent is destroyed when observed, so nobody can spy on quantum-encrypted messages without getting caught. This suggests that everything we know is fleeting, destined to be updated an infinite number of times. Perhaps we'll never know everything about the universe. But perhaps we don't need to know it all to believe in it.

This begs the question: Is it necessary to know everything about a topic before you can experience "belief" in it? Clearly, our ancestors understood the beauty and meaning of objects that reflected light to our eyes, long before we knew the specifics of electromagnetic energies in the visible light spectrum. We too are awestruck by our experiences in the context of our connection to others and to the deeper meaning of the universe. We don't need to know everything about God to believe He exists. We sense, we experience, and we take pride in our ability to discern—even what's subtle—but nonetheless rings true. One valid scientific proof is that our experience of God is useful in our lives. If a routinely used concept is useful in our daily lives, then that's why we have that concept. The brain wouldn't evolve a profound sensitivity to any life-force or universal guiding principle, like God, if that universal concept wasn't representing something real.

The conscious matrix is the ultimate seeker and finder of "one-ness." It seeks unity across ideas, like monotheism out of polytheism. It unites space with time as easily as energy converts to mass. The conscious matrix is responsible for assembling together the human mind—consisting of both the breadth of human intelligence and the depth of the human spirit. Our conscious matrix unites us together, and it launches our spirit out to reach as far as is possible, uniting us with other people, and uniting us with our "one true God." The conscious matrix is both our means to understanding and what inspires us to seek greater understanding.

But if quantum systems destroy old ideas when creating new ideas, does that mean information is lost? No, because the new ideas elegantly incorporate the old ideas within them. That's the attractiveness of quantum mind theory. We're not subjugated to simple-minded ignorance; our conscious matrix doesn't ignore history or facts from the past. Instead, our conscious matrix uses artistry and simplicity to capture the essence of all things, and it has the further capacity to include all the complicated messy stuff into one beautifully-wrapped package. Truly, the conscious matrix is God's gift to us. And only one true God has the capacity to give that. As the Bible says in Timothy 1:7 (KJV), *"For God hath not given us the spirit of fear; but of power, and of love, and of a sound mind."*

CHAPTER 2: NOTES AND REFERENCES

1. Hamilton E. Mythology, Little, Brown, & Co. 1942

   Bulfinch T. Bulfinch's Mythology, Classic Books, 2008.

2. Woolf NJ. Global and serial neurons form a hierarchically arranged interface proposed to underlie memory and cognition. Neuroscience. 1996, 74(3):625-51.

3. Bhasin S, Kennedy JM, Niemeier M. Emotional expression on a profile: feature height, mouth angle, and tilt. Atten Percept Psychophys. 2010, 72(1):187-92.

4. Hawking SW. The Theory of Everything: The origin and fate of the universe. New Millennium Press, 2005.

5. Plato. Phaedo. Translated by David Gallop, Oxford Press, 1996, 2009.

6. Aristotle. On the Soul and On Memory and Recollection. Translated by Joe Sachs, Green Lion Press, 2001, 2004.

7. Laird JD. Feelings: The Perception of Self. Oxford Press, 2007.

8. Epicurius. The Essential Epicurus: Letters, Principal Doctrines, Vatican Sayings, and Fragments. Translated by Eugene M. O'Connor, The Big Nest, 2014.

9. Schwabl H, Klima H. Spontaneous ultraweak photon emission from biological systems and the endogenous light field. Forsch Komplementarmed Klass Naturheilkd. 2005, 12(2):84-9.

10. Unterman J. Justice for All: How the Jewish Bible Revolutionized Ethics, University of Nebraska Press, 2017.

    Newman CC, Davila JR, Lewis GS. (eds.). The Jewish Roots of Christological Monotheism: Papers from the St Andrews Conference on the Historical Origins of the Worship of Jesus. Baylor University Press, 2017.

11. St. Augustine of Hippo. On the Trinity. Translation by Hadden AJ. Veritatis Splendoris Publications, 2012.

12. Sahajananda JM. Fully Human- Fully Divine: Integral Dynamic Monotheism, a Meeting Point Between the Vedic Vision and the Vision of Christ. Partridge, 2014.

    Maller RA. Judaism and Islam as Synergistic Monotheisms: A Reform Rabbi's Reflections on the Profound Connectedness of Islam and Judaism, Hadassa Word Press, 2017

    Harvey P. Buddhism and Monotheism. Cambridge University Press, 2019.

13. Shields PJ, Rovee-Collier C. Long-term memory for context-specific category information at six months. Child Dev. 1992, 63(2):245-59.

14. Descarte R, Meditations on First Philosophy, 1641.

15. Hameroff S. The Future of Consciousness at TEDxTucson, April, 2013

16. Crick F. The Astonishing Hypothesis, 1994.

17. Hameroff S. The "conscious pilot"-dendritic synchrony moves through the brain to mediate consciousness. J Biol Phys. 2010, 36(1):71-93.

18. Rohaut B, Naccache L. Disentangling conscious from unconscious cognitive processing with event-related EEG potentials. Rev Neurol (Paris). 2017, 173(7-8):521-528.

19. Ceylan ME, Dönmez A, Ünsalver BÖ, Evrensel A, Kaya Yertutanol FD. The soul, as an uninhibited mental activity, is reduced into consciousness by rules of quantum physics. Integr Psychol Behav Sci. 2017, 51(4):582-597.

20. Lagercrantz H, Changeux JP. The emergence of human consciousness: from fetal to neonatal life. Pediatr Res. 2009, 65(3):255-60.

21. Hunt HT. A collective unconscious reconsidered: Jung's archetypal imagination in the light of contemporary psychology and social science. J Anal Psychol. 2012, 57(1):76-98.

22. Lala P. Quantum Computing. McGraw Hill, 2019.

3

WE PERCEIVE GOD THE FATHER AS OUR PROTECTOR AND CREATOR

QUANTUM MIND THEORY explains how the conscious matrix perceives or experiences God. The conscious matrix uses two powerful tools—superposition and entanglement—to connect us with the far reaches of the universe. We seek the highest principle in all things, and we're exceedingly gifted at perceiving what's real. Our phenomenal experience of God is most probably based on real physical properties of God. If God truly exists, either as some life-force or personification of that force, then it follows that conscious matrix has adapted to perceive this life-force and to experience God. We perceive God as all-loving. We talk about the "love of God," a special unconditional acceptance and approval that's difficult to get from other people or even from ourselves. "God the Father" sits at the top of the Christian Trinity. Judaism and Islam also depict God as a fatherly protector, and many religions call their adherents the "children of God."

Religion isn't just a college course people study for a few months and then throw away the textbook. Religion is part of many people's daily lives. Besides the repeated rituals and routines, certain life events have widely-practiced religious traditions. Most religions celebrate or memorialize the three major life events: birth, marriage, and death. Of the Trinity, God the Father is most closely associated with the first event: birth. The role of Father explicitly connects God to birth, childhood, and childlike vulnerability in adulthood. There's arguably a human need to believe in a supreme and mighty life-force when we're vulnerable. This belief ensures our survival through infancy, child development, and during adult challenges.

> **A thought to ponder:** *The human infant is born with a unified consciousness that's already connected to God and ready to connect to others. This readiness potential in the infant to "share conscious experience" with the parent or caregiver is necessary for long-lasting bonding.*

Each human being is conceived as a new and completely unique life. All our thoughts throughout our lives are completely unique and our own. No two people think exactly alike, not even identical twins developing from a single fertilized egg. Each brand-new and unique human life can only survive under protected conditions. The embryo and a fetus get that protection from the mother's womb. But after birth what happens? What does the newborn infant have to aid in his or her survival?

The newborn infant is born with a conscious matrix that's already connected with God. Each of us has at birth the most incredible human soul we'll ever possess. When a child is born, most parents can immediately sense the enormity of a new sentient being with them. The look in a newborn's eyes or their broad smile conveys an overwhelming sense of awe and joy that's ready to be shared with others. A brand new life has arrived that was not present the day before; it's an incredible awakening. I remember taking my newborn son, and then a year later my daughter, home from the hospital along with my husband. When we stepped out of the hospital into daylight it was like a brand-new world. My consciousness was elevated in a way I'd never before experienced. That feeling was shared between the three of us: mother, child, and father.

In nature, bonding occurs readily between mother and child. Specific hormones are triggered by the birthing process that switch on the mother's nurturing instincts.[1] These hormones, oxytocin and vasopressin, mediate cuddling and affection in both males and females. Accordingly, these hormones are important for building trust and they increase monogamous behavior. These hormones don't only enhance monogamy in human beings, other animals respond. Some strains of prairie voles are monogamous. These creatures mate for life, share a nest, tend to travel together, and often don't mate again if one of them dies. Oxytocin, vasopressin, and dopamine mediate this complex behavior in prairie voles.[2] But these hormones and chemical transmitters only trigger the behavior; chemicals aren't conscious and don't choose behaviors.

The magical phenomenon of consciousness requires electron particles sheltered inside neurons to entangle with photons, as described in Chapter 1. It's this entanglement that enables consciousness and entanglements that connect people with one another and with the universe. Chemicals may trigger bonding between parent and child, but bonding is the ability to share consciousness. Without the presence of a human soul, the newborn infant wouldn't be able to reach out to touch the soul of the caregiver. This all-important connection wouldn't occur, not even if one had buckets of oxytocin, vasopressin, or dopamine.

The conscious matrix of the newborn starts out as one with God, as needed for its early survival. The human soul is there in the child with little else to diminish its light. His or her pure and untarnished soul enables the infant to touch the soul of the caregiver. And it's well known that a failure to thrive may occur in the absence of sufficient bonding between infant and the mother, father, or other caregiver. This can happen when the child has an impoverished conscious awareness due to brain damage or disease. An unresponsive infant disrupts appropriate bonding between father, mother, and child. On the other hand, some parents are bereft of enough conscious awareness to function as effective parents. This may be because of mental incapacity, extreme poverty, or severe addiction. Particularly in countries where there are food shortages, insufficient nutrition can result in a child dying because the parents didn't provide.

Infants and small children sometimes die as a result of neglect. It's beyond sad to think about it. In the wide range of human experience, some circumstances are so harsh that few might be expected to survive. But the presence of God, that elevated and "enlightened" state of consciousness, can work miracles. Extended family members, people of the church community, and people from various charities may come to rescue a child who's starving or otherwise neglected. The conscious matrix of others sometimes will respond to those in need.

We see God's presence in most births, but why would a loving God let even a single child die? That's a long-standing question of religious skeptics and believers-in-doubt. There are no good answers. But we can instead focus on the children God does save. We can celebrate all those instances. We know of countless human-interest stories where people overcome very slim odds to accomplish the seemingly impossible, like saving a young infant. Yes, people do overcome huge obstacles, and this is typically because of an energized spirit in those so strengthened and inspired. That's evidence of God having a real impact on the human condition. God would probably save every child, if He could.

> **Another thought to ponder:** *A secondary purpose of "God the Father" is to provide support for a fatherless child, entangling the consciousness of the newborn with that of the community. This greater purpose may be one of the drivers of organized religion, insofar as God provides for people who are outcasts and have no home.*

The father's role is equally, if not more, important than that of the mother. In most patriarchal societies, it's the father who will be responsible for providing food and shelter for the mother and child. The father must bond in the absence of the hormones that are triggered in the mother by giving birth. It's here that a "consciousness of God" offers a clear-cut survival advantage. Evolution enabled the conscious matrix to detect the presence of God, particularly at the time of a new birth. The father may be overwhelmed and frightened, but in most instances, he'll happily accept this awesome responsibility.

So besides aiding in the bonding of father to child, another function served by the presence of God is to provide for the fatherless child. If for some reason the biological father doesn't step up to the plate and take responsibility for the child, oftentimes another man will. If no other man will assume responsibility for the child, that child will still be God's child.

We hear that common phrase we're all "children of God." It means all will be provided for regardless of our circumstances. We need not worry; we need not fear; God will provide. We believe God is the Father of all children. The Bible says in 1 John 4:4 (ESV), "*Little children, you are from God and have overcome them, for he who is in you is greater than he who is in the world.*" And Psalm 103:13 (NIV) says, "*As a father has compassion on his children, so the Lord has compassion on those who fear him.*" God will take care of us as long as we respect Him.

When our children were very young, we belonged to an Anglican church in Los Angeles and that's where our children were baptized. In one of the Christmas-season sermons, the Reverend presented a beautiful interpretation of the virgin birth of Christ. Her idea was you didn't need to literally believe the Biblical story of the nativity to be in awe of its majesty. If Jesus was without a father who would claim him, why destroy his destiny by declaring it? Why not accept a miracle instead? That we're all "children of God," is just another way of saying the community will step in and provide, or God will provide. There's always a way, and no one need despair and fear complete abandonment.

Just as a child needs protection, adults need God's protection when they're vulnerable to harm. When a group of people are being persecuted, they often seek God's help to protect them and lead them out of danger. This is illustrated many times over in the history of the Jewish people. Many biblical stories of the Old Testament tell of the unbreakable bond between the Jewish people and God. When the tides turn against them, God provides as the Jews flee Egypt heading for Mt. Sinai. Centuries later, Jews credit God again for protecting them as they flee persecution throughout Europe. Many ask: If God is just and all-loving, why does He allow persecution in the first place? Unfortunately, bad things can happen to good people. When misfortune falls upon us is precisely when we need our faith most.

I'll address this issue more in Chapter 7. But for now, quantum mind theory does predict a solution to this age-old conundrum of how a loving and protective God can allow bad things to happen to good people. The answer lies in connection. God connects directly to us and provides guidance. But we choose our own path, and that's how it's supposed to be. If we choose the wrong path, God provides us with an opportunity to benefit from that experience and choose more wisely in the future. We have the opportunity to learn. But if we don't learn, God's guidance will resurface to aid us again. If we repeatedly ignore history, we'll repeatedly fail to benefit from God's advice. But He'll continue to guide us anyway. It's in our best interest to listen to God as soon as we hear His advice. But even when we do heed God's advice, we have no guarantee that life will work out. Life is complicated. We can't always see the "big picture," but God sees it and tries to help us see it too. So when bad things happen, it's not God's fault. He's usually warned us, or it's the case that the effects on someone else are more devastating, and that obstructed His helping us first.

Belief in God not only provides protection for small children, God is a concept with great utility for all men and women. God keeps people strong and energizes their will to survive, particularly when times are difficult or worse. People who learn about God as children will always have the option to rekindle those beliefs and survive, rather than abandon faith and perhaps die. But at any age, people are invited by most organized religions to join and share in that belief system.

Moreover, no person needs to depend on any organized religion to connect with God. Each human being is capable of finding God through their conscious matrix. All one needs to do is accept their ability to experience God and to believe their perception of a life-force, however that takes form, is their personal portal to God. The architecture of the conscious matrix is already there in our brain anatomy. We just have to let the conscious matrix connect through quantum entanglements to a solution that will lead us out of frustration, away from danger and to safety. We only have to let success and survival happen; our brain is pre-wired to pursue it.

Is our conscious matrix infallible? Of course not, but that it works at all is miraculous enough. God is infallible, but that means sometimes having to say "No" or "I'm busy elsewhere." And we wouldn't want it any other way. All of humanity loves to rise to the occasion and show God we're worthy of our connection to Him.

> ***An idea to examine:*** *Our ability to fully experience God as our fatherly protector lessens our anxieties and fears. This belief also inoculates us from psychological pain.*

Believing in God creates many positive psychological benefits because it puts our unresolved issues in a "box" so we can move on to new problems. The conscious matrix puts a period—or a comma, semicolon, or colon—at the end of each problem-solving session and stores a progress report in memory. This allows us to get back to the tougher problems in our lives at a later time. We have a memory of what's been done already and can pick up where we left off. Our anxiety is lessened when we trust in God and in ourselves to solve our problems. He gives us the strength to deal with them. As stated in 1 Peter 5:7 (NIV), *"Cast all your anxiety on Him because He cares for you."*

Young and old, fear is one of our biggest obstacles in life. Neuroscience has dissected and defined what fear is. Fear is an emotional response triggered by an aversive stimulus that arouses the sympathetic nervous system.[4] Sympathetic arousal is what causes our heart to race, our blood pressure to increase, and a surge of energy to mobilize our muscles to action. It's also called the "fight or flight" response. We try to avoid aversive or negative situations out of fear. But when forced to face a threat or challenge that's inevitable, we'll either fight our adversary or run away. To live in constant fear or a state of hypervigilance isn't healthy. Chronic stress increases circulating levels of hormones such as cortisol, which can eventually cause high blood pressure and organ damage.[5]

Our belief in God helps us cope with fear. Fear is a chief driver of human behavior throughout life. Most small children fear abandonment—not only being separated from a parent or caregiver, but also the loss of an object like a toy. Jean Piaget, the famous French psychologist, discovered how the child's mind develops in discrete stages.[3] Piaget studied the mistakes children commonly make to determine when conceptual abilities first appear. Very young children have no way of knowing that an object suddenly hidden from their view still exists. Piaget identified a phenomenon called "object permanence," which appears at around 6 months. Before that age, infants are inconsolable when a toy or other object is hidden from view. It takes several months for infants to learn that "out of sight" is temporary and that most often objects hidden from view are still there behind the curtain.

Abandonment isn't the only thing feared. Children have both rational and irrational fears. Young children seem to know they're incredibly vulnerable and display a readiness to accept God as an idealized parent figure, the Father. Many modern parents teach their children about God and take their young children to special religious study sessions, like Sunday school classes in the Christian churches. In these settings, children learn about God, how God loves them, and how God will protect them throughout their lives. This early training gives many adherents a lifelong feeling of joy, along with a proven way to cope with fear and feelings of abandonment. One song I remember learning as a child is "Jesus Loves Me." Years later, as an adult struggling with feelings of abandonment, I sang myself to sleep with that song. It worked beautifully because it transported me to a very memorable state of mind that once brought me enormous emotional comfort.

The growing child continues to need varying degrees of protection and nurturing until maturity. During the first ten to twelve years of life, a child needs extensive supervision from parents or caregivers to make some decisions for the child—to guide them. It's also during middle childhood that views about God develop more fully.[6] How a child views God gradually morphs into what will be the adult view. But all along the way, experiencing God in whatever way available helps to quell the child's fear of real or imagined danger and the fear of the unknown.

Older children and adults fear more subtle threats, such as social rejection. Social rejection can be a painful experience. Recent neuroscience research shows how social pain activates many of the same brain centers that are active when injury causes physical pain.[7] Social rejection, like pain due to injury, elicits an immediate withdrawal or escape response. It's important not to let social stress cause us to withdraw from social activities. We need instead to focus on learning new social skills. When we feel loved by God, it gives us strength and courage to face social situations and learn to improve our social skills. This Bible quote is known for giving comfort: Isaiah 40:31 (NIV), *"But those who hope in the Lord will renew their strength. They will soar on wings like eagles; they will run and not grow weary, they will walk and not be faint."*

Another idea to examine: *Our belief in God allows us to learn from fear rather than being paralyzed by it. Firstly, our conscious matrix seeks connection with others to keep us safe. Secondly, our conscious matrix has the capacity to store memories about feared objects. We can then retrieve those memories to avoid feared objects, cope with threat, and ultimately overcome the danger posed.*

Like young children, grown adults can't function optimally without spirit, hope, and faith. We're a community-bound people; we seek out others as a source of added protection. People are social animals, and we heavily depend on others to function optimally and to remain psychologically calm in the face of danger. Religious beliefs and practices celebrate and reinforce the glorious feeling of being bound to others in a community. But what accounts for those elevated feelings one gets when worshiping God with others?

Quantum mind theory offers some explanation for many religious practices and beliefs. Conscious experience is awe-inspiring by definition. Each concept is a genuine "aha moment" when first realized. But not all thoughts are spiritually uplifting, especially when encountered regularly. We quickly habituate to all the beauty that surrounds us. We discount our blessings without gentle reminders of how lucky we are. Religious practice in groups reignites those feelings of awe and directs our thoughts towards high-mindedness, and the group reinforces this elevated experience. Experiencing God in a group garners extra power, further inoculating people from fear and protecting them from suffering the pain of social rejection.

Our belief in God also gives us the courage to look danger in the eye long enough to learn something useful for future reference. If, for example, we're looking at a stranger's face, we see the patterns in the reflected light that are processed through our eyes and finally reach the visual cortex. Next, neurons in our cerebral cortex search for a match with a stored copy of a familiar face, much like facial recognition software does today. This search involves the superposition of quantum states. Reduction occurs when a match is found. But if there's no match, we'll categorize the face as a stranger.

Next, we'll assess the facial expression of the stranger to determine if they mean us harm. When we encounter a feared stimulus such as an angry face or loud noise, this triggers sympathetic arousal—the fight or flight response. Sympathetic arousal inhibits gastric acid production in the stomach—our gut gets a queasy feeling. We might also experience an increase in heart rate and blood pressure. This makes us feel "keyed up." We're ready to learn in this state; we'll absorb information like a sponge.

Why do we bother to learn about things we fear? Why not just run away? We learn because we don't want to run every time we see the face of a stranger who's not smiling. After all, we don't want to always trigger a full-blown fight or flight response. We want to save our energy for real emergencies. So instead of running, we learn a concept to shut it down. The conscious matrix is capable of storing trillions upon trillions of thoughts and concepts. We could argue that any number of these thoughts or concepts could have purpose or utility. God is arguably the most effective calming-concept enabling the human mind to compartmentalize any conflict and move on. The experience of God as an all-loving, all-knowing being has power like no other concept the human mind can experience.

Quantum mind theory enables one to explain how the brain stores memory in a way that ties it to consciousness. We remember our experiences by reactivating a structural matrix deep inside neurons, the physical architecture of the conscious matrix. This structural matrix serves as a "freeze-frame" or snapshot of activation patterns among neurons.[8] At any moment in time, billions of neurons are responding to trillions of inputs. Much of this activity is filtered out. But some activity gets amplified. Passing a certain threshold of energy entangled in the meshwork of filaments inside neurons activates photons in the conscious matrix. The conscious matrix exists slightly removed from the connections between neurons. It has to be arranged like this because quantum entanglements are too delicate to occur at the synapse level. Synapses are far too noisy.

Traditional neuroscience posits that consciousness results directly from synaptic activity, and this rules out delicate quantum states from the equation. This is exactly where the quantum mind model diverges from traditional neuroscience views. Instead of consciousness occurring at synapses, the quantum mind matrix consists of subatomic particles protected in pockets located deep within structural proteins.

As outlined in Chapter 1, photons travel along these structural proteins, using them like waveguides, and this enables entanglement. The theory then says a critical number of particles become entangled, superposition of quantum states provides a selection of choices, and eventually the quantum state reduces, a choice is made, and this is perceived as a conscious experience.[9] The conscious experience punctuates the end of the thought; it can be thought of as the period at the end of the sentence. It also clears the mind for the next thought. The end result is a continuous stream of consciousness we experience throughout our entire lifetime.

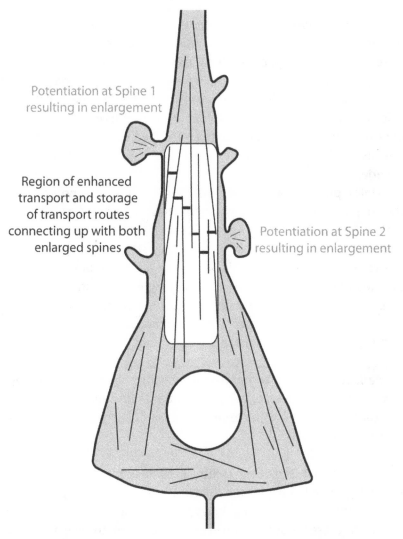

Potentiation at Spine 1
resulting in enlargement

Region of enhanced
transport and storage
of transport routes
connecting up with both
enlarged spines

Potentiation at Spine 2
resulting in enlargement

Quantum mind theory predicts that entanglement alters the architecture in the conscious matrix that "preserves in memory" the co-activation of two synapses. (Reprinted from ref. 10)

But is the quantum entanglement arising in the conscious matrix the stored memory? The answer is no, the entanglement is transient and can't persist indefinitely. But the conscious matrix is capable of storing an architecture that will support a similar entanglement in the future. The conscious matrix is an extensive network deep inside neurons.

Acting as the "inner eye" of the neuron, the conscious matrix captures endless patterns of neural activity. Learning and memory sculpt a physical change in the conscious matrix. Laying down a memory is like taking a still photograph of one moment in time—a solitary experience. Then when we later remember those past experiences, once-entangled particles within our neurons are read-out again. Our "present-state matrix" entangles with a "past-state matrix." The two matrices fuse into one new experience, or more precisely, a new snapshot of that revisited experience.

Unlike photographs we take with cameras, the snapshots stored in the conscious matrix are living records that are updated each time we look at them. We know that a new memory must be recreated each time because in quantum computing, previously stored entanglements are destroyed when observed. This means our memories are continuously updated to include new information. Our experiences are continuously upgraded. Starting from birth and possibly ending never, our conscious matrix stores a lifetime of memories—a cumulative succession of understandings, with each level more profound than the last.

> *One last possibility to ponder:* A newborn child comes already connected to God. Over the years, the human soul is sculpted to accept more ideas about God. We learn about the mind of God throughout life.

The idea that God is our creator predates monotheism. Whereas the biological father begets the child in the flesh, could the child's mind or soul come from God? Why do we have this intuition that God is our father? All these questions swirl in our conscious matrix and might even puzzle us throughout our lives.

There's virtually never any doubt who's the child's mother at birth. But the identity of the father has always been an educated guess. Before there were paternity tests to compare father and son's DNA, there was no sure-fire way to be certain of the biological father's identity. Sometimes it might be obvious that the presumed father wasn't the biological father, for example, if the race of the father didn't match that of the child. But in many instances, it's next to impossible to tell without a paternal DNA test.

The one religious tenet most skeptics cast doubt on is the Immaculate Conception of Jesus Christ. Some skeptics find this story implausible, and use it to discredit all further Christian belief. But what the skeptics fail to appreciate is how it's the moral of the story that's important. It's a provable fact people weren't absolutely certain of how fertilization and conception worked until the late nineteenth century. At the very least, these skeptics are being harsh in their criticism given that it wasn't uncommon to believe a virgin birth might be possible at the time the story was written. How many faulty theories have scientists had to revise over the centuries? And I dare not question the veracity of this Bible story; that would be hugely disrespectful to millions of believers. That's beside the point I'm trying to make.

My point is only to consider other possible interpretations. One possible interpretation is that when we say "God is the creator of man," we're really talking about the creator of our conscious matrix—creator of our souls, not our bodies. This is where interpretations get tricky. If the conscious matrix is merely a product of our brain, then God has no fatherly place in our creation, mind or body. But what if, as quantum mind theory would suggest, our human soul is equivalent to peak experiences mediated by the conscious matrix, which are already entangled with some fundamental life-force at birth, or what most people call God? That would mean our conscious matrix is quite possibly entangled with God from conception or earlier. A newborn infant has consciousness written deeply into his or her eyes or infectious smile. Infants are born to connect. If God created our conscious matrix, then He is indeed forever connected to us through it and He is rightly our father and creator, not only metaphorically, but literally.

During one's lifetime, the body and mind are inextricably linked. Our human consciousness is revised over and over again with each new experience. But in the end, we're reduced to the essential consciousness with which we're born. Where this conscious energy goes next is still a mystery. If, for the sake of the argument, we view ourselves more as souls than as bodies, then one can make a solid case for our souls being created by God. If we're created in God's image, and that reference is mainly concerning our mind and soul, then what is the mind of God like?

Researchers have discovered differences in how children and adults view the mind of God.[11] Adults have different "implied" versus "expressed" views. Young children express views on the mind of God that adults only imply indirectly. For example, children believe God is all-knowing in the sense that God can literally see and hear everything going on in the mind of any child. A child sees God almost as a person with magical powers. As a child gets older, their views on God start to gradually change. Adults see God more abstractly, at least in their descriptions. Adults view the mind of God to be similar to, but separate from, the human mind. Adults recognize that God's mind is infallible and omnipresent, whereas our minds have limits.

These different beliefs yield different practical outcomes. The very young child tells God everything. The adult might hold a few things back, but fully realizes God eventually will find out. This trend towards decreased disclosure suggests our earliest experience of God might be the purest experience. This would mean our first experiences of God will serve as a lifelong "ultimate-peak-experience" point of reference. As the child matures into adulthood, real life experience become more ordinary and mundane as history repeats itself. It takes self-reflection and religious practice for older children and adults to relive and regain the intensity of their youthful experience of God.

We shape our attitudes and ideas about God over the course of our lifetimes. And for the most part, organized religions dedicate themselves to discovering how to best increase our willingness to be open to the experience of God. Most theologies praise introspection; theologians encourage looking inward for answers. Science takes the nearly opposite course. Psychology, as a science, condemns introspection as a flawed method. Instead of inner reflection, science is based on hypothesis, followed by testing, followed by interpretation. But when arguing what's better—science or religion—we go full circle to reach quantum physics. At the quantum level, the observer is inextricably linked to the matter under observation. If the conscious matrix is observing natural phenomena, then it's fundamentally linked to those phenomena in unity.

We've been taught that God's mind is like ours, except He has more answers. And what we come to learn in life bears out this truth. We come to see our limits time and again. And we seek His infinite wisdom time and again, and our prayers are answered. Solutions come in due time.

CHAPTER 3: NOTES AND REFERENCES

1. Carter CS. The role of oxytocin and vasopressin in attachment. Psychodyn Psychiatry. 2017, 45(4):499-517.

    Carter CS. Neuroendocrine perspectives on social attachment and love. Psychoneuroendocrinology. 1998, 23(8):779-818.

2. Young KA, Liu Y, Wang Z. The neurobiology of social attachment: A comparative approach to behavioral, neuroanatomical, and neuro-chemical studies. Comp Biochem Physiol C Toxicol Pharmacol. 2008, 148(4):401-10.

3. Piaget J, Inhelder B. The Psychology of The Child. Basic Books, 1969, 2000.

4. Kozlowska K, Walker P, McLean L, Carrive P. Fear and the defense cascade: Clinical implications and management. Harv Rev Psychiatry. 2015, 23(4):263-87.

5. Rodrigues SM, LeDoux JE, Sapolsky RM. The influence of stress hormones on fear circuitry. Annu Rev Neurosci. 2009, 32:289-313.

6. Heiphetz L, Lane JD, Waytz A, Young LL. How children and adults represent God's mind. Cogn Sci. 2016, 40(1):121-44.

7. Eisenberger NI. The pain of social disconnection: examining the shared neural underpinnings of physical and social pain. Nat Rev Neurosci. 2012, 13(6):421-34.

8. Woolf NJ. A structural basis for memory storage in mammals. Prog Neurobiol. 1998, 55(1):59-77.

    Woolf NJ. Microtubules in the cerebral cortex: role in memory and consciousness. In: Tuszynski, J. (ed.) The Emerging Physics of Consciousness. Springer, Berlin, 2006.

9. Woolf NJ, Hameroff SR. A quantum approach to visual consciousness. Trends Cogn Sci. 2001, 5(11):472-478.

    Hameroff SR, Penrose R. Orchestrated reduction of quantum coherence in brain microtubules: a model for consciousness. In SR Hameroff, AW Kaszniak, AC Scott (Eds.), Toward a science of consciousness; the first Tucson discussions and debates, MIT Press, Cambridge (1996), pp. 507-540.

10. Woolf NJ, Priel A, Tuszynski JA. Nanoneuroscience: Structural and Functional Roles of the Neuronal Cytoskeleton in Health and Disease, Elsevier, 2009.

11. Nyhof MA, Johnson CN. Is God just a big person? Children's conceptions of God across cultures and religious traditions. Br J Dev Psychol. 2017, 35(1):60-75.

    Richert RA, Saide AR, Lesage KA, Shaman NJ. The role of religious context in children's differentiation between God's mind and human minds. Br J Dev Psychol. 2017, 35(1):37-59.

JESUS CHRIST DIED TO ASSURE US IMMORTALITY

THROUGHOUT THE AGES, all of humanity has struggled with the fact that we live only to die. Some of us only see hard work until the day we die, and it's a bitter pill to swallow. We know what happens to the flesh, but we yearn to know what happens in our conscious matrix when we die. What happens to the human soul?

Billions of human souls cherish their personal experiences of God to give them the faith—the belief that it's all worth it. And through our beliefs, the "faithful" gain a glimpse of a wondrous afterlife. Hindus and Buddhists believe in reincarnation, where the soul passes to another living being—to a different person or different kind of animal. Christianity and Islam teach that the soul goes to heaven if the person is right with God. Christian teachings of Jesus Christ reveal much about what will happen after death, if one's a believer.

The entire New Testament of the Christian Bible is dedicated to the teachings of Christ. Many books have been written that attempt to interpret these biblical passages. In one such book, *The Passion of Jesus Christ: Fifty Reasons Why He Came to Die,* John Piper lists over fifty reasons why Christ died for our sins.[1] Among these reasons, Jesus had to die in order to be resurrected. It couldn't have happened unless he suffered painful persecution and death. Jesus died to show people how much he loved us, and to tell us God will forgive us all sins if we believe. But most amazingly, Jesus promises we'll meet God in heaven and live with Him forever. That Jesus died for our sins and to grant us immortality seems contradictory and requires all the reasoning power our conscious matrix can muster. How can death result in life? Who can understand these kinds of ideas?

Those who study theology address these kinds of questions. For centuries, higher-learning institutions—the colleges and universities—put equal emphasis on the humanities and the sciences. But today there's a trend to convert the humanities into social sciences, and to all but eliminate theology. The Ivy League Divinity Schools (Harvard, Dartmouth, Yale, Princeton, Brown, and University of Pennsylvania) have become modern to the extent that many divinity professors are no longer even religious. The result is science dictates our philosophical thinking. But is science the correct discipline to interpret the humanities? Is science prepared to dictate theology? Was mankind meant to be one polarized, single-minded, group-think population?

Psychology, as a discipline, takes a mechanistic view of how most people will behave in one situation or another. Psychologists typically study behavior in well-controlled experiments that only reveal responses in those specific situations. Even psychological inquiry that relies on naturalistic observations has its limitations. It's not always clear how results from psychological investigations apply to real-life situations; and in many cases, they don't apply. People encounter situations in real life that are quite varied, and each new situation presents an entirely novel set of challenges.

Theology, although not an experimental science, is an academic discipline very much devoted to examining human behavior in the real world. Theology far outstrips psychology in its relevance. Theology examines human responses to life's most difficult challenges. Theology involves introspective reflective thought, whereas psychology forbids it. The two disciplines are at odds from the start, beginning with their mission statements. And sometimes life requires introspection. It's what people do, especially when life gets difficult.

Quantum mind theory is a scientific approach to understanding how people think. And it opens the door to introspection because in quantum systems, the observer is an integral part of the system. Quantum mind theory predicts that the human soul is the above-threshold activation or "enlightenment" of the conscious matrix. If this theory proves correct, then perhaps theologians are best equipped to study the workings of the conscious matrix system, not psychologists. We still have a lot to learn about how one person's soul connects with the soul of another, how our souls ultimately connect to God, and how our souls might persist after death.

> **A thought to ponder:** Our belief that "God will grant us immortality" motivates us to perfect our behavior. It motivates us to entangle our present conscious state with a "perfect behavior" goal state, despite our admitted shortcomings.

We know that as human beings we are flawed, we are imperfect, and we make mistakes. We aim to improve our behavior to maximally enhance our survival, while taking care not to hurt others. To this end, one purpose of believing in God is to visualize "ideal behavior." When we experience God in our lives by practicing a religion, meditating, or simply acting ethically or morally, we're able to imagine and imitate perfect behavior.

Most people believe that if you live a good life—obey the rules and follow the laws—you'll earn eternal contentment in the afterlife. Life reinforces this lesson over and again. When we behave appropriately in situation X, we're rewarded with Y. If we don't behave, we're punished with Z. Learning works and behavior adapts. But we can only learn so many cause-and-effect relationships, so we seek rules that apply to general situations. The golden rule is to treat others as we'd like to be treated. Life tends to throw us constant curve balls in which unseen circumstances continuously arise. We cope with life by generating personal rules of behavior that are flexible enough to apply to diverse situations. We might learn how to perfect our moral behavior, but the concept of fairness initially comes from within our conscious matrix. We generally know the right thing to do, as the Bible says in James 4:17 (ESV). *"So whoever knows the right thing to do and fails to do it, for him it is sin."*

Whereas psychology explains behavior in a stimulus-response manner, theologians emphasize the human being having an inner conscience. That inner conscience is built into the conscious matrix at its highest level. As mentioned in earlier chapters, our brains are hierarchically organized. Sensory information comes in through multiple channels to reach the cerebral cortex and then is passed on to higher levels. Each higher level is capable of conscious realization of something more abstract. We go from reading letters and words on a page to abstracting their meaning, comprehending a story, and finally understanding the implications or the "moral" of the story. These highest abstract concepts are only realized because our brains have evolved a particular structure that enables language, symbolism, and higher moral principles. The template for this understanding is already there. We're born with a conscious matrix that is pre-loaded with a few software packages.

> **Another thought to ponder:** People are able to calm themselves by imagining a "perfect place" called heaven.

Quantum mind theory suggests that whenever our conscious matrix imagines this perfect place where there's no conflict, we gain a moment of peace, a quieting of the mind. Heaven on earth is a state of mind, a calm and tranquil place to entangle our consciousness with the universal oneness. Heaven is also where we envision our loved ones go when they die. We imagine seeing our loved ones in heaven someday, and that helps us cope with loss and move on.

Regarding the afterlife, scientists and religious skeptics can't prove the entanglements our minds and souls make with other particles in the universe don't survive our death. Nor can they prove our souls don't entangle once again with pieces of the souls of our loved ones. It's theoretically possible; we just haven't explored these possibilities or developed the appropriate scientific jargon to discuss these possibilities in any detail. No one would have believed in biblical times that paternity DNA tests would be invented. Yet we're embarking on science that can resolve paternity questions long after the father's death from decades-old saliva samples on saved envelopes.[2] Will we soon be able to do paternity tests on remains from people who lived millennia ago?

In fact, there's simple proof that our souls do stay entangled with others after our death. We live on many years after death in the hearts and minds of our loved ones because our conscious matrices have entangled with theirs. Certainly, one can argue those are just old memories. But when our loved ones get together, remember us and talk about us, that process creates new entanglements in which we're further extended in time forward. Belief in religious prophets—Muhammad for Muslims—or belief in the son of God, Jesus Christ, for Christians—ensures eternal life for followers and believers. As populations of religious adherents grow and continue to worship, so too does the size of the collective entanglement. Belief is enlightenment in the conscious matrix; and it has the intrinsic energy to perpetuate a deceased person's strong beliefs past their death, possibly forever.

The human mind faces many struggles in life. The discipline of psychology teaches us to label emotional discomfort and restlessness of thought as disorder or disease. We have countless diagnoses today of anxiety disorders, depression, attention deficit disorders, posttraumatic stress disorder, just to name a few. Typically, the remedy is to take a medication that alters the levels of neurotransmitters. This approach has proven successful when the mental condition is severe. For example, antidepressant drugs do improve mood in severe depression. However, it's becoming increasingly clear that antidepressants do little more than serve as a placebo for mild depression.[3] Our conscious matrix needs healing sometimes, and a pill can't do that.

The theological route to understanding human suffering and struggle is introspection. If we believe the human mind is little more than connected neurons that spew chemicals in response to stimuli, then it follows that introspection wouldn't yield any useful result. But we reach a much different conclusion if we view the human mind and soul as an incredible instrument that's remarkably accurate in its ability to sense the deeper order of the universe. Scientists would do well to ponder how on earth they come up with their hypotheses, some of which are profoundly brilliant, if their minds and souls are little more than machines? Perhaps they think God lives only within them or that they are God. Ordinary people know better.

> *A possibility to consider: We all live forever in the hearts and minds of others. The entanglements we make with other people survive long after the death of our bodies. This is analogous to pieces of our soul dispersing throughout the universe.*

We remember our loved ones long after they die. They become a part of us. I remember the first time I realized my mother might someday die. I was about four or five years old, trying to fall asleep at my grand-mother's house while looking around the dark room. My grandmother had some odd pictures on the wall. I could barely make out the images, but in full daylight it was clear the picture was of two ladies sitting in fine long dresses with long sashes hanging down embellished with tassels. In the darkness, and in my very young mind, it looked like the ladies had very thin legs, and they looked sickly. "Oh no," I thought in agony, "My mother might get sick someday and die. What will I do?"

My mother was (and still is) the dearest, sweetest person I've ever met. I couldn't imagine living without her. Long after I forgot that childish fear, thirty-some years later, my mother was taken with breast cancer that metastasized to her brain and eventually caused her death. My heart was broken, and I was stricken with grief upon learning my mother would likely die soon. Immediately, I remembered my childhood fear. It was a silly fear, but it became a reality many decades later. It took two years for my mother to die, and during that time I was able to cope with the inevitable. Since I was married and had two children of my own, there was plenty to keep me busy. Still, no one would take the place of my mother, whom I loved and still love dearly. Even though we didn't often have a chance to talk, she was and has remained always present in my heart.

At the time my mother died, I was already a professor and researcher in neuroscience. I was researching the molecular basis of learning and memory. We'd just discovered how experience alters the organization of microtubules in brain cells, serving as a memory storage mechanism we now call the "conscious matrix." It occurred to me my mother would never leave me, that she'd live forever in my heart and in my mind, stored permanently in my conscious matrix. This scientific knowledge gave me comfort. And the more I thought about it, the more I concluded she really would still be with me. It wasn't just some sentimental meta-phor. Since I already lived in a different city from my mother, and I only talked to her occasionally, it really wouldn't be all that much different when she died. All of what she meant to me existed in my conscious matrix. Nothing physical, not even her death, would take away that exhil-arating feeling of love and bonding. It's been twenty-five years since my mother passed away, and I still agree with this conclusion. I don't need to look at endless pictures of my mother. To me pictures are less precious than the memories of the feelings. In my mind and in my consciousness, I can still experience my mother just like I did when she was alive. Loving and knowing a person is to experience their soul, the "essence" of that person, even in their absence. My mother's soul lives on after her death. I'm living proof of that.

Another example of people living after their death is when someone is reconstituted by a biographer or screenplay writer who writes a book or makes a movie about that person. Most of the time, books and movies are only created about people who accomplish great deeds (or infamous people who commit great wrongs) or people who are particularly beautiful, talented, or in some other way remarkable. But how does the woman who was a wonderful mother live for all eternity? She may have rarely gone out of her house, instead staying home to cook, clean, and care for her family.

Many people love their mothers as much as I do. The "universal mother" is one of Carl Jung's archetypes that's stored in the collective unconscious.[4] Each person's love of their mother energizes that collective unconscious archetype. This shared experience has real power; it's a game-changer and life-giver. To the extent that individual consciousness might be entangled light energy emitted in complete darkness of the skull-encased brain, the collective unconscious might be gazillions of tiny lights flickering eternally in the boundaries of space-time, like endless arrays of candles lit for a night-time vigil.

There are some in the artificial intelligence community who believe that "someday" we'll be able to upload our consciousness onto a computer. If that's ever possible, we might then be able to insert the "consciousness template" of that particular person into a new person. That person even could be a clone of the original made out of that person's harvested DNA. Perhaps all this will be possible someday. DNA encodes intergenerational information, a sequence map for every specific protein making up that person. But the conscious matrix, made of filaments, enables us to retrieve the memories of a lifetime. That's all our intrapersonal and interpersonal information, an entire encyclopedia of our mind stored in a matrix.

The conscious matrix provides a physical framework to house memories and create archival histories. Could a quantum computer in the future capture all this quantum information stored? Could it be a copy of the entirety of our mind, our living soul? Your guess is as good as mine, and only time will tell us the answer. By combining current technologies with those of the future, can we ever expect to upload a person's conscious mind and insert that information into a clone of that person's body? Will we ever be able to artificially reproduce a person and their mind? And, even if we could, would we ever want to do that?

We already know identical twins who share nearly the same DNA aren't clones of one another. Twins may think alike, but they're separate people who have unique thoughts and memories. But cloning is possible and, for the sake of argument, let's imagine cloning an identical copy of a person named John. Then let's upload John's conscious matrix at age forty. John's conscious matrix at this point in his life would likely have an architecture supporting over a gazillion quantum entanglements. We'd likely need a quantum supercomputer to upload and store all this information, but let's assume we could. Then we'd need a technology to transfer the uploaded information onto the clone's brain tissue. If we did all that, would the newly assembled person be John? Would this newly created person have John's soul? If John had a wife, would she recognize the uploaded clone as her husband?

And let's look down the road a bit. Let's speculate that the new John clone was in every way the same as John at the time of upload. The clone felt like John; he acted like John; he had John's "essence" captured down to the smallest detail; he even fooled John's wife. Even if all this were true, would the John clone still be an identical replica of the original John one year later? For John's clone at forty-one years old to match the original John at age forty-one, all their experiences would've had to be identical during the past year. Identical lives for one year would be impossible to duplicate; too much goes on during one year to render the two Johns to remain exactly the same one year out. Such an undertaking, even if possible, would be absurd. This example is likely to forever remain just a thought experiment. Apart from the fact it would be nearly impossible to repeat John's life and experiences, there's no need. What purpose would it serve to duplicate John for a few moments? John and all his experiences occurred once. One existence; one life is enough of a miracle. One life is all that's needed.

Let's try going down a different road. If we accept that our minds and our souls live in a quantum realm, it means our inner reality exists at the quantum level, where space and time are irrelevant. Therefore, it's conceivable we're all immortal in an infinite space-time. Our souls may, in all reality, last forever. Once released from our mortal bodies, our souls may be capable of jumping or leaping from universe to universe, in a "multiverse" of human souls.[5] Or it may be quite simple. We may be immortal in our own minds, and since that's the only reality we'll ever know, we may exist for all eternity in the sense that we'll never experience "not" being alive. And then again, maybe it isn't important to know what happens after we die. Maybe we waste a lot of time contemplating the future when we don't have enough understanding to propose a sufficiently advanced concept. What faith brings to the table is an acceptance that even though we don't know everything, that's okay. It's okay not to know what's going to happen next. We can enjoy the moments we have now.

The big question is: Can our soul survive death and remain intact? That's the Christian story of Jesus' resurrection. Jesus rose on the third day and his soul was reunited with God the Father in Heaven. Some Christians read this story as a metaphor meaning good people rise up in the end: if you've lived a good life, you'll be remembered and forever held in high esteem by all who knew and loved you. Other Christians believe the story of resurrection literally. Who's right? We can't say definitively. The sum total of quantum entanglements stored in the brain proteins upon death could move or somehow attach to some force field. We simply don't know. When the brain dies, the proteins start to deteriorate. Dead brain cells no longer emit ultra-weak photons, so no new entanglements are possible. But where do the previously stored entanglements and their energies go? We simply don't know. But many believe in Jesus and his promise of immortality. As the Bible says in John 11:25-26 (NIV), *"Jesus said to her 'I am the resurrection and the life. The one who believes in me will live, even though they die; and whoever lives by believing in me will never die. Do you believe this?"*

> **An idea to examine:** *To understand death, we first need a defini-tion of life. We can start by first looking at what makes a cell alive. Cellular life is the continuous struggle between success and failure to match a state of perfection.*

The cell's job is to maintain homeostasis, the biological "steady state." This oversight job ensures metabolism continuously maintains optimal levels of the materials that sustain life. Low levels of light are emitted by all cells as a by-product of metabolism. When the cells of the body die, there's a burst of metabolic activity (a Hail Mary pass), followed by a slow decrease and discharge of the cell's energy.[6] The cells die when the body stops functioning, metabolism ceases, and as a result, no new light is emitted.

Somewhat surprisingly, scientists still don't know what the essen-tial ingredient of life is. Early descriptions identified a few key elements essential to life: carbon, hydrogen, oxygen, and nitrogen. But life is more than the correct mix of elements. Life possesses the ever-mys-terious "spark." Accordingly, scientists decided to try electricity to jolt elements into forming life-giving molecules, and it proved successful. In 1952, Stanley Miller and Harold Urey mixed water, methane, ammonia, and hydrogen in flasks maintained at conditions typical of earth's atmo-sphere.[7] Then they subjected the flasks to continuous electrical sparks simulating lightning. What resulted was somewhere between 11 and 20 amino acids—the building blocks of proteins, which are the foundation of living cells and complex organisms.

But complex molecules aren't alive any more than are elements. It's the way molecules combine that makes a cell functional and alive. There are lists of functions a cell performs that define life. A living cell must be able to grow, reproduce, and maintain a steady state of metabolism. Metabolism is the sum total of chemical reactions inside a living cell. According to the hypothesis here, life is many things, but the absolute proof of ongoing life is light: a faint emission of single photons that signal the cell is actively performing its metabolic functions.[8]

Living things are made of four types of carbon-based molecules: carbohydrates, fats, proteins, and nucleic acids (the materials of DNA).[9] Metabolism takes place inside the cell where the mitochondria make energy out of glucose. Many foods in our diet (proteins, carbohydrates, and fats) are broken down or converted into glucose. The circulatory system supplies the cell with glucose and other essential nutrients. Glucose is able to enter all cells and then enter the mitochondria. The mitochondria are called the powerhouses of the cell because they make the energy cells use. There's one important catch, however. Cells can only produce energy in the presence of oxygen. This is why multi-cell organisms need a circulatory system linked to the lungs, to bring oxygen taken in through our lungs to all cells. We need nutrients and oxygen to live. If metabolism is critical for life, then we should be able to understand death by looking at what happens to the cell when it dies.

Cell death is a huge topic in biology and is a goldmine for research in health and disease. Cells die by two paths: programmed cell death and necrotic cell death.[10] Programmed cell death is ongoing during early development. The body produces more cells than it needs, and then decides which cells will live or die. Take, as an example, the nerve cells that activate our muscles to move our bodies. There's one neuron for every muscle fiber. Whenever a neuron sends a message to the muscle, it contracts. Our bodies optimize the neuron-to-muscle match-ups. Many neurons compete with each other to reach and control each muscle fiber. The neuron that makes the best connection survives, while those neurons making less satisfactory connections die.

Programmed cell death also plays a role in neurological diseases like Parkinson's disease and Alzheimer's disease.[11] But scientists still don't understand what triggers programmed cell death in these diseases. Neurological diseases alone don't cause death, but instead lead to direct causes of death. Typical direct causes of death include halted heart function (heart attack or cardiac arrest) or halted breathing (asphyxiation). Once the heart stops beating and the diaphragm stops contracting to bring in new breath, the living human being dies. Cells are deprived of oxygen and begin to undergo necrosis—cell death by lack of nutrition. In necrotic cell death, the cell membrane disintegrates, disrupting every chemical reaction. Without the optimal environments created by these membranes, metabolism is severely disrupted, and eventually, all the cells of the brain and body die and decompose.

When the mitochondria lose their ability to function, the cell gets into real trouble. Being the powerhouse of the cell, responsible for converting glucose into energy, the cell goes into a death spiral. The mitochondria respond with a last burst of energy, a final emission of light, and then go dark. It's almost a biblical prophecy come true: light giveth life, and death taketh light away.

> *One last possibility to ponder:* When we die, the conscious matrix disintegrates. But the energy of our final thoughts disperses into the universe as an intact cloud.

Assemblies or coalitions of neurons synchronously experience entanglement of electrons in proteins buried deep inside the conscious matrix, and these entanglements are linked by photons. We directly experience that synchrony as inner consciousness, it's an inner light that exposes or "highlights" information processing in select neural networks. That light is our inner consciousness, our mind's eye. Our inner eye is linked to the universe. The steady state it measures is our success and failure to match a state of perfection: a state where all our needs are met in harmony with the needs of others and in lock-step with the overall order in the universe. It's precisely when we come closest to experiencing this harmony that the amount of light emitted in our neurons is highest. Some people experience that light when they die.

When a person dies, the heart stops beating and we stop breathing. This results in a lack of oxygen and nutrients being provided to every cell in the body, including the brain. The brain is a special organ in the body and it has a special uptake mechanism ensuring it gets the lion's share of glucose. What happens to the brain when we die? Depending on the cause of death, there may be a surge of activity prior to flat-lining. Researchers at the University of Michigan simulated the conditions of cardiac arrest in rats and measured their brain activity. They were surprised to find an initial burst of enhanced electroencephalogram (EEG) activity, indicative of heightened states of consciousness.[12]

Is there conscious experience after death? This question is intriguing enough to warrant a five-million dollar grant from the Templeton Foundation being awarded to University of California Professor John Fischer. In his book, *Death, Immortality, and Meaning in Life*, Fischer reviews cases of reported near-death experiences.[13] Among people who are close to death, ten percent report near-death experiences. There are certain common themes such as traveling down a tunnel towards a bright light, seeing deceased friends and relatives, and experiencing a life review.

After reviewing the literature on near-death experience, one scientist found consistent correspondences between the nature of experience and brain areas demonstrating abnormal EEG activity.[14] The brain is often damaged following cardiac arrest, general anesthesia, or mind-altering drugs. The region of the brain that's damaged affects the near-death experience. Damage to different parts of the temporal and parietal lobes were associated with intensified emotions, life review, and out-of-body experiences. On the other hand, general anesthesia and hallucinogens (like ketamine, LSD, and cannabinoids) triggered joyful, vivid near-death experiences. Interestingly, some of the people reporting near-death experiences had flat EEG records, indicating little or no electrical activity.

In a large study examining 344 patients who were resuscitated following cardiac arrest, eighteen percent reported a near-death experience.[15] Few factors correlated highly with the presence or absence of experience except death in the next thirty days. People who would die within a month were significantly more likely to have a near-death experience. There's no clear explanation for this anomalous result.

After-death experiences, described by patients who've been resuscitated, suggest consciousness is possible up to three to five minutes after cardiac arrest.[16] This is hard to reconcile given that the brain cells die in twenty to thirty seconds. The only thing we can conclude is that whatever is left in the way of brain cell machinery and metabolism can still perturb the conscious matrix and create experience. This period may extend even longer than minutes. Experiments done on pig brains show life-giving metabolism can be revived up to four hours after death.[17] These resurrected pig brains regained metabolic activity but not electrical activity.

In a recent article, one scientist argues that near-death experiences can no longer be written off as imaginations or hallucinations triggered by lack of oxygen.[18] Consciousness after death, with a flat-line EEG, is scientifically possible. For at least a few minutes, metabolism continues in dying neurons, suggesting the conscious matrix takes its cues from metabolism, not from the EEG. Since metabolism triggers single photon emissions, the conscious matrix should experience increased enlightenment as the cell discharges its final bursts of energy right before the cell decomposes. Where this energy goes next, after the cell decomposes, is a matter of speculation. Some researchers suggest quantum mechanics allows for our consciousness to fuse with the universe,[19] an idea similar to ones suggested in this book.

Skeptics sometimes turn into believers after personal near-death experiences. Neurologist Eber Alexander wrote the best-selling book, *Proof of Heaven*, after having his own encounter with the "other side."[20] Alexander describes his near-death experience as entering a beautiful, incredible, dream world. Carried on the wings of butterflies, he felt a profound knowing that he was loved and cherished, and that he had nothing to fear. There's nothing in biology that directly contradicts the Bible, particularly if one's interpretation isn't extremely literal. Our consciousness can live on after our death; it's simply not clear in what form. It might live on in a form similar to how it started at birth: a pure and highly energized soul without specific content.

What do the major religions teach about resurrection? John 3:16 is the most widely quoted verse in the Bible: *"For God so loved the world, that he gave his only begotten Son, that whosoever believeth in him shall not perish, but have everlasting life."* Jesus has some two billion followers today. The collective consciousness associated with a vast number of followers is truly astonishing.

Practicing Christians not only believe Jesus is the son of God, but that Jesus died so we might be forgiven our sins and live forever in the love of God. This is a beautiful and uplifting message, and sharing this message among billions of living souls is an exalting experience. But no matter how exalting, no matter how much inner light is shone, does this strong belief connect the billions of living believers with the billions of believing souls that have since departed? I'm not sure how to test that.

Let's consider more features of Christian belief to make a connection. Belief in Jesus Christ is a highly personal experience. The individual Christian accepts Christ as their personal savior. Jesus connects or entangles with each and every person who believes in him. It's been slightly more than two millennia since Jesus Christ was born. According to Christian belief, many billions of souls have already been united with that of Jesus and enjoy eternal life. Moreover, through quantum entanglement believers in Christ today may link with souls of the deceased who remain immortal by their faith.

If there's any tangible evidence that those souls are truly immortal, it might be found in the strength of Christianity today. All religious beliefs wax and wane. All religious beliefs have their strengths and weaknesses; none are perfect. Christianity is strong in some parts of the world, and that's tangible evidence that the souls of deceased believers are still alive in the collective unconscious of Christians. What if your belief and faith was all that survived? That's not such a bad possibility, considering what the strong belief could help others do in the future. Maybe that's the answer: faith survives when people die, and faith is the best thing we have and we'll never lose it. Faith is immortal. That might be part of the answer, but it's not the whole answer. At least my conscious matrix tells me there's more.

CHAPTER 4: NOTES AND REFERENCES

1. Piper J. The Passion of Jesus Christ: Fifty Reasons Why He Came to Die. Crossway Books, 2006.

2. Russell JG. Artifact testing on its way. The Legal Genealogist, November, 2018. https://www.legalgenealogist.com/2018/11/04/artifact-testing-on-its-way/

3. Baumeister H. Inappropriate prescriptions of antidepressant drugs in patients with subthreshold to mild depression: time for the evidence to become practice. J Affect Disord. 2012, 139(3):240-3.

4. Jung C. The Archetypes and the Collective Unconscious. Princeton University Press, 1969.

5. Greene B. The Elegant Universe: Superstrings, Hidden Dimensions, and the Quest for the Ultimate Theory. WW Norton, 2010.

6. Slawinski J. Photon emission from perturbed and dying organisms — the concept of photon cycling in biological systems. In: Popp FA, Beloussov L. (eds) Integrative Biophysics. Springer, Dordrecht, 2003.

7. Miller SL, Urey HC. Organic compound synthesis on the primitive earth. Science. 1959, 130(3370):245–51.

8. Wijk RV, Wijk EP. An introduction to human biophoton emission. Forsch Komplementarmed Klass Naturheilkd. 2005, 12(2):77-83.

    Niggli HJ. Biophotons: ultraweak light impulses regulate life processes in aging. J Gerontol Geriat Res. 2014, 3:143.

9. Metzler DE, Metzler C. Biochemistry: The Chemical Reactions of Living Cells (2nd Ed.). Elsevier, 2004.

10. Green DR. Cell Death: Apoptosis and Other Means to an End (2nd Ed.), 2018.

11. Majd S, Power JH, Grantham HJ. Neuronal response in Alzheimer's and Parkinson's disease: the effect of toxic proteins on intracellular pathways. BMC Neurosci. 2015, 16:69.

12. Borjigin J, Lee U, Liu T, Pal D, Huff S, Klarr D, Sloboda J, Hernandez J, Wang MM, Mashour GA. Surge of neurophysiological coherence and connectivity in the dying brain. Proc Natl Acad Sci U S A. 2013, 110(35):14432-7.

13. Fischer JM. Death, Immortality, and Meaning in Life. Oxford Press, 2019.

14. Konopka LM. Near death experience: neuroscience perspective. Croat Med J. 2015, 56(4):392-3.

15. van Lommel P, van Wees R, Meyers V, Elfferich I. Near-death experience in survivors of cardiac arrest: a prospective study in the Netherlands. Lancet. 2001, 358(9298):2039-45.

16. Parnia S. Understanding the cognitive experience of death and the near-death experience. QJM. 2017, 110(2):67-69.

17. Youngner S, Hyun I. Pig experiment challenges assumptions around brain damage in people. Nature. 2019, 568(7752):302-304.

18. van Lommel P. Near-death experiences: the experience of the self as real and not as an illusion. Ann N Y Acad Sci. 2011, 1234:19-28.

19. Beck T, Colli J. A quantum biomechanical basis for near-death life reviews, J. Near-Death Stud, 21(3) 2004.

20. Alexander E. Proof of Heaven. Simon & Schuster, 2012.

5 THE HOLY SPIRIT PERMEATES OUR QUANTUM REALITY

LIFE IS FILLED with spirited experiences ranging from the depths of despair to the heights of ecstasy. Each of us has a conscious matrix that houses this inner spirit. The human spirit is synonymous with the human soul and is often described as something non-material, ethereal, and other-worldly. The word "spirit" derives from the Latin word *spiritus*, meaning breath. Having a healthy spirit is fundamental to being alive and well.

Our conscious matrix has the unique capacity to connect us internally and with another person's inner spirit, while also connecting us to nature and to a higher-being or God. In this sense, spirituality is a multidimensional superposition of connections: internal connections to make peace with ourselves, connections with others to form social bonds, connections with nature, and our fundamental connection with God to form a perfect union with all forces in the universe. Spirituality and religion overlap, with the main difference being religion is structured with traditions, rituals, and practices. Some people love the structure and fellowship of organized religion. Other people like to interpret things for themselves. Spirituality, expressed outside of traditional religion, is a way many people find meaning in life. They find understanding by looking within and directly connecting to a higher-being.

The major religions incorporate spirituality in what many call the "Holy Spirit." In Christianity, the Holy Spirit is part of the Trinity. God the

Father, Jesus the Son, and the Holy Spirit form a triune—all of whom are God but none of whom are equivalent to one another. To put it simply, they represent three different perspectives of God or three paths to understanding God. Symbols for the Christian Holy Spirit include the dove and tongues of fire. The dove is a symbol of good intentions and of love. The tongues of fire signify the Holy Spirit's ability to "take over" the speaker and enable them to speak a different language. This practice among Pentecostal and Charismatic Christian congregations represents their belief that the Holy Spirit exists among us and can enter us. Scientists can't explain speaking in tongues and have simply put a technical label on it: *glossolalia*, the Latin word for tongue.

The Holy Spirit appears in other religions too, but with different meanings. In Judaism, the Holy Spirit is equivalent to wisdom and divine prophecy. Muslims only occasionally mention the Holy Spirit. The angel Gabriel acts as the spirit when he delivers messages from God to the prophet Muhammad. Muslims don't believe in the Holy Trinity, and that distinguishes Muslim belief from Christian belief. The Hindu concept of "Advaita" is closest to that of the Trinity, and is the one aspect of Hinduism that links it to Christianity. In Buddhism, the Holy Spirit is likened to a unified consciousness that enables a person to chart their path to God.

Among the remaining religions of the world, most have some concept that equates with spirituality. Moreover, of the over one billion people who claim to be areligious, agnostic, or atheist; many believe in some kind of spirituality. The belief in spirituality, not limited to the confines of a particular religion, seems to be more of a universal concept than does a belief in God. One could argue the differences in belief are merely semantic, with different people referring to the same concept with different words. However, it's not that simple.

Practical life outcomes depend on one's specific beliefs, intensity of belief, and level of adherence to one's beliefs. Having beliefs and living by those beliefs results in better physical and mental health, but other factors play a role too. People have different lifestyles. People make different major life choices and this modifies their life experiences. Belief and lifestyle, in combination, contribute to health and well-being.

Let's examine the conscious matrix for clues about how we can optimize our spirituality or religious practice. Regardless the religion practiced or level of personal spirituality expressed, human beings tend to think about their souls from time to time. We know the brain and its hundreds of billions of neurons have particular metabolic needs. We meet those needs with food and rest. But our souls have needs too. What constitutes the basis of that need? Does quantum mind theory give us any clues about how to satisfy the needs of our souls?

> *A thought to ponder:* The conscious matrix needs to be re-energized. When we're tired or weary, brain activity lessens, brain metabolism slows, and the light produced can fade. We need spiritual rejuvenation to function optimally; it's a biological need like that of sleep.

Whereas all cells of the body need food, water, and oxygen, sleep is something unique that only brain cells need. Human beings have an absolute need to sleep and its function is to restore mental vitality. Sleep deprivation impairs our ability to process information, destroys our general good mood, and tires us out for vigorous physical activity. While humans can survive extended sleep deprivation lasting several days, it's considered torture by some experts. At the extremes, prolonged and severe sleep interruption can cause disability or even possible death.[1]

Sleep restores our minds by turning down the volume of input to our brain cells and this slows down metabolism.[2] It gives our neurons a vacation from the myriad inputs arising from all sights, sounds, touches, and bodily movements occurring during the day. If we're really sleepy, we may not be able to keep our eyes open. But if we're ready to fall asleep, lying down in a quiet, dark environment will usually do the trick. The lack of sensory input and not having to maintain an upright posture is enough if you're tired already.

Sleep occurs when neurons self-hypnotize to a relaxed beat, measured as a pattern in the EEG. During the day, we exhibit lots of beta waves—high levels of EEG activity that keeps a fast, irregular pace. When we relax, alpha waves appear in the EEG, and this slows down our thoughts. When we fall asleep, delta waves—the slowest of all—appear in spurts and eventually take over. We're virtually unconscious during delta-wave sleep. Most people doze off and spend a little over an hour in dreamless delta-wave sleep.

What happens next is most intriguing. If we're merely taking a nap during the day, then under those circumstances—the light shining around the curtain edges or the ticking clock—any of those kinds of interruptions will typically break the hypnotic trance and wake us up. But in the dead of night, instead of waking up, we usually shift into 10-15 minutes of dream sleep and then fall back again into deep sleep. We repeat the 90-minute cycle, except that later in the night our dreams get longer.

Dream sleep is a magical time when we experience an altered state of consciousness. Dreams exquisitely explore the inner recesses of our minds to create a virtual reality. We see and hear things that exist only in our mind. We experience action without moving our bodies. What is it in our brain that enables us to have a movie-like animated experience not based on any real visual or sound input? Neuroscientists don't know the exact answer, but they have a few hypotheses. The most prominent dream sleep theory is Alan Hobson's idea that neurons fire spontaneously and randomly at dream onset, and then our brains make a story out of that activity.[3] Dream sleep has an EEG pattern that's similar to that of a person who's awake. Hobson's theory fits with the EEG records during dream sleep, but it alone doesn't explain how the brain makes a story out of random spontaneous activity. Quantum mind theory provides a possible answer to the second question.

Dreams prove consciousness depends on far more than sensory input alone. We have a conscious matrix embedded within our neurons. When our senses are stimulated, brain activity increases metabolic activity, and this triggers the release of photons. But what reaches consciousness? Consciousness isn't so much focused on the sensory stimulus; it's focused on the connections with other ideas stored in the architecture of the conscious matrix. Sensory stimuli, real or imagined, merely trigger metabolism and emit photons which "turn on the lights" to highlight quantum entanglements representing memories past. Dreaming merely stimulates "story fragments" stored in memory and we put them together as new stories. But, unlike a random read-out of meaningless story fragments, the way the pieces fit together has rhyme and reason. Many of our dreams are lifelike and the stories seem authentic.

Is there any valid reason our dreams make sense on some level, that they're realistic enough to seem real? The answer lies in the defined architecture of the conscious matrix. This architecture isn't merely the road to all possible connections. Our conscious matrix makes a quantum level connection according to certain "rules of order" that traverse the universe. Our conscious matrix has an inner wisdom we can directly access. Our job is merely to get regular sleep to restore our conscious matrix to its full potential.

> **Another thought to ponder:** *Religious practices and personal spirituality rejuvenate the conscious matrix in a way other human activities can't. These practices also help us access our inner wisdom.*

In addition to sleep that rejuvenates neurons by enabling periods of reduced metabolism, the conscious matrix needs spiritual rejuvenation. Each day takes a toll on our minds and souls, especially when we encounter life's most difficult challenges and stressors. Stress comes in many forms. The busy routine of a young single mother who has to balance work with motherhood produces one kind of stress, chronic and unrelenting. A sudden-onset type of stress is grief following the loss of a loved one. Surprisingly, positive events are stressors too. We feel stress when we experience any major change in our lives. Getting newly married, even though it's a happy event, is often associated with high levels of stress. We fear the unknown. When we're faced with one or more types of stress that go beyond our ability to cope, we might seek counseling from a religious or spiritual authority, or from a health professional. Or we might cope by turning inward—looking to our conscious matrix for answers.

What enables our "conscious matrix" to sort out life's problems or create stories out of nothingness? We seem to have an almost unlimited capacity to piece together memory fragments in new and sometimes meaningful ways. The theories of Sigmund Freud created a new approach in psychiatry that focused on dream analysis and interpreting symbolic content.[5] Although dream analysis is no longer popular in modern psychiatry, dreams can provide insight to anyone. August Kekule (1829-1896), famous for many discoveries in chemistry, is well-known for his having dreamed the solution to an important chemical structure, the benzene ring. The night before he solved the chemical structure, he dreamed of a snake circling around to bite his tail. That solved the problem he'd been stuck on: the benzene structure has a ring-shape.[6]

What kinds of things make a story meaningful or worthwhile? Good stories have plots that make sense, and there's the proverbial "moral-to-the-story." The "rules" about what we expect or want to happen are pre-wired in our conscious matrix. We make abstractions in a certain order: from simple to complex. We store these abstractions at successive levels, each one more complex and far-reaching than the lower level abstractions. Curiously, the highest-level abstractions and concepts have the ability to restructure those ideas that lie subordinate. Psychologists call this "top-down processing." But who or what tells the topmost level how to organize information?

Believers might answer it's God who instructs those "highest principles." Believers might also guess that God defines the "rules" at the highest level of the hierarchy. Skeptics might instead say we simply need a new "theory of how the brain works" to explain how the human mind operates. It's up to each person to decide what they truly believe. And we must have the courage to be authentic in our beliefs. It's better to be an honest skeptic than a disingenuous believer. It's normal and healthy to doubt our faith, and many who do have their faith return even stronger. The struggle is a defining part of life.

What we believe affects our mood, outlook, and ability to cope. Religious beliefs and spiritual practices have largely positive benefits on health outcomes, coping with life, and managing stress.[6] Certain mental health conditions, like depression and anxiety, are lessened by religious practice or spirituality. This is because many religious practices and spiritual rituals revitalize our conscious matrix. Religion and spirituality have positive effects on mental health, which in turn increases our odds of having better physical health and a higher quality of life. As stated in Romans 15:13 (KJV), "*Now the God of hope fill you with all joy and peace in believing, that ye may abound in hope, through the power of the Holy Spirit.*"

Tending to the human soul isn't simply placating those stricken with illness and disease. Spiritual therapy directly heals the root cause of some illnesses. Depression and anxiety are actual injuries within the human soul. This is scientific fact, not a metaphor. The conscious matrix is continuously updating its structural architecture to store new conscious thoughts and memories. This makes the conscious matrix the major site of neuroplasticity within neurons, and constant changes make them vulnerable to damage.[7] Structurally "plastic" neurons comprising the conscious matrix are physically damaged by high levels of stress and anxiety.[8] Excess stress and anxiety literally annihilates parts of the conscious matrix; it kills parts of our human soul. We can heal our conscious matrix; those neurons will recover with time passed. But healing will only occur if we remove ourselves from the stressors.

> **An idea to examine:** *The practice of meditation or mindfulness improves one's mood, decreases depression, and relieves anxiety because it enables the conscious matrix to rejuvenate.*

Western medicine long ignored the health benefits of Eastern culture, religion, and practices like meditation. That has dramatically changed in recent years. The relationship between meditation and overall health, particularly mental health, is now widely accepted. With very few exceptions, meditation produces a positive effect on health. The most consistently changed features include a decrease in heart rate, lowered blood pressure, decreases in oxygen consumption, and a decrease in anxiety.[9]

There are different kinds of meditation arising from different schools of thought. In *Transcendental Meditation*, the person sits upright with eyes closed and focuses his or her thoughts on a particular word or phrase. It may be a word assigned by a mentor or teacher, or it could be some issue the meditator wants to address. As meditation proceeds, the person feels relaxed, as if they "transcended" into their inner consciousness. The sensation is relaxing all the way to the deepest core of the mind, and this allows tension to melt away. This method is proven effective to improve some health measures. The American Heart Association, for example, recommends Transcendental Meditation to lower blood pressure.[10]

"Transcendental Meditation opens the awareness to the infinite reservoir of energy, creativity, and intelligence that lies deep within everyone." That's a popular quote of Maharishi Mahesh Yogi. Those who teach the practice of Transcendental Meditation believe you gain insight into the universe and gain control over your body by accessing your innermost consciousness. Perhaps the most dramatic example of this philosophy is Yogic flying, a special, heightened form of Transcendental Meditation. According to its founder Maharishi Mahesh Yogi and his followers, yogic flying enables one to experience the "unified field of all the laws of nature." Yogi and his adherents further believe this unleashes one's peak creativity and intelligence.

Although skeptics doubt meditation can produce actual levitation as the yogic flyers profess, the idea of the spirit rising is an interesting one that frequently appears in various religious teachings. An alternate explanation is that the practitioner feels "as if" they're flying. The sole intent of discussing this here is to examine the belief, not to examine or resolve any controversy about levitation.

Another type of mediation is based on a psychology concept called "mindfulness" or "bare attention." From a historical point of view, mindfulness draws heavily from the Buddhist practice of *Zen Meditation*. This variation of meditation is rooted in the more demanding practice of *Vipassana* meditation.[11] Vipassana meditation involves rising early and meditating all day long. Sustained practice of Vipassana mediation over weeks or months increases attention and target detection; and it changes EEG patterns.[12] Although beneficial, this form of meditation requires a lifestyle that's not available to most people, unless you're a Buddhist monk.

Mindfulness mediation is a modified version of the ancient practice that many people are able to add to their daily lives. The emphasis of mindfulness meditation is to observe what happens in each moment, focusing only on content in that moment. It's controlled and purposeful introspection. Teachers of mindfulness mediation instruct you to notice your surroundings without making any judgments. The aim of this meditation practice is to facilitate your ability to experience raw consciousness. Mindfulness is learning how to access our conscious matrix directly, without distraction.

There's evidence that mindfulness meditation reduces anxiety and depression while it forces our conscious thoughts stay in the present.[13] Daily practice prevents mind-wandering and rumination, the tendency to review unpleasant experiences over and again with no progress or solution in sight. A variety of mindfulness-based therapies, all of which are based on the Buddhist traditions of meditation, are found to work as well as traditional cognitive behavioral therapy and antidepressant drugs in treating anxiety and depression. This is a major advance, since anti-depressant drugs have side-effects, and cognitive therapy requires continued visits with a therapist. Once trained, a person can assume the role of their own practitioner, administering mindfulness therapy without other interventions or as an add-on to other therapies.

Mindfulness meditation combined with cognitive therapy, stress reduction, and pain reduction therapy has been administered to veterans with post-traumatic stress disorder, resulting in favorable outcomes.[14] When assessed for brain activity, patients treated with mindfulness-based therapies show increased activity in the prefrontal cortex and decreased activity in the amygdala, a small almond-shaped structure that triggers rage among other autonomic system responses. Rage is a negative emotion that can interfere with daily activities. According to quantum mind theory, the conscious matrix can override lower brain centers like the amygdala. In this manner, the conscious matrix can tame the beast within us. Mindfulness can aid in this effort, and quelling rage and anger gets easier with consistent practice.

The applicability of quantum mind theory to mindfulness is a topic of great interest. An intriguing idea is that mindfulness triggers retro-causality and this promotes healing.[15] In quantum mechanics, a measurement affects the particle under study in bizarre ways, including effects on past states. Retro-causality is undeniably present in human memory. Each time we revisit or remember the past, we entangle past experience with our present state. At some future time, we'll recall that past experience again, at which time the memory will be subtly sculpted and altered yet again. That's what memory is: an entanglement made in the past, updated by entanglements occurring with each successive view. Memories are the sum total of all those entanglements, each version leaving a small trace.

The human memory has no intrinsic time-keeper; timing is only relevant to the present. Memories of people, places, and things blur together their ever-changing characteristics into one essential thing or concept. This is why eye-witness accounts of past events are unreliable; particularly after repeated interrogations.[16] We can use the changeability of memory to our advantage, however, when coping with trauma or painful memories. Mindfulness increases the favorability of past events by subtly updating those memories, integrating those times with more pleasant circumstances experienced after the event. It's as if the conscious matrix comes to a realization: "Yes, that was a terrible experience. But over the years I've learned to appreciate the good times. I now feel confident most future events will be positive."

While meditation and mindfulness are finding their way towards full integration and acceptance in Western medicine, an important hurdle is how to mix the East and West together successfully. Quantum mind theory is a useful tool to sort out what kinds of practices help and how to successfully combine them. What works best for the individual finding their inner wisdom, calm, and peace will usually predict a good health outcome and an optimal response to other medical interventions. The different peoples of the world have different cultures and religions, but we all share in having a conscious matrix that seeks the best for ourselves and for others too.

> **Another idea to examine:** *Religious inspiration and elation, when shared among members of a group, attains levels of increased intensity that's greater than the sum of intensities of individual conscious matrices. The strength of the collective consciousness is greatly augmented by traditional religious practices.*

People in groups tend to think alike. Psychologists talk about the "collective consciousness," another term for shared conscious experience. Scientific research shows that people may use mirror neurons to share conscious experience.[17] Other theories that explain like-mindedness in groups include group-think, herd behavior, and the social mind. As a general rule of thumb, the more like-minded the believers, the stronger their shared belief. Religious beliefs, like all strongly held beliefs, are polarizing. Group-think theory explains how strong ideas acquire even more strength as they circulate among the like-minded.[18]

The word "religion" derives from the Latin *religiare*, which means to bind together. The conscious matrix of one person doesn't operate in isolation. We're continuously receiving energy from others, or being drained of it. Religious practices set up beliefs and rituals that favor people deriving positive energy from one another. The Holy Spirit might be viewed as a positive energy force field that exists among us. Chanting together, praying out loud in a group, singing hymns in church—all these practices encourage entanglements or oneness of belief among many. As Thessalonians 5:11 (KJV) states, *"Wherefore comfort yourselves together, and edify one another, even as also ye do."*

Buddhist chanting has become popular in the United Kingdom and the United States (U.S.). This increasingly popular practice is based on Nichiren Buddhism that originated in Japan 700 years ago. The Soki Gakkai International is a religion order based on Nichiren Buddhism. [19] This religious order claims over twelve million adherents worldwide. A chant is performed daily. *"Namu Myoho Renge Kyo"* is repeated over and again. In a large group, the chant takes on a vibration that overwhelms the senses and fills the spirit. I've experienced it firsthand, and it's hypnotizing and elevating. Simple as it is, the combined chanters make it sound eerily musical. The belief is that chanting can unite the individual with the unifying principle of the universe. Chanting likely entangles the conscious matrices of chanters with one another, next with the highest unifying principles of the universe, and finally with God. At least this is what it feels like is happening.

Christians, Jews, and Muslims also pray in large groups in churches, synagogues, and temples. It's not uncommon for people to kneel, lie down, or simply hold hands and then join in prayer. Christians and Jews have a tradition of praying before meals, and Muslims pray before doing most things. In church, there are regularly recited prayers the congregation might know from memory—the Lord's prayer, for example. The Eastern Orthodox, Roman Catholic, and Protestant Episcopalian Churches use the *Book of Common Prayer*, which contains the Nicene Creed. [20] Praying in a group often increases the spiritual experience above that attained by individual prayers recited silently.

That multiple conscious matrices expand the power of prayer to another level has been duly noted. In Judaism, a quorum of ten people is required for public worship and joint prayer. [21] This quorum is called a minyan or assembly. The quorum rule teaches us humility and unity. It matters not how learned or devout the members of the minyan are, only that there's a sufficient number to indicate the faith in the community is strong. A famous quote says, "Nine rabbis do not constitute a minyan, but ten cobblers can."

Christians gather in congregations or churches without any minimum number of participants required. Nonetheless, there's a tradition to recruit new membership. Christians are known for sending missionaries into foreign lands and for knocking on doors attempting to gain new members. Christians are motivated to recruit new members and believe their message of kindness, charity, and altruism will resonate with non-Christians. This message has gained many converts, but not all people are receptive. In the chapters to come, I'll discuss how quantum mind theory explains how different perspectives of spirituality and God are deeply tied to one's culture and environment. Religion is a personal choice, and when people are allowed their free will, most people choose the religion or spirituality that best supports survival and success based on their personal experiences tied to their culture. Our conscious matrix is wired to find the best way to meet our spiritual needs so that we maintain optimal spiritual, physical, and emotional health.

In his book *Quantum Christianity*, Jim Groves argues that the basic principles of quantum physics prove that many of the Christian teachings are valid and true.[22] Groves points to quantum entanglement for explaining the omnipresence of God. He cites wave-particle duality theory to support the many depictions of God and of miracles described in scripture. Of the three perspectives of God in the Trinity, Groves argues the Holy Spirit is most consistent with quantum physics theory.

Quantum mind theory reveals how our conscious matrices might communicate between individuals through known neural mechanisms like mirror neurons. One person's conscious matrix energizes that of another person if they're "in tune" with each other. Sharing deeply held beliefs enables one person to energize another. Those energies accelerate with group activities like chanting, singing hymns, and praying in groups.

Religious practices that revitalize our conscious matrix also might be invitations to divine intervention, asking for help to achieve our dreams and feel compassion. Unfortunately, religion also creates strong beliefs that can precipitate wars and promote dehumanization of people outside of that particular faith. In this book, I focus on the positive outcomes of religion and spirituality because there's a net positive force of religion, and I believe it to be overwhelming and life-giving. Nonetheless, in Chapter 8 we'll look at how quantum mind theory explains "good versus evil" using the quantum phenomena. An independent evil force may not actually exist; evil might best be explained as deviations away from the natural path taken by the conscious matrix, which is inherently good. As the Bible says in Psalm 37:27 (NASB), *"Depart from evil and do good, so you will abide forever."*

> ***One last possibility to consider:*** *When we combine religious and spiritual philosophies of the East and West, we realize that the human spirit is real and determines our health and well-being. The conscious matrix will solve problems that arise in populations, like how to provide health care for everyone.*

Religions worldwide are involved with showing concern for people's general well-being and for providing health care. In the Western world, Judaism and Christianity teach principles of kindness, charity, and altruism within the context of family, and this extends to other members of their religion, and to all people worldwide. These religious groups create intra- and interconnected communities that encourage caring behavior towards one another. Christian and Jewish religious groups have long-standing roles in building hospitals and medical schools and providing funding for medical research. More recently, however, the secular government has taken over health care and medical research in the Western world.

For decades now, ignoring religion and spirituality has been a trend in modern Western health care settings. This is despite many scientific research studies showing that practicing a particular religion or having a well-developed spirituality results in better health outcomes. Religions teach their traditions, which include ways to develop coping skills and better deal with illness. Religious beliefs come into play, especially when dealing with terminal illness. And people who belong to a religion or who profess spirituality often live longer.[23] Not all studies agree on this result, however. In some cases, religious belief has no greater a positive effect than does a placebo. But remember that placebo effects are small but real effects. Just having someone care about you produces the modest "placebo" effect. We need to value these small effects because when multiplied over billions of lives, small effects add up to something big.

And when we look closer at select beliefs on specific health conditions, we see stronger and more reliable effects.[24] Regular church attendance is positively correlated with lower blood pressure. Most impressive is the effect religion has on improving outcomes in depression and lowering chances of recurrence. Overall, religion and spirituality increase measures of happiness. One hypothesis is that religion and spirituality have a positive effect on cardiovascular health because these factors decrease stress and depression and this, in turn, decreases inflammation.

Whether the beliefs come from the East or West, effects of religion on health outcomes vary with age. First of all, there's an influence of chronological age and country of origin on religious beliefs and spirituality.[25] As shown by the World Values Survey, responses from people living in the thirteen most-populated countries indicate people over sixty years of age are significantly more religious than are people under sixty. Irrespective of age, China has the fewest religious people (12.9%), followed by Japan (25.4%), and Thailand (33.0%), whereas Pakistan has the most (99.8%), followed by Nigeria (95.8%), and Turkey (85.0%). The U.S. has numbers right around average. Worldwide, a simple majority of people (65.1%) express religious beliefs and slightly more (76. 8%) express spirituality and a quest for the meaning of life.

Today there are close to one billion people who are over sixty years of age. The world's population of those over sixty is expected to double to two billion by the year 2050. This poses high health care costs that are only going to increase. Now is an especially important time to consider the ability of religion and spirituality to prevent or diminish disease and health problems, and to increase the number of quality years in the lifespan.

In the U.S., approximately 12% of our health care dollars go towards treating patients in the last year of life.[26] Although this amount isn't crippling, it could become so if health care costs increase as the aging population also increases. According to the Centers for Medicare and Medicaid Services, the U.S. spent $3.5 trillion in the year 2017 on health care. Nearly half of U.S. health care is paid by the federal, state, and local governments (e.g., Medicare, Medicaid, Children's Health Insurance Program, and insurance subsidies). The rest is paid by out-of-pocket costs incurred by patients and employers who provide health insurance for their employees.

According to the Organization for Economic Co-operation and Development, health care in the U.S. cost over $10,000 per person for the year 2018, nearly ten times more than health care cost in Mexico, and twice as much as health care cost in Japan.[27] Yet life expectancies don't correlate with health expenditures. According to a World Health Organization 2015 report, Japan ranks #1 in life expectancy at 83.7 years, the U.S. ranks #31 at 79.2 years, and Mexico ranks #46 at 76.7 years. How can health care cost around $1,000 per person per year in Mexico and yield roughly the same life expectancies as the U.S., where health care costs ten times as much?

The answer might be that countries like Mexico and other nations in South America and Asia rely more on holistic medicine. Holistic medicine treats the whole person—the mind, body, spirit, and emotions. Holistic medicine empowers people to take care of themselves and potentially reduce cost. Although Western medicine originally rejected holistic medical practices, that's no longer the case. Surprisingly, this relatively recent acceptance hasn't lowered health care costs in the U.S. This can be taken as an indirect proof that we need to revitalize our collective consciousness on health care. Our spiritual needs are being neglected. We have spiritual needs; that's not a delusion. The hard numbers speak for themselves—the U.S. is spending huge amounts of money while simultaneously ignoring our spiritual needs in health care. Taking care of our spiritual needs will lead to major savings on health care costs; it's a testable hypothesis.

There's increasing and mounting evidence we need to rely on all possible health care avenues: (1) traditional medicine, (2) holistic medicine, and (3) enhanced quality of life through meditation, mindfulness, and other spiritual approaches. Only by blending these three wisdoms together can we satisfactorily meet our future health care needs.

Here's the moral conundrum: Human life is priceless, yet the possible cost of preserving human life is theoretically infinite. One can imagine a new device that might keep a person alive for one more second, one sixtieth of a minute. The cost of this treatment is $1 billion. Most people wouldn't opt for this treatment, not for themselves nor for their loved ones. It's a ridiculous amount of money to spend for one more second of life. This example proves most people don't believe we should spend any conceivable amount to keep a person alive; there are limits. But we're reluctant to admit this, let alone name an amount. Instead, we evade the issue.

But there's another way to morally address this issue. The moral approach is to let every person make the choice about what they want done or not done at the end of life. If we take religious teachings as our guide, each person would gauge their right to live at any cost against what's best for their families and their religious communities. And beyond our religious groups, we might consider effects on the community as a whole. Belief in an afterlife actually helps find the right balance. We live on—at the very least in the hearts, minds, and souls of our loved ones as entanglements that can still grow after we depart. Our deeds live forever, and the end-of-life choices we make affect the well-being of generations to come.

This book isn't about solving any of these problems. This book is about how the conscious matrix connects us to all three perspectives of God. The Holy Spirit lives in the quantum realm that surrounds us. When we're united as one with the Holy Spirit, all things are possible. Solutions are coming. As it says in Matthew 10:28 (NKJV), *"And do not fear those who kill the body but cannot kill the soul. But rather fear Him who is able to kill both soul and body in hell."*

CHAPTER 5: NOTES AND REFERENCES

1. McRae M. Can you actually die from sleep deprivation? Science Alert, May 2018. https://www.sciencealert.com/health-risks-death-from-sleep-deprivation

2. Kayaba M, Park I, Iwayama K, Seya Y, Ogata H, Yajima K, Satoh M, Tokuyama K. Energy metabolism differs between sleep stages and begins to increase prior to awakening. Metabolism. 2017, 69:14-23.

3. Hobson JA. REM sleep and dreaming: towards a theory of protoconsciousness. Nat Rev Neurosci. 2009, 10(11):803-13.

4. Freud S, Dream Psychology: Psychoanalysis for Beginners. James McCann, 1921.

5. Rothenberg A. Creative cognitive processes in Kekulé's discovery of the structure of the benzene molecule. Am J. Psych. 1995, 108: 419-438.

6. Mueller PS, Plevak DJ, Rummans TA. Religious involvement, spirituality, and medicine: implications for clinical practice. Mayo Clin Proc. 2001, 76(12):1225-35.

    Skevington SM, Gunson KS, O'Connell KA. Introducing the WHOQOL-SRPB BREF: developing a short-form instrument for assessing spiritual, religious andpersonal beliefs within quality of life. Qual Life Res. 2013, 22(5):1073-83.

7. Woolf NJ, Butcher LL. Dysdifferentiation of structurally plastic neurons initiates the pathologic cascade of Alzheimer's disease: toward a unifying hypothesis. In: Cholinergic Systems (Eds.: M Steriade, D Biesold). New York: Oxford University Press, 1990, pp. 387-438.

8. Gulyaeva NV. Functional neurochemistry of the ventral and dorsal hippocampus: stress, depression, dementia and remote hippocampal damage. Neurochem Res. 2019, 44(6):1306-1322.

    Mah L, Szabuniewicz C, Fiocco AJ. Can anxiety damage the brain? Curr OpinPsychiatry. 2016, 29(1):56-63.

    McEwen BS. Stress and the aging hippocampus. Front Neuroendocrinol. 1999, 20(1):49-70.

9. Sampaio CV, Lima MG, Ladeia AM. Meditation, health and scientific investigations: review of the literature. J Relig Health. 2017, 56(2):411-427.

Park SH, Han KS. Blood pressure response to meditation and yoga: a systematic review and meta-analysis. J Altern Complement Med. 2017, 23(9):685-695.

10. American Heart Association: Transcendental Meditation proven approach to lowering blood pressure, doctors may consider in clinical practice, May 2013, Cathlab Digest. https://www.cathlabdigest.com/American-Heart-Association-Transcendental-Meditation-Proven-Approach-Lowering-Blood-Pressure-Doctors

11. Nyanaponika T. The heart of Buddhist meditation. Samuel Weiser, 1973.

    Nyanaponika T. The vision of Dhamma: Buddhist writings of Nyanaponika. BPS Pariyatti Editions, reprinted 2000.

12. Slagter HA, Lutz A, Greischar LL, Nieuwenhuis S, Davidson RJ. Theta phase synchrony and conscious target perception: impact of intensive mental training. J Cogn Neurosci. 2009, 21(8):1536-49.

    Lutz A, Slagter HA, Rawlings NB, Francis AD, Greischar LL, Davidson RJ. Mental training enhances attentional stability: neural and behavioral evidence. J Neurosci. 2009, 29(42):13418-27.

13. Gu J, Strauss C, Bond R, Cavanagh K. How do mindfulness-based cognitive therapy and mindfulness-based stress reduction improve mental health and wellbeing? A systematic review and meta-analysis of mediation studies. Clin Psychol Rev. 2015, 37:1-12.

    Sharma M, Rush SE. Mindfulness-based stress reduction as a stress management intervention for healthy individuals: a systematic review. J Evid Based Complementary Altern Med. 2014, 19(4):271-86.

    Parsons CE, Crane C, Parsons LJ, Fjorback LO, Kuyken W. Home practice in mindfulness-based cognitive therapy and mindfulness-based stress reduction: a systematic review and meta-analysis of participants' mindfulness practice and its association with outcomes. Behav Res Ther. 2017, 95:29-41.

Gotink RA, Meijboom R, Vernooij MW, Smits M, Hunink MG. 8-week mindfulness based stress reduction induces brain changes similar to traditional long-term meditation practice – a systematic review. Brain Cogn. 2016, 108:32-41.

Kuyken W, Hayes R, Barrett B, Byng R, Dalgleish T, Kessler D, Lewis G, Watkins E, Brejcha C, Cardy J, Causley A, Cowderoy S, Evans A, Gradinger F, Kaur S, Lanham P, Morant N, Richards J, Shah P, Sutton H, Vicary R, Weaver A, Wilks J, Williams M, Taylor RS, Byford S. Effectiveness and cost-effectiveness of mindfulness-based cognitive therapy compared with maintenance antidepressant treatment in the prevention of depressive relapse or recurrence (PREVENT): a randomised controlled trial. Lancet. 2015, 386(9988):63-73.

Hofmann SG, Gómez AF. Mindfulness-based interventions for anxiety and depression. Psychiatr Clin North Am. 2017, 40(4):739-749

14. Khusid MA, Vythilingam M. The emerging role of mindfulness meditation as effective self-management strategy, Part 1: Clinical implications for depression, post-traumatic stress disorder, and anxiety. Mil Med. 2016, 181(9):961-8.

15. Di Sia P. Mindfulness, consciouness, and quantum physics. World Scientific News. 2018, 96:25-34.

16. Loftus EF, Greenspan RL. If I'm certain, is it true? Accuracy and confidence in eyewitness memory. Psychol Sci Public Interest. 2017, 18(1):1-2.

Wixted JT, Mickes L, Fisher RP. Rethinking the reliability of eyewitness memory. Perspect Psychol Sci. 2018, 13(3):324-335.

17. Combs A, Krippner, S. Collective consciousness and the social brain. J Consciousness Studies. 2008, 15:264–276.

18. Janis IL. Groupthink: The Desperate Drive for Consensus at Any Cost. Thomson Wadsworth, 2015

19. Soki Gakkai International (SGI) webpage: http://www.sgi-usa.org/about-us/

20. The Book of Common Prayer and Administration of the Sacraments and other Rites and Ceremonies of the Church. Church Publishing, 1789

21. Millgram A. Minyan: The Congregational Quorum https://www.myjewishlearning.com/article/minyan-the-congregational-quorum/

22. Groves J. Quantum Christianity. Mountain Door Books, 2011.

23. Hummer RA, Ellison CG, Rogers RG, Moulton BE, Romero RR. Religious involvement and adult mortality in the United States: Review and perspective. Southern Med J, 2004, 97:1223–1230.

    Mishra SK, Togneri E, Tripathi B, Trikamji B. Spirituality and religiosity and its role in health and diseases. J Relig Health. 2017, 56(4):1282-1301.

24. Tartaro J, Luecken LJ, Gunn HE. Exploring heart and soul: effects of religiosity/spirituality and gender on blood pressure and cortisol stress responses. J Health Psychol. 2005, 10(6):753-66.

    Koenig HG. Depression in chronic illness: does religion help? J Christ Nurs. 2014, 31(1):40-6.

    Kilbourne B, Cummings SM, Levine RS. The influence of religiosity on depression among low-income people with diabetes. Health Soc Work. 2009, 34(2):137-47.

    Abdel-Khalek AM, Lester D. A significant association between religiosity and happiness in a sample of Kuwaiti students. Psychol Rep. 2009, 105(2):381-2.

Shattuck EC, Muehlenbein MP. Religiosity/spirituality and physiological markers of health. J Relig Health. 2018. https://doi.org/10.1007/s10943-018-0663-6.

25. Zimmer Z, Jagger C, Chiu CT, Ofstedal MB, Rojo F, Saito Y. Spirituality, religiosity, aging and health in global perspective: A review. SSM Popul Health. 2016, 2:373-381.

26. Aldridge MD, Kelley AS. The myth regarding the high cost of end-of-life care. Am J Public Health. 2015, 105(12):2411-5.

27. OECD (2019), Health spending (indicator). http://www.oecd.org/els/health-systems/health-data.htm (Accessed on 03 September 2019)

QUANTUM SUPERPOSITION: THE
ESSENCE OF DEEPER UNDERSTANDING

THE CONSCIOUS MATRIX is the stairway to our inner beliefs. When asked, people often respond that they don't know what God is, that faith requires you to trust without knowing. Many religious people claim to be content not knowing. But ironically, most of those same people will be able to tell you quite clearly what God isn't. It seems people hold multiple perceptions of God, knowing none are entirely correct. "We see God indirectly through His works," it's often said. When pressed with the question, people commonly express their vision of God as an all-knowing and benevolent man-like figure or as the abstract concept of a "higher-power" or "supreme-being."

Curiously, this exact kind of uncertainty typifies quantum mechanical theory. Wave-particle duality is a paradox. At the smallest scale, when dealing with subatomic particles and the smallest units of energy, things become quite uncertain. We can describe an electron, for example, as a wave or as a particle. So which is it? It's not clear an electron is either a wave or a particle; it may exist as cloud of possibilities. Until the position or velocity is measured, the electron exists in a *superposition* of multiple possible states. When there's any kind of measurement, the superposition is forced to one state; this is called reduction of the wave-function. But it gets more complicated than that. The observer is part of the quantum system. It's like that old adage: If no one's in the forest when a tree falls down, is there any sound? There will be vibrations, but "sounds" are vibrations in the audible range that require an observer, so the correct answer is "No."

If our conscious matrix operates in accordance with quantum mechanical theory, our intuitions concerning God are in a kind of superposition. Whenever we "experience God," there's a reduction of multiple quantum states. The result is we know God exists, and we know what kinds of thinking and what type of events produce our experiences of Him. We know and we believe (if we're believers), even though we can't describe exactly who or what He is.

> *A possibility to consider*: God is all the wisdom in the universe. God has all the answers to quantum mechanics and to all the mysteries of biology and human behavior. Every human being seeks this wisdom; it's an inborn drive, the quest of the human soul. Viewing God as a person affords some advantages in the seeking process.

People have an inborn need to understand. We seek to understand why we do things. We seek to understand why others do things. Understanding helps us deal with complex situations. When we get the plot of the story, when we're able to read another person's intentions, when we simply get it—that instantaneous understanding is a magical moment. Understanding enables us to cope with difficult situations and adapt our behavior for success. Believers look to God for answers and he provides. As the Bibles says in Luke 11:9 (NASB), *"So I say to you, ask, and it will be given to you; seek, and you will find; knock, and it will be opened to you."*

Our view that God is a person-like entity enables us to talk to Him like a friend or parent. Perhaps that's why so many people retain a vague notion that God is a person, or something like a person. This belief persists in a significant number of people, even after higher education. Skeptics who claim "belief in God" is declining in America are mistaken.

One way to assess religious beliefs is to take surveys or polls. Gallup, Rasmussen, and Pew Research Center take polls periodically asking Americans about their views about God and religion. Overall, ninety percent of Americans believe in God or some kind of higher-power, most Americans feel religion is important in their lives, and most feel connected to a local church or religious group.[1]

But what's the breakdown between literal or metaphorical believers? A Rasmussen poll conducted in December, 2012, found sixty-four percent of Americans polled believe in God as described in the Bible.[2] There was a significant effect of age in how Americans answered this question. For people under forty years of age, only fifty-three percent responded they believe in "God of the Bible," whereas seventy-three percent of those over sixty-five years responded yes to that same question. Americans, however, are divided when it comes to believing if the Bible is the "literal word" of God. A Gallup poll conducted May, 2017 found only twenty-four percent of Americans believe the Bible is the "literal word," whereas seventy-one percent believe the Bible is the "inspired word" of God or some mix of literal and inspired.[3]

Pew Research Center looked at education level and religious belief in a series of surveys. Pew found that among the seventy-one percent of Americans who identify as Christian, obtaining a college education doesn't diminish their faith or decrease their attendance at church services.[4] Faith in God transcends higher education for many religion groups in America. An impressive ninety-five percent of Muslims, ninety percent of Evangelical Christians, ninety percent of historically black Christians, eighty-eight percent of Mormons, and eighty-two percent of Orthodox Jews claim an "absolutely certain" belief in God after obtaining a college degree. Catholics, Mainline Protestants, and Non-Orthodox Jews showed lower baseline levels of belief in God, and this lower percent was decreased further by higher education. After college, only twenty-three percent of non-Orthodox Jews responded they believe in God with absolute certainty, compared to forty-five percent of Jews without a college education.

Many people believe in seemingly impossible "miracles" of a religious nature, whereas those same people would totally reject seemingly impossible events in ordinary life. There are at least three reasons why people might hold literal beliefs in Bible stories. The first explanation is that religious traditions teach obedience. Most of us are taught our religious traditions as children. We're taught to obey our parents at the same time we're taught to obey God, who is all-knowing. As a result, we learn to obey what our parents have taught us even when they're not observing us. Since God can see us all the time, we internalize that idea and behave accordingly.

The second reason, which also accounts for many believers, is that holding onto literal beliefs of a religious nature is a useful heuristic. It's easier to talk to God if we personify him. When we go about our daily living, we can have a conversation with a living God. When we teach about God, it's much easier if we present Him as a person. It also makes more sense to pray to a personified God, than to a universe force.

The third possibility, however, is the most intriguing. It could be that we need an inextricably-linked combination of both literal and metaphorical interpretations to convey the deeper meaning of God in all His roles. In the expression of religious ideas, we see examples of both literal and metaphorical concepts used alternatively to capture the deeper meaning. As shown in Table 1, literal concepts—based on concrete examples—produce high levels of obedience. Young people and the innocent respond best to literal conceptualizations. One simply lacks the ability to think deeply on matters with which they've had no experience. Metaphorical concepts—based on abstractions—convey complex stories that can have multiple interpretations. These concepts are more useful to older and more experienced people, who have acquired wisdom through living. People who have dealt with many difficult life challenges are high in conviction. They believe what they believe and are unlikely to be convinced otherwise.

Different Ways to Perceive God

Literal Belief	Metaphorical Belief
• High obedience	• High conviction
• Concrete examples	• Abstract concepts
• Simple story lines	• Complex story lines
• Youthful perspective	• Mature perspective
• Faith based on trust	• Faith from wisdom

The inspirational power of Bible stories comes from the interplay between the literal and the metaphorical. Not all literal examples are deep enough to effectively explain the subtle nuances of meaning. But only those metaphors that reflect realistic situations and teach a lesson survive the ages. Shallow or contrived stories that don't inspire fall by the wayside. In order to grow spiritually as individuals or as a religious group, the stories passed down must bridge the literal and metaphorical, the young and old, and the innocent and wise. The effectiveness of the literal-metaphorical superposition is measured in its ability to trigger reflection and to positively impact life outcomes. The most enduring of the Bible stories give us understanding—these stories shed light where there was only darkness.

A thought to ponder: *God is both a literal "being" and a metaphorical "concept" fused together by quantum superposition. We think of literal and metaphoric perspectives as distinct. But when descriptors are reduced to their quantum mechanical essence, the resulting experience is all that matters. We can reach God, the experience of God, through either literal or metaphorical interpretations. Neither interpretation is real; God, the experience, is what's real.*

Belief in God is a product of the conscious matrix: our thinking and feeling mind. How our mind makes a concept is therefore relevant to understanding how we access our belief in God. Language is the way we usually express most of our thoughts and concepts. Some concepts represent real, concrete objects or actions. In contrast to the concrete, other concepts are abstract, representing categories of objects or actions. The highest-level concepts are rules governing our actions and our life plan. There's not just one route to accessing our highest concepts. Likewise, for believers, our minds reach God by many routes, each of which might be taken in any number of circumstances.

We can start with simple examples of meaning. How do we identify the meaning for ordinary words? The mental lexicon doesn't operate like a mental dictionary.[5] Instead, it acts like a quantum mechanical system where many possibilities reduce into a decision, or more realistically, a series of decisions. The decision process goes something like this: Is this string of letters a word? If yes, what are the possible meanings? Does the context of the word (the whole sentence) suggest a meaning? Does the larger context (the setting or story) suggest a different meaning?

Looking at how the mental lexicon actually works illustrates how the mind constantly selects the best answer based on huge databases of information storing past experiences in a specific architecture. That architecture upon which our conscious matrix operates has the keys to the car; we only have to jump in and start the engine. Our brains are wired to find the routes to experience God. And on a deeper level, our biology is custom-made to house the quantum entanglements that link us to the greater universe. As mentioned in other chapters, measurable distances between pockets housing electrons free to entangle in the conscious matrix aren't random. The grand plan placed them at exactly the correct distances to enable conscious experience, and ultimately to experience of God.

Understanding how our conscious matrix works is more like poetry than science. In her book, *Intersecting Sects: A Poet Looks at Science*, Alice Major discusses the parallels between meaning in poetry and quantum uncertainty.[6] Metaphors, by nature, lead the reader to consider many meanings before choosing. Poetry relies heavily on metaphor, not because it aims to confuse, but because only by first savoring the many choices of possible meanings can one truly appreciate the depth of simple words. A word is just a word, but if you give a word many subtly different meanings, it becomes magical. If we apply her logic to religious doctrine, our use of metaphors to describe the glory of God is in no way trivializing God. Quite the opposite, metaphor opens the door to subtler, deeper meanings, and to reflection.

In his honors thesis on religious metaphors, Tyler Kibbey explains how certain linguistic theories of metaphor enable us to understand the typical religious metaphor.[7] The goal in religious metaphor is to seek the deeper meaning in ordinary life events. Kibbey cites the metaphor "time is money" to make this point. Time is a very complex concept that even quantum physics struggles to define in simple terms. Money is banal and concrete. By equating these two examples representing separate linguistic domains, we immediately grasp the deeper meaning. Our time spent (or our labor) is worth something concrete, yet not. Our time is worth some set wage, while at the same time being absolutely priceless.

> **Another thought to ponder**: *The "creation versus evolution" contro-*
> *versy persists today with religious believers on one side and scientific*
> *skeptics on the other side. This controversy, as it exists in the public*
> *domain, is an example of a "literal versus metaphorical" superposi-*
> *tion in quantum mind theory.*

Everyone has their own opinion about the "creation versus evolu-tion" debate. Or at least that's what it would seem. But in reality, lots of people sit on the fence, or hold completely different views depending on the situation or to whom they're talking. I've seen it first-hand. Having held a faculty position in a science department for over twenty-five years, I saw many colleagues who firmly believed and even taught the Darwinian theory of evolution (or it's more recent interpretations) who would nonetheless defer to a religious spouse at a social gathering. I often thought it must be much easier for male scientists because they could be "scientifically correct" religious skeptics with no consequences if they were wrong. They all had their dutiful spouses keeping their places safe in heaven. Based on countless examples of this sort, I ask with all sincerity: Is it hypocrisy or quantum mind superposition? And being a female scientist, I understand the delicacies of wearing two hats.

The former director of the Human Genome Project, Francis Collins, believes Evangelical Christianity and the theory of evolution aren't at odds.[8] His saying so doesn't make the issue go away, but the path he took to his conclusion is instructive. Collins converted to Christianity after having been an atheist. What really changed things for Collins was going to medical school and interacting with dying patients. Collins turned to the writings of C.S. Lewis, where he found cogent, intelligent arguments for the existence of God and of moral laws. In the end, Collins elegantly concludes you can be a good scientist and a good Christian at the same time. This entails some juggling of the time scale as stated in the Bible, and some other tweaks. Collins argues that some forty percent of scien-tists profess belief in God, far above that claimed by some out-spoken skeptics, who view science and religion as incompatible.

For many people, the more we learn from science, the more in awe we stand of what we don't know. The "raw feels" experience of God is the closest parallel to that awe. This paradox of belief/disbelief, a superposition of states, keeps the depth of spirituality going. Remember what the living cell needs to be alive? The living cell exists in a constant struggle between an optimal state and varying less optimal states. Metabolism is like the beat of the drum: strike, rest; strike, rest; strike, rest. Without rests between strikes, there's no beat. Without occasional skepticism or doubt, our beliefs wouldn't be as deep as they might be. We grow spiritually when our faith is alive. In fact, many students at Christian colleges say doubting their faith occasionally is part of the process; it strengthens belief in the long run.[9]

It's nearly impossible to always be content with our life. Paradise is best suited to be a dream or a goal state. We might occasionally experience exhilaration, but we don't seem to be able to linger there too long. The planning and remembering of vacations are often more pleasurable than the actual experience. We live our lives in pursuit of eternal happiness, but that's not real life as we know it. Life is a struggle; it's a journey. All we can do is fill that journey with as many peak experiences as possible, energize our souls at every peak, and pray that our inner light sustains us through the darkest valleys. Experiencing God or developing our personal spirituality keeps our inner light shining bright.

> *An idea to examine*: *The "virgin birth of Jesus" is a deeply held religious belief among Catholic and Protestant Christians. The discovery of DNA and the accuracy of paternity tests are at odds with this teaching. This "duality of belief" is another example of superposition of states conveying deeper meaning in religion.*

Pew Research Center polled Americans asking about their belief that Jesus was born of a virgin.[10] The results showed that a majority of Americans believe this religious tenet. More women believe this than men. More blacks believe this than whites, with highest levels of belief being expressed by white Evangelicals (ninety-seven percent) and black Protestants (ninety-four percent).

Although the following question wasn't asked in any of the surveys, it's likely that the response would be "no" if asked whether virgin births are possible outside the special case of Jesus. Christians believe Jesus is the son of God, so it follows logically that Mary didn't conceive in the typical way. Given the way people are sensitive to questions about paternity, this science/religion duality isn't publicly debated to the same extent as the "creation versus evolution" debate.

Not only Catholic and Protestant Christians, but Muslims also believe that Mary was a Holy and Sacred woman, who was born without "original sin" as are the rest of humanity.[11] Original sin is a concept of disobedience. We are born imperfect and will make mistakes; it's in our natures. Mary, the Virgin Mother, is considered the highest among the Saints. Mary is the mother of Jesus, who is conceived as a duality mingling "human and divine," making Mary a duality, being both a mother (like most other ordinary women) and holy (by giving birth to the Son of God).

This belief has an enormous impact on women in society. By sanctifying Mary, all mothers retain some connection to this duality: human/divine. The story of the virgin birth of Jesus is religious metaphor that juxtaposes ordinary roles—motherhood and childcare—with the divine aspects of being someone's beloved mother. The metaphor—to ascribe divinity to motherhood—is a call to see poetry in every mother's daily life and her struggles. How many mothers have toiled hard almost to the point of losing faith and strength, only to have their faith restored by the church? The Catholic and Protestant Churches connect strongly to the women in their congregations because women, many of whom identify with their most common role as mother, are glorified by the story of the Virgin Mary and her Sainthood.

Is there a heuristic value of believing in a woman's virtue or purity without question? There are many examples of where this appears to be true. For example, we probably wouldn't dare to ask our fathers whether our mothers were virgins when they married. It's considered disrespectful. For the most part, questioning the virtue of anybody's mother is off the table. And this isn't so much for her sake, but for the sanctity of her children. It most cultures, a woman's virtue is strongly upheld unless she strays too far from cultural norms.

Despite our tendency to act like this never happens, false paternity is relatively common. Researchers find that one in twenty-five children aren't the biological offspring of the presumed father.[12] It's not unusual for another man to marry a pregnant woman abandoned by the biological father. In this case, there's no initial deception. But later on, some deception may occur, as the couple may choose to keep the matter secret from others, spare the child knowing, and never inform the biological father (if he's out of the picture anyway). This can sometimes raise ethical issues later on. It's another case entirely when a married woman becomes pregnant from an illicit affair and never tells her husband about the affair (or why little Johnny looks quite a bit different from the other children). This deception usually takes a toll on the woman if she never tells anyone. Lingering guilt can cause anxiety and interfere with her coping with the normal ups and downs of life.

The Catholic Church has been helpful in releasing anxiety by offering confidential confessionals, where people can vent their guilt and thereby relieve some of the psychological pressure. Protestant Christians don't have confessionals, but may rely on techniques of modern psychology to deal with anxiety and guilt. Denial, or believing the illusion that "everything is okay," is sometimes healthy. Used wisely and sparingly, illusions decrease anxiety and facilitate successful coping with stressful circumstances.[13] Compared to many of the anti-anxiety medications which tend to be addictive and troublesome, a little bit of "kidding ourselves" about our problems may be a good thing, as long as serious problems with a clear solution aren't being ignored.

What does quantum mind theory predict? It predicts people will believe what makes their life work out best. When it comes to suspicions regarding the past virtue of mothers, paternity, and sexual matters, it might be beneficial to believe the best of people we love. Even if we have hard evidence of transgressions, it might be best to evaluate the whole picture. Married couples do forgive adultery and worse. Whether or not you can forgive and forget is a personal choice. Your inner consciousness knows what you want, what you can handle, and what's best for you. Religious authorities, friends, and family can help you decide, but only you know your heart. Only you can talk this matter over with God (or consult the higher-life force). And the way to connect is with our conscious matrix. That's why good spiritual health is so important. It's like having a body that's toned and in shape. We need a smooth-running conscious matrix when spiritual challenges come our way.

> ***One last idea to examine***: *The resurrection of Christ and his joining God, the Father, in heaven is widely believed even though heaven has no actual established location. Belief in heaven transcends our learning more about the universe because this belief was never meant to be about astrophysics. This belief is about sacrifice bringing about delayed reinforcement, and more deeply than that, this belief is about altruism.*

How many people believe they're going to heaven? Where is this wonderful place? How do you get in? Pollsters have asked people about specific religious beliefs concerning heaven. A Rasmussen poll conducted March, 2016 found seventy-seven percent of Americans believe Jesus Christ died for our sins and rose from the dead and reunited with God in heaven.[14] In a poll conducted June 2017, sixty-two percent of Americans believe in an afterlife that includes heaven.[15]

When college-age students at Michigan State University were interviewed on YouTube video,[16] most stated they believe they're going to heaven and gave the following reasons: (1) I believe in God. (2) I've accepted Jesus Christ as my personal savior. (3) I attend church regularly. (4) I'm basically a good person. Only a few were unsure, mostly because they thought they were too young to be judged. Nonetheless, it's clear most people think if they behave themselves, they'll go to heaven.

But is this correct biblically? How many will go to heaven according to the Bible? The book of Revelations states only 144,000 will be asked by God to join in eternal life in heaven. Even biblical scholars have questioned whether this is "literal" or "symbolic." Muddling the issue further, the Bible offers multiple meanings of heaven. The first is as God's dwelling place as described in Psalm 103:19 (NKJV), *"The Lord has established His throne in heaven, and His kingdom rules over all."* In this first context, the Bible describes heaven as a new place where there are no tears and no pain. Heaven is a place of perfect peace, with houses, vineyards, and gardens. But in other passages, the Bible describes heaven as the infinite universe. Psalm 8:3 (NKJV) says, *"When I consider Your heavens, the work of Your fingers, the moon and the stars, which You have ordained."*

The Bible seems to offer "literal" juxtaposed with "metaphorical" descriptions of heaven. How does this fit with the quantum mind theory?

Superposition of concepts, ranging from concrete to abstract, percolate in the conscious matrix until we settle on one idea and reduction occurs. So we simultaneously blend the sky (the atmosphere we see in the day) with the universe (the stars we see at night), and ultimately blend that with God (the all-knowing, father-like figure who watches over us). These ideas are merely routes to the experience of God. Believing in God is the simultaneous experience of all these wonderful things. It's the beauty of nature, the light of day, the dazzle of stars at night—fused into one elated experience.

Intuitively, this interpretation makes sense. We know we often feel joy and awe as we look up to the heavens or the sky. If there are clouds forming, or if there are mountains or sea nearby, the views can be nothing short of spectacular. It's not difficult to see how the mind fuses the concept of sky with the concept of the infinite universe. And then lastly, our minds fuse those concrete concepts (sky and stars), with the abstract concepts of transcendence and an all-powerful being. We think of heaven while gazing at a beautiful sky, sunset, or sunrise. This beauty and this context trigger our experience of God; it literally lights up our inner consciousness, sending photons dashing through our conscious matrix.[17]

During our lifetimes, we may only get an occasional glimpse of how intense experience can enlighten our conscious matrix. Perhaps we leave as we came, as pure experience. It could be that our conscious matrix moves into another universe, one we've never experienced but that has similar things to ours, like houses and gardens. We simply don't know, but we can imagine. As Emily Dickenson eloquently wrote:

THE BRAIN is wider than the sky,
For, put them side by side,
The one the other will include
With ease, and you beside.

The brain is deeper than the sea,
For, hold them, blue to blue,
The one the other will absorb,
As sponges, buckets do.

The brain is just the weight of God,
For, lift them, pound for pound,
And they will differ, if they do,
As syllable from sound.

Poem by Emily Dickenson (1830 – 1886)

When we die our brain architecture that holds our conscious matrix deteriorates. Our bodies, our organs, and all the cells within us deteriorate upon death because metabolism stops. There's no more inner light generated without metabolism. But our conscious matrix connects with the universe. How it does that isn't known, but we sense something comes next. Is the Bible right about heaven? Are there no tears and no pain? If our conscious matrix still connects to the universe after our metabolism ceases, then there would be no pain. The situation would be completely new. And without the struggle of metabolism, there would be infinite peace. Is heaven someplace real or ethereal? Or could heaven be a complex combination of both everything we dream about and the vast expanse of space-time? Only quantum mind theory can deal with this level of complexity. And we've only scratched the surface.

Perhaps the real and practical purpose of heaven, at least in religious teachings, is to direct our behavior while we're living. Christians, and people of other religions, try to live good and moral lives, in part, because we want to go to heaven. But living good and moral lives pays off much sooner than that. Healthy behaviors promote our own health and well-being. That's job one. And since people are highly social beings, we need to be continuously concerned about how our behavior affects others. We live in families and communities. Our actions must be carried out, not only in our own self-interest, but also with consideration to our families and to the larger community. When viewed in those larger contexts, sacrifice for the greater good and altruism are necessary objectives. Religious teachings help us meet those more complicated goals.

Our moral development has six ascending stages, as outlined by Lawrence Kohlberg.[18] Moral reasoning starts as a simple skill set for choosing behavior to avoid punishment or obtain rewards. A deeper moral understanding develops over the years. At the highest levels of moral reasoning, social norms and mutual benefit sometimes have to be tossed aside for the more "transcendent" moral principle. Quantum superposition is the only theory that can fully explain the Kohlberg model.

6 Stages of Moral Development

Stage	Age Range	Goal State
Obedience/ Punishment	Infancy	Avoid punishment
Self-Interest	Pre-school	Gain rewards
Conformity	School-age	Gain approval from others
Social Order	School-age	Understand rules of social behavior
Social Contract	Teens	Understand mutual benefit and reciprocity
Universal Principles	Adulthood	Understand moral behavior transcends rules and mutual benefit

Adapted from Kohlberg, 1973

According to Kolhberg's model, young children are only equipped to choose right from wrong; they can only deal with situations where the choices are clear and simple. Adults will be placed in dilemmas where no choice is perfect, and they might have to pick the choice that does the least harm to other people. And in some cases, the situation may require that some people are more critical to save than others (protecting the leader in war as an example). Quantum mind theory explains simple and difficult moral conundrums as a superposition of choices. Sometimes none of the choices are savory. In those extreme cases, we may need to consider virtually every experience we've ever had—long and hard—to make a decent decision.

Some of the college kids in the YouTube video answered they didn't know if they were going to heaven, saying that it was too soon to judge. Although undecided, their answers showed profound insight. We simply don't know what life will throw at us. And we don't always know what life has thrown at others. Some situations we might have to face in life won't allow for an easy way to heaven. But is heaven all we're after? In addition to a final resting place, can heaven be a metaphor that fills one's journey through life with deeper meaning instead of emptiness? This is where theologians excel above scientists when dealing with moral dilemmas. But to their credit, scientists discovered quantum mind theory. The more we discover through science, the more we know how little we understand about the universe and the human soul. But there's great beauty and joy in the journey of discovery—it's the experience that matters.

CHAPTER 6: NOTES AND REFERENCES

1. Fahmi D. Key findings about American's belief in God. Pew Research Center. April, 2018. https://www.pewresearch.org/fact-tank/2018/04/25/key-findings-about-americans-belief-in-god/

    Religion important to most Americans. Rasmussen Reports, October, 2017. http://www.rasmussenreports.com/public_content/lifestyle/general_lifestyle/october_2017/religion_important_to_most_americans

    Fifty-seven percent think Churches essential to healthy communities. Rasmussen Reports, June, 2013. http://www.rasmussenreports.com/public_content/lifestyle/general_lifestyle/june_2013/57_think_churches_essential_to_healthy_communities

Americans feel most connected to a local religious group. Rasmussen Reports, March, 2013. http://www.rasmussenreports. com/public_content/lifestyle/general_lifestyle/february_2013/ americans_feel_most_connected_to_a_local_religious_group

Eighty percent say religious faith is important to their daily lives. Rasmussen Reports, April, 2010. http://www.rasmussenreports. com/public_content/lifestyle/general_lifestyle/april_2010/80_say_ religious_faith_is_important_to_their_daily_lives

2. Sixty-four percent believe in God of the Bible. Rasmussen Reports, December, 2012. http://www.rasmussenre- ports.com/public_content/lifestyle/general_lifestyle/ december_2012/64_believe_in_god_of_the_bible

3. Chapman MW. Gallup: Only 24% of Americans believe the Bible is the literal word of God. CNSNews.com, May 2017. https://www.cnsnews.com/news/article/michael-w-chapman/ gallup-only-24-americans-believe-bible-literal-word-god

4. In America, does more education equal less religion? Pew Research Center. April, 2017. https://www.pewforum.org/2017/04/26/ in-america-does-more-education-equal-less-religion/

5. Libben G. The quantum metaphor and the organization of words in the mind. Cultural Cognitive Science 2017, 1:49–55.

6. Major A. Intersecting Sets: A Poet Looks at Science. University of Alberta Press, 2011.

7. Kibbey TE. Religious metaphor and structural complexity. Chancellor's Honors Program Projects, 2017. https://trace.tennessee.edu/ utk_chanhonoproj/2032

8. Religion and science: conflict or harmony? Pew Research Center. May, 2009. https://www.pewforum.org/2009/05/04/ religion-and-science-conflict-or-harmony/

9. Silliman D. Doubt your faith at an Evangelical College? That's part of the process. Christianity Today, August 2019. https://www.christianitytoday.com/news/2019/august/evangelical-students-faith-crisis-christian-higher-ed-cccu.html

   Carter JL. The patterns of religious struggle among undergraduates attending Evangelical institutions. Christian Higher Education. 2019, 18(3):154-176.

10. Masci D. Most Americans believe in Jesus' virgin birth. Pew Center Research. December, 2013. https://www.pewresearch.org/fact-tank/2013/12/25/most-americans-believe-in-jesus-virgin-birth/

11. Hopler W. Who is the Virgin Mary? The life and miracles of the Blessed Virgin Mary, Mother of God. Learn Religions. January, 2019. https://www.learnreligions.com/who-is-the-virgin-mary-124539

12. Surprise! 1-in-25 Dads are not the real father. LiveScience, August, 2005. https://www.livescience.com/375-surprise-1-25-dads-real-father.html

13. Taylor SE, Armor DA. Positive illusions and coping with adversity. J Pers. 1996, 64(4):873-98.

14. Three quarters of Americans believe Jesus rose from the dead. Rasmussen Reports, March, 2016. http://www.rasmussenreports.com/public_content/lifestyle/general_lifestyle/march_2016/three_quarters_of_americans_believe_jesus_rose_from_the_dead

15. Most Americans believe in the afterlife. Rasmussen Reports. June, 2017. http://www.rasmussenreports.com/public_content/lifestyle/general_lifestyle/june_2017/most_americans_believe_in_the_afterlife

16. Asking people: "Do you think you're going to heaven?" YouTube October 13, 2013. https://www.youtube.com/watch?v=u92Me3iOmjU

17. Looper S. A theology lesson from quantum physics: What beaming a photon to space has to do with salvation. Christianity Today, October 2017.

18. Kohlberg L. Stages and aging in moral development-some speculations. Gerontologist. 1973, 13(4):497-502.

7

GOOD AND EVIL: HOW CAN A LOVING GOD ALLOW BOTH?

YOU WAKE UP each morning and can't avoid reading or hearing news of some shockingly tragic event. Evil things happen all the time: war, murder, corruption, deception, and betrayal. Why do bad things happen? But even more perplexing is this question: Why do bad things happen to good people? People from all walks of life, but particularly religious people, often ask with all sincerity: How can a loving God allow people to suffer? If God is truly all-knowing, all-loving, and all-powerful, then how can He let the faithful down? One of the tenets of faith is to trust God even in the darkest hours.

Does quantum mind theory offer an explanation for this paradox? All our conscious matrix can do is take a look at ourselves, another look at others, and finally shoot a large panoramic view of the world. When all the images are collected and compared, the conscious matrix computes how we all connect. In the grand scheme of the universe, there's no absolute good nor is there absolute evil; it's all relative and a matter of perspective. In the final analysis, what's good is what works and connects people together best.

The universe runs according to laws that determine its nature and order; deviations from those laws of nature result in disorder. Life is a constant struggle. Metabolism is the core biological principle of life. The living cell struggles between an optimal set-point and counters constant deviations to bring the cell back to center. If we apply that biological principle to human life, then optimal set-points are beliefs that tell us how to behave in a way that helps us connect to others and to the "greater good." To say it another way, the function of beliefs is to generate better life outcomes. We expect good behavior to be rewarded with better health, more happiness, and stronger relationships with family and friends. As our behaviors continuously deviate from those ideals, we expect to encounter poorer life outcomes. And we need not be too hard on ourselves when we err. We're nearly guaranteed to make mistakes just by being alive. As continuously active beings, the odds of our behavior being perfect 100% of the time are extremely low. Given the many complex variables, life outcomes are never entirely predictable. How things work out, on any given occasion, is largely a matter of statistical probabilities. Even if we were to possess the highest moral principles possible—achieved through personal reflection and years of intensive religious study—we'd still only succeed at obtaining the reward we seek some of the time. Rewards occur on a statistical basis.

Consider the following scenario: If I estimate my behavior is good almost all the time, let's say ninety-five percent of the time, under those circumstances, I might expect a good outcome roughly ninety-five percent of the time. That seems fair enough. What also seems fair is that when I make an occasional mistake, I might be lucky and not suffer poor consequences. I'll attribute my good fortune to my average record of mostly good behavior. But if on another occasion I might be doing everything right and I get a bad outcome, I'll probably think it's unfair. But it's fair if you consider the average ratios between behavior and outcome; they match perfectly. There's no doubt people who live by good moral principles have better life outcomes, on average. There's just not a one-to-one relationship between our behavior and the immediate outcome because we don't live in a vacuum; we interact with others in most situations.

So bad things can happen to good people. It's not God's fault. Believing in God and living according to moral principles helps reduce the odds of bad things happening to us. Virtuous beliefs and upright behaviors give us the best chance possible, most of the time. When bad things happen is precisely the time we need to renew our faith and keep our odds in the positive range. But that's not always easy. A particular challenge to our faith is when decent people are hit hard, or hit repeatedly with devastation.

Sometimes tragedies that strike are so horrendous we find them nearly impossible to comprehend. For example, few people can cope with a family member having been murdered, especially a child. How does one ever wrap their mind around this kind of devastation? And then, if the murderer is acquitted, it may seem like there's no justice in the world. It may seem like there's no God. But some families so struck down by a tragedy do heal, oftentimes after many years of pain. Some families do forgive, and their faith does return. But sometimes people can't forgive or forget, and their souls suffer. Sometimes that suffering turns into rage, and to revenge, which may cause the cycle to repeat itself. The only way to break the cycle is to face the perception of evil, look at it objectively, and not give in to allowing it to destroy you.

There are tools afforded by quantum mind theory. One such tool is to see "good/evil" as a paradoxical duality. Is there really such a thing as evil, or is evil just one of many deviations away from good? We constantly read and hear about horrific events, but we assure ourselves most are statistical anomalies. We like to think most people are good; otherwise, we'd be living in constant fear. Most of our friends and acquaintances seem to be good people. We tend to reserve judgment for people who we don't know, or people who aren't like us or who don't share our values. But are some people truly evil? The more we learn about people who mean to do us harm, the more we realize that one common denominator is how they have a completely different perspective than we do. Oftentimes, these people who mean us harm are very troubled or in pain. Knowing what makes people deviate from good intentions can help us avoid being victims. As stated in Romans 12:21 (NKJV), "*Do not be overcome by evil, but overcome evil with good.*"

The most extreme example of "pure evil" is war. How does one nation declare war with another nation with the conscious intent of annihilating the people of that nation? How do the leaders of nations get the people to back them and join in military battles that slaughter massive numbers of people?

> ***A possibility to consider:*** *War is an example how the "good" versus "evil" dichotomy boils down to a matter of perspective. Both sides of a conflict believe they're right. As quantum mind theory would predict we only see our perspective, much like the figure-ground illusion. That's how people justify doing harm to others; they dehumanize and vilify their victims by ignoring their humanity.*

Who's right and who's wrong? It's not always easy to decide because we usually can't see the other person's perspective. Here lies much of the cause of human strife; here's why people struggle and wage war. We simply don't see eye-to-eye with everybody. We hold different views of the world because we make different interpretations and draw different conclusions. The world is what it is; all the value judgements exist only in our minds. Different perspectives cause people to focus attention on what's important to them and ignore other people's needs as background noise. This is part of human psychology as illustrated by the figure-ground illusion:

Vase or boy facing boy?

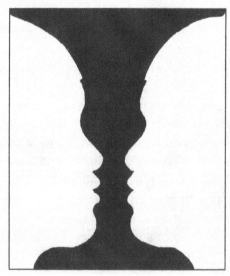

The figure-ground illusion. *Two interpretations are possible: a black vase or two faces looking at each other. Our conscious matrix selects which image to focus attention upon, and which image to ignore as background.*

Our conscious matrices are designed to make value judgements, and they are precision instruments in doing so. We live in pursuit of our well-being in harmony with the grand order of the universe. Our values and conclusions clash when our self-interest is juxtaposed with the self-interest of another. We can't throw our self-preservation instincts to the wind to appease others. Not all people want to be friends; some people genuinely wish to do harm against us. How is this possible?

Let's start with a simple question: If all people on earth have conscious matrices that are connecting them to the grand order of the universe, how is it that we have conflict and war? One might think the grand order of the universe would bind us all together. In many situations, it does. International communication is at an all-time high. More people than ever are traveling the world. Through the Internet, lots of people are connecting with people across the globe, on social media and playing video games together. This level of global interaction has made us more connected than ever before. The Internet also changed how much we know about other cultures. We can search almost anything and get a quick answer.

So why would people want to do us harm? Usually the answer is competition for limited resources. There might be some valued resource—food, energy, textiles, minerals, technology, or human labor—that two or more nations are competing to obtain. One strategy is to barter or negotiate. We'll give you this if you give us that. When that fails, threats may ensue. When negotiations, repeated threats, and other avenues fail, that's when wars sometimes break out.

It's not easy to get people to kill one another. Most of the major religions strongly condemn killing, except for in times of war or when killing is in self-defense. Occasionally, however, wars are fought over religious, ethnic, or political differences. Around eight percent of wars have been fought in the name of religion.[1] How do you get good people to kill each other? The answer psychologists arrived upon is: dehumanization.[2] It's common to dehumanize the enemy. Characterizing the enemy as animalistic or barbaric diminishes their humanity, so you don't connect with them as fellow human beings. Nation states, when they declare war on another nation or on a group of people as in genocide, typically circulate propaganda beforehand to ignite fear and hate of the group being dehumanized.

Quantum mind theory predicts war goes against the way our conscious matrix works. Our conscious matrix seeks to firm up our connection to the universe. This is completely opposite to war, where whatever is gained never seems to justify the mass destruction or loss of life. People across the globe are becoming increasingly aware of war's repeated failure to achieve a good outcome. People *en masse* are rejecting war. But submission to an aggressor isn't the answer either. Submission is giving into the war game; it's playing the game. Negotiation, repeated negotiation, and more tries at negotiation—that's the only way to resolve international conflicts without war.

Once we've identified conflict as a figure-ground problem, real progress can be made. It's first necessary for both sides to see the others' point of view. An important ground-rule in negotiation is honesty and straightforwardness. If there's deception in the process, then the negotiation has to restart. Deception is a war tactic. Deception is the antithesis of sincerity and a deal-breaker for success in negotiations.

A thought to ponder: People use lies and deception to get what they want more quickly. Ironically, the end result of deception usually prevents or delays a good outcome. But people sometimes lie for good reasons. Quantum mind theory predicts that it's the intent that determines the level of destructiveness of a lie.

Good Lie/Bad Lie

Type of lie	Consequence to receiver
White lie: "You don't look fat."	Person feels better.
Hiding shame: "I didn't go off my diet and eat ice cream."	Person doesn't find out something irrelevant to them.
Hiding guilt: "I didn't have an affair with your wife Mary."	Person is deceived, but is spared hurt.
Falsely accusing another: "Mary is having an affair with John, not me."	Person is deceived and hurt. Calls into question the motives of the liar.

Lies and deception aren't good; we know this intuitively and are taught it as well. But are all lies equally bad? Lies fall on a continuum ranging from possibly beneficial to outright malevolent. A "white lie" is what we commonly call a lie meant not to hurt somebody's feelings. The classic example is telling a person who asks that they don't look fat. Many people discount the many white lies they tell, and deny that those examples are really lies. Adults also exclude the many falsehoods they tell their children: like Santa Claus brings gifts, the tooth fairy leaves money, and so forth. Is this right or wrong? Most people would agree that white lies are sometimes the most appropriate thing to do. So we're left to assume not all kinds of lying are evil; it has more to do with the intent of the lie.

The next level of lying is hiding shame. We're not always proud of our behavior. But do we have to admit all of our short-comings? Is it anybody's business? Ordinarily, no one is the wiser and we haven't hurt anyone, but lying to hide shame may have damaging consequences to ourselves. And hurting ourselves isn't good at all. Shame is a dangerous emotion that triggers feelings of unworthiness, dishonor, and disconnection.[3] Using our conscious matrix as our good/evil decider button, this one gets a "mostly okay." But people need to be cognizant and question whether they're experiencing too much shame or inappropriate levels of shame.

Outright lies, ones purposefully crafted to hide guilt, are judged to be wrong by most people. The likely interpretation is that a person is hiding guilt to avoid punishment. It signals that the liar knows they've done something wrong and won't admit it. Usually, lies crafted to hide guilt eventually become known. It's somewhat surprising that people tell outright lies because human beings show a trait called "harm aversion," a concern about causing harm to others.[4] But when people are given a choice to deliver mild electric shocks to another person or receive those shocks themselves, most people demonstrate "moral hypocrisy," in which they judge others more harshly than they judge themselves.

The very worst kinds of deception are outright lies designed to damage the character of another person or group of people. These are vicious lies, conceived with full intent to do harm. These are the lies of character assassination, sometimes used in heated political campaigns. These are also the kinds of lies and deception used to dehumanize an enemy in mobilizing war. The motive is to cause loss to the person targeted, and in the extreme cases, to cause death. In a political campaign, one side may try to destroy the other side so they lose the political race. In war, one nation wishes to annihilate another nation. Hate speech prevails. Reason goes out the window. How does our conscious matrix allow this? Is there a kind and just God anywhere to be found?

The real truth is our conscious matrix doesn't allow deception to continue for long. The conscious matrix is the ultimate lie detector. It knows when the human soul is bereft of any value. There's little light in the conscious matrix when corruption takes over. The pursuit of perfection is displaced by chaos, and anger replaces joy. Time nearly always reveals the truth. God is always nearby; we just have to wait patiently at times for Him at arrive and make His presence known.

> **Another thought to ponder:** *Corruption and criminality are real. These occur in persons or groups who create and live in a delusion that they're doing nothing wrong. Sooner or later, this delusion falls apart.*

Although it seems likely that a true evil force doesn't actually exist in nature, corruption and criminality are very real. How do people ignore their own conscious matrix? Shouldn't we always feel that link to the universal laws of order? Why doesn't our inner knowledge of fairness and justice always prevail? Hypocrisy is one of the great downfalls of mankind.

Psychologists call this kind of hypocrisy the "fundamental attribution error."[5] We judge ourselves as inherently innocent. If we make a mistake, we blame the situation. For example, if we cheat on our taxes, we claim it's because the tax is too high or unfair. If our neighbor cheats on his taxes, that's another story. When judging others, we attribute questionable behavior to weakness of character. He cheats on his taxes because he thinks he's better than everyone else, we might claim. Or we might simply call him dishonest.

In his book *The Lucifer Effect: Understanding How Good People Turn Evil,* social psychologist Philip Zambardo explains how groups of people can grow increasingly insensitive and corrupt.[6] Zambardo designed and conducted the Stanford Prison Experiment where he randomly assigned ordinary students to either the role of prison guard or prisoner. Within a week, the prison guards developed into brutal, sadistic tyrants. Quite oppositely, those students randomly assigned to be prisoners displayed increasingly submissive and beaten-down demeanors. Zambardo concluded that people can be corrupted by social dynamics; people become what the situation demands.

As discussed in Chapter 6, obedience to God is taught in most of the major religions, a concept that's readily grasped, especially by young children. Even as adults, we obey authority figures, and that can sometimes get us into trouble. What happened in Zambardo's prison experiment, and in similar studies, is that people obey all too well. Stanley Milgram conducted another obedience experiment in which college-student participants were instructed to deliver painful shocks to actors, who weren't really receiving the shocks.[7] Surprisingly, many students complied and delivered shocks they perceived to be dangerous and painful to the other person. When asked why they did it, many of the student participants replied "because the experiment told me to do it." It also mattered that the experimenter was viewed as a person of authority. Obedience can be a dangerous thing, especially if we believe and follow directions from the wrong person.

How do criminals live with themselves knowing they're hurting other people? It seems that social dynamics and dehumanizing the victims are two ways those living outside of the law justify their behavior. A classic example of glorifying theft is found in the tale of Robin Hood.[8] The main character of many popular ballads and legends, Robin Hood is the great hero of English folklore of the Middle Ages. With his team of Merry Men, Robin Hood steals from the rich to give to the poor. Why is this stealing celebrated? For one, Robin Hood stood up against injustice. Prince John usurped the presumed "rightful place" of King Richard, to whom Robin Hood remained loyal. Secondly, times were so desperate in the Middle Ages that many men did have to steal in order to survive. This begs the moral question: Is theft sinful if it's done to eat or feed your family? Even though these kinds of conundrums exist, the better solution is to address the underlying problems causing food insecurity, not to condone stealing.

But glorifying criminality continues in modern times. During the late nineteenth and early twentieth centuries, the American mafias organized in major cities such as New York City, Philadelphia, Boston, and Chicago.[9] Organized criminals formed what they called "families." These criminal organizations justified rampant law-breaking, up to and including atrocious murders, using social dynamics and dehumanizing the victim. Not real blood relatives, crime families were composed of bosses and underbosses in complex hierarchies where authority was absolute. It wasn't unusual for disobedient members to be killed. These murders were typically justified because the lower-ranking person "didn't obey the boss," and the boss was the ultimate authority figure.

Many people in crime syndicates were capable of callous and barbaric behavior, especially around their criminal confidants. Nonetheless, some of these criminals would assume the role of decent people in public social settings. When with their children and wives, many crime bosses and their associates functioned as members of regular society. Given that organized crime could be very lucrative, many known criminal bosses became members of high society, mingling with celebrities and politicians.

Many TV shows and movies have been made about the crime families. One particularly popular TV show, the *Sopranos,* delves into the problems faced in the real lives of these people.[10] Tony Soprano, the main character of the show, essentially lives a double life: a duality of criminal and decent family man.

Tony Soprano faces the constant strain of this duality, to the extent that he's seeking therapy from a psychiatrist. His discussions with his therapist are a big part of the show. He's tormented by the duality; it's making him depressed, giving him incredible anxiety, and finally triggers a panic attack. When Tony is hanging out with his partners in crime, he's one person—perhaps his truest self. Tony feels free when he's able to talk about criminal activity with his buddies. They have their secret society and no one will let that information out of the circle. They talk about crime all the time and have no apparent guilt about it because the "group" condones this behavior. Reading between the lines, it seems they worked out justification of their criminality a long time ago.

But Tony has psychological conflict, especially around his wife Carmela and their two children. The wife and children are indirectly affected by the duality created by the incompatibility of criminal/normal social spheres. Carmela mostly stays in a state of denial regarding Tony's criminal associations. Even though she knows enough to be wary, she very much enjoys her affluent lifestyle. Tony and Carmela's children struggle too. The other kids know Tony is one of the crime syndicate bosses. Tony's kids have to repeatedly deny the obvious and claim their dad runs a legitimate business.

The Sopranos was one of the all-time best TV shows and won many awards. Audiences loved the show. One possible reason is that people relate to the struggle between right and wrong, especially when it lingers long in superposition of multiple quantum mind states. Superposition creates tension and makes for great drama. A superposition of opposites—like good versus evil—especially energizes our conscious matrix, giving rise to many thoughts. Viewers might be asking themselves: "What's really so bad about being a criminal when you get to live the good life?" People sometimes wish so much to live the "good life" that they're looking for an easy way and a suitable justification to get there.

But the bitter reality is that even if we're willing to leave our conscience at the door (like Tony tries to do), it doesn't ensure we'll end up fabulously wealthy like the Sopranos. Tony is callous with his crime buddies, but that's a façade. Tony is absolutely tormented by his double life. The psychological discomfort destroys Tony's ability to enjoy the good life. That's the underlying moral of the TV hit. Although the audience loves to see Tony win big, they love to see justice prevail even more. People think Tony deserves to suffer. The quantum superposition reduces in favor of that truth. Crime doesn't pay, even when it does.

Syndicated crime organizations seem to have all but disappeared in America, but street gangs are on the rise. The Federal Bureau of Investigation (FBI) reports over 33,000 gangs exist in the U.S. with over one million members, who commit robbery, murder, drug and human trafficking, among other heinous crimes.[11] Oftentimes these young men are recruited when they're very young. The same sort of duality exists with gangs of young men in America, as described above for syndicated criminal organizations. The gang becomes like family, with rituals for gaining membership and oaths of loyalty. A life of crime is admixed with a sense of belongingness. Fortunately, many gang members leave the gang life as they get older.

Criminal syndicates and gangs exist because of vices like illegal drug use and prostitution. People are willing to buy on the black market what's prohibited through conventional sales in stores or for purchase on the Internet. In this manner, two kinds of evil fuel each other's existence.

> **An idea to examine:** *Vice is a distractor to the conscious matrix. When we're free of vice, our conscious matrix seeks the best outcome for ourselves, for our loved ones, and for our communities. Vice makes us slaves to lesser attractions. Vice interferes with finding inner peace and real solutions.*

Vice is defined in at least three different contexts: religious, legal, and psychological. These different domains or contexts show some overlap in what's considered vice. Vice has at its core some notion of excess. Vice also encompasses, as a fundamental core property, being the polar opposite of virtue. According to Christian theology, the seven virtues are chastity, temperance, charity, patience, kindness, diligence, and humility. Conversely, the seven deadly sins or vices are wrath, greed, sloth, pride, lust, envy, and gluttony. Religion condemns vice as moral weakness and seeks to save the soul of the person attracted to vice.

A legal definition of vice has some overlap with religious views, but with a distinctly different goal. Like religious organizations, law enforcement views vice as a transgression of morality. But the goal of law enforcement is to prevent and punish participation. Vice squads in police departments work to curtail illegal gambling, prostitution, and narcotic drugs sales. Violators are imprisoned. True rehabilitation is rarely pursued in the corrections system.

Psychologists view vice mainly as addiction problems. Drug and alcohol addiction are considered as psychological disorders or conditions that can be treated and controlled.[12] The fifth edition of the Diagnostic and Statistical Manual (DSM-5) lists ten drugs associated with substance-abuse disorders. Street drugs and addictive prescription drugs are chemically similar to chemical messengers our brain cells make. We crave those substances because of the effects they have on our conscious states. Prostitution is sometimes viewed as a "sex addiction" problem, although that label is controversial.

Neuroscience attempts to explain addiction as being chemically mediated, centering the problem on the chemical messenger dopamine.[13] Dopamine is the main chemical operator of the reward system of the brain, located in the bottom middle of the brain stem. The theory is simple: The dopamine reward system is the pleasure center, so addiction must involve some problem in the dopamine system. Cocaine and other stimulants mimic dopamine in the brain, they ramp up activity in the reward center—more than ordinary experiences would. But many additional brain areas and chemicals contribute to addiction.

Acetylcholine is a major player in nicotine addiction.[14] Nicotine is found in tobacco and our natural craving for nicotine is the reason why most people who smoke tobacco products have trouble giving up the habit. Nicotine also stimulates dopamine and this might be why it's addictive.

Narcotics are potent pain-killers derived from opium. Opium comes from the poppy plant, and it's the raw product for the opioid drugs. Both illegal and prescription opioid drugs are very addictive.[15] Opioid drugs include heroin, morphine, codeine, and oxycodone. Opioid drugs mimic chemical messengers naturally found in our nervous system. Our "natural opioids" reduce the perception of pain and produce analgesia. Our natural opioids deal effectively with mild to moderate pain. Natural childbirth, for example, triggers the release of high levels of natural opioids to reduce the pain. But our natural opioids aren't strong enough to endure very painful procedures, such as surgery. This prompted pharmaceutical companies to develop the opium-derivative drugs to combat pain.

Opioid drugs agents are very effective after surgery and don't typically cause addiction with short-term use, especially not in emotionally healthy people with busy active lives. But some people are vulnerable and become addicted to opioid drugs, particularly if they're already in emotional pain, such as occurs with stress or clinical depression.[16] Social rejection is another source of emotional pain, and it activates the same brain areas as does physical pain.[17] Persons who suffer chronic pain or emotional suffering are vulnerable to opioid addiction. Opioid addiction is very serious because it can literally take over a person's life, causing a person to lose voluntary control.[18]

Severe alcohol addiction is even more devastating than opioid addiction, at least when it comes to withdrawal symptoms. Detoxifying from heavy alcohol addiction requires hospitalization. Many people can enjoy moderate alcohol use with no negative effects. But for some, alcohol abuse and alcoholism occur upon exposure. There's a genetic component contributing to alcoholism, but genetics only partly explains why alcoholism occurs in some people and not others.[19] Alcoholism is widespread, affecting over three million people in the U.S. alone.

Alcoholics Anonymous has a twelve-step program that's effective in helping people recover from alcoholism.[20] The first step is recognizing that the alcoholic has a problem. The rest of the steps involve turning to God through prayer, meditation, and humbly asking for help. The program also provides abundant social support through meetings, and each new member is assigned a personal sponsor or mentor who is farther along in the program.

What's the best way to view addiction? Should we classify addictions as medical disorders or flaws of moral character? There are valid arguments for both.[21] Quantum mind theory suggests addictions are both, that there's a duality of causes: one physical and one spiritual. Addictions are characterized by cravings, followed by loss of control. Addictions involve obsessive thoughts and compulsive behaviors. When the conscious matrix is fixated on the substance of abuse, this state detracts from its optimal functioning. We can't search for solutions to other issues that arise in life, nor can we can access inner wisdom through reflection. We can't function optimally when our brain is focused on escaping the psychological discomfort through the use of drugs or alcohol.

Quantum mind theory further predicts that the success of Alcoholics Anonymous is based on its spiritual component. We can resist the urge toward excessive use of drugs and alcohol if we allow our conscious matrix to find solutions to our underlying problems. If we're suffering, then getting in touch with our spirituality may be the best way we have to solve our problems. Only our inner consciousness holds the key to identifying the root causes of our angst; it's our personal struggle. Only strengthening our connection to God can help us. As the Bible says in Luke 10:9 (NIV), *"Heal the sick who are there and tell them, 'The Kingdom of God has come to you.'"*

But the biological underpinnings of addiction are also strong. We can't ignore that our brains and bodies are susceptible to stressors that occur in life. We should resist the urge to blame ourselves for our biological vulnerabilities, but there are ways to overcome biology. We can be prudent and responsible by not allowing stress levels to exceed our capacity to cope. We can remove obvious stressors, reduce expectations of ourselves, and expect less of others. And sometimes we just need to give things time to work out.

We don't need to lose ourselves in drugs or alcohol to escape. We possess our own express-lane on the highway to inner peace. Our brains and bodies are capable of making natural chemicals similar to all the drugs sold or prescribed. The light inside us will release those natural chemicals, but only if we let light inside us shine. Quantum duality connects spirituality with biology better than either approach alone. It's all about the connection.

> **One last idea to examine:** *A good operational definition of "good" is connectedness. We function best when our conscious matrix is optimally connected to our inner-self, to the inner-self of others, to nature, and to God. Disconnectedness breeds chaos, unhappiness, and destruction.*

Many examples of evil have been discussed in this chapter: vilifying and dehumanizing others, deceit, hypocrisy, criminality, and succumbing to vice. In each of these examples, there's an obvious disconnect between the person and others, and perhaps even more evident, there's a disconnect between the person and God and His universal laws of moral behavior. The solution that logically follows is to increase connectedness to overcome these human weaknesses.

The way to fight off submitting to criminal activity, negative authoritarian control, or vice is to keep a good connection with our conscious matrix. Listen to what our inner communicator has to say. We can reliably trust our opinion about a situation more than we should trust any other opinion because we're the only person who knows everything about anything that's ever happened to us. Only we know how much weight to give each experience we've had in moving forward. That's not to say we shouldn't seek guidance from others. When we're faced with a dilemma in uncharted territory, when we have no previous experience or knowledge, then it's wise to seek advice from an expert. But even then, we should check their credentials and then take our own instincts above that of outside advice.

Brain chemistry alone can't explain human consciousness or addiction. Chemical signals relay information, and these chemicals also modify information, to amplify or depress it. But chemical circuits aren't conscious. All that brain chemistry is capable of doing is to provide input to the conscious matrix. The conscious matrix translates those chemical messages into quantum entanglements. When a person gets addicted to street drugs such as heroin or cocaine, their inner consciousness, their soul is taken over by the drug. Quantum mind theory can address this process.

Believers in God have faith in their intuition and insight in a way non-believers don't. Spiritual people have also honed their instincts to make the best choice and trust themselves. People who rely completely on science forget that testing hypotheses only checks out one narrowly-defined idea at a time. Our conscious matrices can cycle through many ideas before settling on one. A quantum superposition reduces every 300 milliseconds.[22] As such, we're capable of testing hundreds of thousands of "quasi-scientific" hypotheses each day. Our conscious matrix is our inner scientist, just as much as it's our inner spiritual guru. That's the dual nature of our conscious matrix.

Looking at life as an "endless string of opportunities" energizes us to meet each new challenge. When our spirit is full of light, we're able to successfully triumph over those obstacles. Our inner strengths and our belief in God or in a higher-power increase the light shining in our conscious matrix. Rather than relying on deception and criminality as a short-cut to success, we can build our inner character through self-reflection. By strengthening our conscious matrix, we enhance our ability to experience God or our personal spirituality. A strong conscious matrix that's well-connected to others allows us to see purity, goodness, and justice as the first choice, saving us time in the long run by eliminating short-cuts to nowhere.

We need more people like Father Greg Boyle, who tirelessly reaches out to young gang members, inspiring these young men to want a better life. After thirty years ministering to gang members in Los Angeles, Father Boyle was struck with the realization that his wanting to save these young men doesn't work; the young gang members have to want it.

Boyle tells the story of Louie, a nineteen-year-old gang member making serious money selling drugs on the street.[23] But when Louie's brother commits suicide, Louie has an epiphany, realizing there's more to life than crime. Louie has a dream where he and Father Boyle are in a dark room and then Louie turns on the light switch. Struck by the symbolism of the dream, an emotional Louie says to Father Boyle: "...the light is better than the darkness." Father Boyle fully sees the significance of Louie's change of heart. Boyle rightly concludes: "It's the connection and the kinship that heals people." Gang members need connection outside the gang to make real progress. Despite the comradery within the gang, belonging to a gang renders one profoundly disconnected away from all the good and decent people who are their victims.

Life is a journey, a wonderful adventure. The road may be long, and it may have bumps and curves to navigate, but we should honor and respect the challenge. We need to spend more time enjoying the challenge of solving our problems and helping others to find their way when we're able. We're capable of solving nearly any problem thrown at us if we allow our conscious matrix to reach into the depths of wisdom each of us possess. It's our conscious matrix that connects us: (1) to ourselves to achieve intrapersonal understanding, (2) to others to achieve interpersonal understanding, (3) to nature and all its glory, and (4) to God to achieve spiritual enlightenment and oneness with the universe.

A person with a strong and healthy spirit is difficult to corrupt, and each of us has the potential to be that spiritually healthy person. God is all-knowing and all-powerful, and He trusts us to find Him wherever and whenever distractions try to take us off our path. As stated in Ephesians 4:29 (KJV), *"Let no corrupt communication proceed out of your mouth, but that which is good to the use of edifying, that it may minister grace unto the hearers."*

CHAPTER 7: NOTES AND REFERENCES

1. Axelrod A, Phillips C, eds. Encyclopedia of Wars. 2004, Vol.3. Facts on File. pp. 1484-1485 Index entry for "Religious wars" category.

2. Haslam N. Dehumanization: An Integrative Review. Personality and Social Psychology Review. 2006, 10(3): 252–264.

3. Lamia MC. Shame: A concealed, contagious, and dangerous emotion. Psychology Today. April, 2011.

4. Yu H, Siegel JZ, Crockett MJ. Modeling morality in 3-D: Decision-making, judgment, and inference. Top Cogn Sci. 2019, 11(2):409-432.

5. Jones EE, Harris VA. The attribution of attitudes. J Exp Social Psychol. 1967, 3(1):1–24.

6. Zimbardo PG. The Lucifer Effect: Understanding How Good People Turn Evil. New York: Random House, 2007.

7. Milgram S. Behavioral study of obedience. J Abnormal Social Psychol. 1963, 67(4):371–8.

8. McSpadden JW. Robin Hood. Cricket House Books, 2010.

9. Kenney DJ, Finckenauer JO. Organized Crime in America. Wadsworth Cengage, 1994.

10. Gabbard G. The Psychology of the Sopranos: Love, Death, Desire and Betrayal in America's Favorite Gangster Family. Basic Books, 2002.

11. Federal Bureau of Investigation: What we investigate: Gangs. https://www.fbi.gov/investigate/violent-crime/gangs

12. American Psychiatric Association. Diagnostic and statistical manual of mental disorders, 5th ed. Arlington, VA, 2013.

Grant JE, Chamberlain SR. Expanding the definition of addiction: DSM-5 vs. ICD-11. CNS Spectr. 2016, 21(4):300-3.

13. Blum K, Chen AL, Giordano J, Borsten J, Chen TJ, Hauser M, Simpatico T, Femino J, Braverma ER, Barh D. The addictive brain: all roads lead to dopamine. J Psychoactive Drugs. 2012, 44(2):134-43.

14. Subramaniyan M, Dani JA. Dopaminergic and cholinergic learning mechanisms in nicotine addiction. Ann N Y Acad Sci. 2015, 1349:46-63.

15. Kreek MJ, Levran O, Reed B, Schlussman SD, Zhou Y, Butelman ER. Opiate addiction and cocaine addiction: underlying molecular neurobiology and genetics. J Clin Invest. 2012, 122(10):3387-93.

    Smith DE, Roy AK III, Fried L, Chen TJH, Chapman E Sr, Modestino EJ, Steinberg B, Badgaiyan RD. Genetic addiction risk score (GARS)™, a predictor of vulnerability to opioid dependence. Front Biosci. 2018, 10:175-196

    Stoicea N, Costa A, Periel L, Uribe A, Weaver T, Bergese SD. Current perspectives on the opioid crisis in the US healthcare system: A comprehensive literature review. Medicine. 2019, 98(20):e15425.

16. Manchikanti L, Giordano J, Boswell MV, Fellows B, Manchukonda R, Pampati V. Psychological factors as predictors of opioid abuse and illicit drug use in chronic pain patients. J Opioid Manag. 2007, 3(2):89-100.

    Meghani SH, Wiedemer NL, Becker WC, Gracely EJ, Gallagher RM. Predictors of resolution of aberrant drug behavior in chronic pain patients treated in a structured opioid risk management program. Pain Med. 2009, 10(5):858-65.

    Trevino CM, deRoon-Cassini T, Brasel K. Does opiate use in traumatically injured individuals worsen pain and psychological outcomes? J Pain. 2013, 14(4):424-30.

17. Eisenberger, NI. The neural bases of social pain: Evidence for shared representations with physical pain. Psychosomatic Medicine. 2012, 74(2):126–35.

18. Hyman SE. The neurobiology of addiction: implications for voluntary control of behavior. Am J Bioeth. 2007, 7(1):8-11.

19. Morozova TV, Mackay TF, Anholt RR. Genetics and genomics of alcohol sensitivity. Mol Genet Genomics. 2014, 289(3):253-69.

20. Monico N, Thomas S. The 12 Steps of Alcoholics Anonymous. October, 2019. https://www.alcohol.org/alcoholics-anonymous/

21. Morse SJ. Medicine and morals, craving and compulsion. Subst Use Misuse. 2004, 39(3):437-60.

22. Woolf NJ, Hameroff SR. . A quantum approach to visual conscious-ness. Trends CognSci. 2001, 5(11):472-478.

23. Boyle G. Father Greg Boyle: I thought I could "save" gang members. I was wrong. America Magazine: May 2017.

OUR CONSCIOUS MATRIX PERCEIVES GOD THROUGH A CULTURAL AND POLITICAL LENS

OUR CULTURE REFLECTS our geographical roots and our traditions. The borders that separate people don't just define different nation states, sometimes the people of two neighboring countries think entirely differently from one another. Countries have different governments and different dominant religions. Religions still practiced today started spreading across the globe five millennia ago—around 3,000 years Before the Common Era (BCE). Religions and governments bind people of one or more cultures together, but only if the conscious matrix is willing.

What's the optimal relationship that should exist between government and religion? History suggests nearly every type of relationship exists or has existed.[1] Throughout history, governments have sought greater control over people by manipulating religious beliefs. If the government can join in a power-partnership with the prevailing religious authorities, that provides greater power to both religious and political elites over the people.

Conversely, when governments are threatened by the people's religious beliefs, the government may try to shut those beliefs down. But as history has proved many times, people believe what they believe. No matter how hard governments try to dictate religious beliefs, and no matter how strongly the state forbids religious practice, not even the most powerful governments succeed in forcing the people to believe in a certain way. Eventually, the people go back to their old ways of believing, even if it takes many years to overcome religious oppression. As the Bible states in Psalm 112:6 (NIV), *"Surely the righteous will never be shaken; they will be remembered forever."*

Even though governments can't completely hijack our strongly held beliefs, our conscious matrix is nonetheless subtly influenced by political agendas. As explained in many chapters of this book, our conscious matrix connects us to a deeper level of truth and justice. These essential universal truths are so pervasive and powerful that our conscious matrix can access these truths even during times of persecution and oppression. That our faith can never be destroyed, and that our faith reappears every single time government attempts to abolish it, is living proof of our access to those universal truths.

So once again we encounter a duality, a quantum superposition of mental states. Quantum mind theory predicts that while we're attracted to new ideas, we'll always try to incorporate new ideas with what we already believe. We're vulnerable to political influences; we're susceptible to what other people around us believe. But those new ideas have to work out for us or else we're going to discard them. We might give a popular new political idea a chance, even trying it out for many years. But if we learn after many years of living in a political system that our conscious matrix isn't fulfilled, then we'll abandon those ideas and that political system. It's our God-given right to pursue life and happiness. And we'll look within, making full use of our conscious matrix to rediscover those beliefs that succeed in bringing contentment, inner peace, and joy.

A possibility to consider: Religious beliefs spread through contiguous geographical areas and spread across continents through migration. Governments oftentimes try to manipulate religion and migration with political agendas.

The five major religions of the world spread across the globe triggered by a few key events.[2] Around 3,000 BCE Hinduism had its start in and around the Indus River Valley, and it began spreading through what is present-day India. Two millennia later, around 1,000 BCE, Abraham was born in Mesopotamia, and Judaism began to spread around the Mediterranean Sea in what are currently Israel, Jordon, Syria, and Lebanon. Next, in 563 BCE, Siddhartha Gautama was born and later became the Buddha. His birth and development heralded the start of Buddhism, which spread to China.

The next events change the picture dramatically and mark the beginning of the Common Era (CE), alternatively called the Christian Era. In 33 CE, Jesus was crucified by the Romans. The crucifixion of Jesus Christ lead to the birth of Christianity, and it quickly spread throughout Europe. Then in approximately 500 CE, the prophet Muhammad was born in Mecca and this was the start of Islam. Islam spread throughout the Middle East, Northern Africa, and parts of Asia. Finally, in the fifteenth century AD, Europeans traveled the Atlantic Ocean and discovered the continents of the Americas. These Europeans spread their religion, Christianity, to North and South America. In the late 1800s, Christianity spread to Africa. Then, in 1948, Israel was declared a Jewish state. Many Jews emigrated from Europe to Israel. This map takes us up to where most of the major religions are concentrated today.

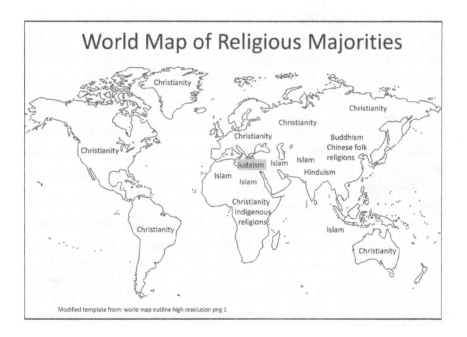

But the world map of religions is continuously evolving, even today. Migration and conversion are the two mains ways religions can spread. Governments can intervene in naturally occurring trends by enforcing policies that protect existing religious practices against outside influences or that foster growth of outside religions by encouraging immigration. Parties of the government may take opposite approaches if they have opposing agendas. Alternatively, governments can attempt even greater control over the people by denying or limiting religious freedoms.

During the past two centuries, the trends have been for governments worldwide to increase their hostilities toward religion. Even recently, there's been increased promotion of atheism, agnosticism, and secularism. Pew Research Center analyzed data from 2007 to 2017 and found that over fifty countries show high levels of religious restriction, including China, Indonesia, and Russia.[3] Governments can restrict religious practices by enacting laws to limit religious freedom, banning religious practice in public, closing places of worship, and harassing people professing or practicing a disfavored religion.

Religious oppression affects countries large and small. The most populous nation of the Asia-Pacific region is China, with a population of 1.4 billion people. China is currently a communist country and the communist party requires party members to be atheist.[4] The Chinese government discourages religion, and will only allow its citizens to register in one of the five state-approved religions: Buddhism, Taoism, Islam, Catholicism, and Protestantism. Any religious practice permitted is closely monitored by the government. Not surprisingly, many surveys record a high level of atheism among the Chinese. For example, a 2015 Gallup poll reported as much as ninety percent of the Chinese population claimed atheist or areligious views.[5]

But there's a duality of belief, whereby the Chinese report contradictory views depending on the way the questions are posed. In the Chinese Family Panel Studies, for example, over eighty percent of Chinese people surveyed admit to practicing a Chinese folk religion, with additional upticks in Buddhism and Christianity in most recent times.[6] This duality of belief shows state-supported atheism as an agenda is ineffective at changing people's deeply held beliefs. People will say they're atheists in one forum and then admit to religious practice in another situation.

Many Chinese resolve this dual belief by viewing their folk religions as "spirituality," which they claim to be distinct from religion.

India is the second most populous country in Asia, with a population of 1.3 billion people. In marked contrast to China, religious practice is widespread in India, and the country is proud of its heritage as the birthplace of four major religions: Hinduism, Buddhism, Jainism, and Sikhism. A majority of people in India identify as Hindu (eighty percent), followed by Muslim (fourteen percent), Christian (two percent), and Sikhism (one-and-a-half percent).[7] The government of India supports freedom of religion; nonetheless, there are restrictions on religious conversions. Christians and Muslims have even been arrested for proselytizing.[8] The prevailing religious climate in India seems to be pro-religion, with particular support for traditional Indian religions, especially Hinduism. The vast majority of the world's Hindu population lives in India.

In contrast to Hinduism being practiced mostly in one country, there are forty-five to fifty Muslim-majority nations throughout the Middle East, Northern Africa, parts of Asia, and Indonesia. Many of these countries self-identify as Islamic nations, where Islamic practices are encouraged and sometimes even mandated by Islamic law, or what's called Sharia law.[9] Islam is the fastest growing religion today. Indonesia has the largest Muslim population at 225 million, but not all people of Indonesia are Muslims.

Apart from Indonesia, Islamic nations discourage other religions in their lands. Islamic nations form a large geographically contiguous region spanning the Middle East, Northern Africa, and adjacent parts of Asia. All these nations are Muslim-majority, with one exception. Israel, a Jewish state, is centered in the Middle East between Egypt, Syria, Jordan, and Lebanon. The Jewish people claim Israel as the homeland promised to them by God, as written in the Bible. In Genesis 12:1-2 (NIV), *"The Lord had said to Abram: 'Leave your country, your people and your father's household and go to the land I will show you. I will make you into a great nation and I will bless you. I will make your name great, and you will be a blessing.'"*

World religions are currently in flux. Just like each of us has a conscious matrix, the collective consciousness made up of various religions and states are in a superposition of conflict. Multiple conflicts arise between governments and religion, between religions, and between the politics of neighboring countries. This gets even more complex when multiple nation states enter into alliances and escalate hostilities with yet other nation states. Whenever there's a superposition of opposing ideas, neither of which wins out immediately, a conflict percolates. These conflicts can persist for decades, centuries, and even millennia. The struggles can be bitter and painful, but there can also be immense joy when a resolution is found.

As quantum mind theory would predict, people are receptive to new ideas and will consider them, but only to compare and contrast with their long-standing beliefs. Once comparisons are made, people tend to select religious practices and political ideas that historically fit the geography of their country and the history of their people. Hence, government policies that seek to protect existing religions seem to prove more successful than do policies seeking to change the religious composition of a nation or region.

It's human nature to be curious about different ideas and to seek and love diversity. But people function optimally and have their spirits revitalized when they live and worship with like-minded people. Our culture and histories determine which beliefs work best for us. It's as if our biology matches the climate and the geography of our native land. This begs the questions: Do certain beliefs go with certain people based on their biological adaptations to certain lands? Do people settle in certain geographical regions based on their DNA? The following sections will probe those issues.

> *An idea to examine:* Israel, a Jewish state centered in the Middle East, has a history of conflict with the Islamic nations surrounding it. Quantum mind theory predicts that the strong faith of the Jewish people and belief in their "right to be in Israel" gives them negotiating power. The Arab-Israeli conflict is a superposition of states that can only be resolved through both parties negotiating and reaching a local solution.

Judaism is considered a major religion to this day because of its place in history. Judaism was the first Abrahamic religion, the first monotheist religion of major significance. Judaism has increased in number of adherents, but not nearly as much as Christianity and Islam have expanded. Compared to over 2 billion Christians, 1.5 billion Muslims, and 1 billion Hindus, there are only 14–18 million Jews worldwide. That's less than 0.2 percent of the world population. Today, nearly half the Jews live in Israel. The other significant majority of Jews live in the U.S. The rest of Jews live throughout the world in a collective called the "Jewish diaspora."

The way in which Jews have grown is different from the way in which other major religions—Christianity, Islam, and Hinduism—have grown in numbers. The Jews have kept their numbers small and focused more on increasing their influence. And with this approach, the Jews have indeed succeeded. Are the Jews God's chosen people, as some have claimed? This question has survived three millennia; that alone seems to mean something profound.

Jews, small in number, nonetheless make a major impact on the world. Jews succeed in some endeavors at higher rates than other groups. An astonishing number of Nobel Prizes have been awarded to Jews, nearly one-quarter of the total.[10] And after only 100 years since many Jews immigrated to the U.S., their small religious group (two percent of the U.S. population) comprises twenty-five percent of the 400 wealthiest Americans.[11] Sometimes Jews are proud of their accomplishments; other times, they'll deny them. Why? Most Jews will say out of fear of persecution.

Jews have a history of repeated persecution. First as slaves of the Egyptians, Jews were forced to leave their homeland. Much of the Old Testament of the Bible chronicles the trials and tribulations of the Jews searching the desert for a home with God's help. The Holocaust is one of the worst cases of genocide in the history of mankind, in which Adolph Hitler and the Third Reich rounded up and executed six million Jews in World War II.

During Jewish persecution in Nazi Germany, the U.S. took in the largest number of Jewish refugees escaping persecution, over 100,000 between 1933-1939.[12] The U.S. remains to this day an ally of Israel and has offered unwavering military protection over the years. Conflicts between Israel and the surrounding Islamic nations are ongoing. Part of that conflict involves the partitioning of the city of Jerusalem, which is considered a Holy city to Christians, Muslims, and the Jewish people. Why are the three Abrahamic religions in conflict? A common origin in Abraham would seem to be a binding factor, a way to find unity and peace.

Mild to moderate conflict might not be all bad. Conflicts reflect dualities, superposition of states. Human beings seem profoundly inclined towards the "familiar versus novel" paradox. We tend to be attracted to the familiar when it comes to religion. Familiar is what best matches our geography, genetics, ancestry and beliefs. But we're also attracted to what's novel; we're excitedly open to new ideas. We like to travel to foreign lands and we like to meet people from far-away places. As a result, nearly every nation today has some mix of all the major religions, even the communist countries. Maybe it's God's plan that we seek novelty to learn how to improve our own culture. When we're challenged to think differently, it provokes our conscious matrix to question our own beliefs. We only grow spiritually when we're free to question things around us. We can only refine and improve our beliefs if we're allowed to think "outside the box" once in a while.

We tend to naturally accept people who think differently from us, up to a certain point. When conflicts escalate too far or threaten our own culture, that's a problem. There must be some solution that can be negotiated between those conflicted in the Middle East so all these excellent cultures can thrive and survive. The three Abrahamic religions: Judaism, Christianity, and Islam all arose from one common origin. That's a significant basis for some common ground. What's the obstacle we're not seeing? God has given us intelligence we can use to solve this dilemma. The best chance of finding a solution is honest negotiations free of deception. We must all pray for a peaceful resolution.

> *A question to ponder: If people of different religions can't get along, should nation-states abolish all religion? Quantum mind theory predicts that any attempts by government to abolish religion are doomed to fail. This is because religious belief comes from within; our conscious matrix connects us to God. No person or state can take that away.*

Institutionalized atheism is a historical example of government banning religion. Eastern Orthodox Christianity was the predominant religion in Russia before the revolution. The communists took over Russia in 1917. Five years later in 1922, Russia abolished all religious practice for the next seventy years. After the revolution was won, Vladmir Lenin installed atheism in what became the Soviet Union.[13] The takeover was brutal. Churches were converted into government buildings and re-purposed. Hundreds of bishops and thousands of priests were murdered. The process was meant to eradicate all remnants of religion in order to take control over the people.

Lenin was inspired by a widely read pamphlet, *The Communist Manifesto,* written in 1848 by Karl Marx.[14] Marx advocated for class warfare between the wealthy business owners (the bourgeoisie) and the working class (the proletariat). Marx believed the former took advantage of the latter, and he further believed the ruling class used religion as a way to manipulate the masses. Marx called religion "the opium of the people."

Curiously, Karl Marx used the concept of "class consciousness" to argue his thesis that capitalist economies were built on class struggle. Marx believed this would inevitably lead to class warfare and the abolition of capitalism, with socialism or communism rightfully taking its place. Marx remains to this day influential in the social sciences, and many agree with his conclusion. But viewing Marxist ideology from the biological perspective, Marx fails to see the obvious: struggle is the definition of vitality, of life. If you take away metabolic struggles, you have cell death and a dead organism. If you remove "class struggle" from the economy, you have a dead economy. Everyone shares equally in the poverty and the misery. And misery abounds in communist countries where food is scarce and the state all but kills the very things that elevate the human soul. Communism is incompatible with religion.[15]

The Soviet communist leaders were wrong in their thinking that once religious organizations were dismantled, religious belief would disappear, never to return. They miscalculated and guessed the source of religious belief arose from outside the person rather than from within. Stamping out religious institutions wasn't working. So in 1936 and 1937, Joseph Stalin again rounded up tens of thousands of clergy members and had them shot to death.[16] But none of these measures survived the test of time.

Millions of people in Russia today worship at Eastern Orthodox Christian churches, and a wide variety of other religions are practiced in smaller numbers. The Pew Research Center surveyed several thousand people in 2015/2016 and found that seventy-one percent of Russians identify as Eastern Orthodox, along with even higher percentages in neighboring Eastern European countries, like the Ukraine, Serbia, and Moldova.[17] And in Poland and the Czech Republic, affiliation with Catholicism has returned to high levels (eighty-seven percent and seventy-two percent, respectively).

If history proves anything, it shows that people have an indisputable inner faith or spirituality. Government attempts to force people to be Godless atheists doesn't work in the long run. Quantum mind theory predicts this failure because the conscious matrix is connected to universal principles of moral behavior. Most importantly, the conscious matrix provides a direct connection with God and the ability to "experience the presence of God."

People have their different cultures. These cultures are based on personality traits determined by the people's DNA and the different climates and terrains to which their ancestors adapted. People's religions suit them. And given enough time for restrictions to relax, people go back to their original religious beliefs. People like their old familiar religions and people like to worship in groups. Worshiping in groups creates fellowship, provides connection to others, and at the same time strengthens one's personal connection to God.

> *Another idea to examine: In this twenty-first century, Americans show correlations between their religion and their politics. Liberalism in America is associated with much higher levels of secularism, whereas conservatism in America is associated with high levels of Evangelical Christian religious belief. These two factions are fighting for the soul of America.*

After 225 years of relative peace among religious groups, religious struggles have hit the U.S. hard. On September 11, 2001, the World Trade Towers were struck down in what was characterized as an attack by Islamic terrorists.[18] Since 9/11, there's been political strife in the U.S. between the two major political parties. To an extent that had never occurred before, conservatives on the political right and liberals on the political left began to intensely disagree. Major points of disagreement include immigration policy and religious freedom.

Although overlap occurs, there are marked differences in religious beliefs when comparing conservative and liberal Americans. In a 2015 survey, Pew Research Center assessed religious and political beliefs.[19] The results showed that large majorities of Evangelical Christians, black Protestants, and Mormons are politically conservative. Catholics and mainline Protestants tend to be moderate. And a majority of atheist, Jewish, Hindu, and Buddhist people identify as liberal. Liberalism is becoming the new secularism, even though many on the left believe in God or are spiritual.

Christians in the U.S. have a very favorable opinion of Israel and of Jewish people; this is particularly true of Evangelical Christians. Liberals in America claim to support Israel but make policy decisions that seem opposite to that goal. In some cases, liberals in America seem more energized to fight against conservative Americans, fomenting intense disapproval of not only conservative politics, but of conservative religious beliefs. It sometimes appears as if some of the most secular liberals in America want to destroy Christianity.[20] I'm shocked at how many liberal politicians and journalists openly criticize conservative attitudes on religious freedom and illegal immigration. Many liberal candidates running for office campaign on government-paid abortion, open borders, and unlimited welfare to illegal immigrants and refugees.

Many conservative Christians are concerned there isn't enough money to fund welfare benefits to illegal immigrants, and that it's deceptive to encourage people with false promises. The U.S. can't afford to sustain what's promised them. Conservatives are also concerned about our being able to continue to enjoy our much beloved principles, particularly freedom of religion. Many conservative Christians are concerned with Sharia law coming to America because it opposes some of our religious practices and limits Christian culture.

The most extreme liberals in the media are alienating many Christians in America, calling conservative Christians bad names—like racist—without justification. As a result, many conservative Christians no longer listen to mainstream media or seek out as much entertainment because of high levels of liberal-bias and painful slurs of people's religious beliefs. The U.S. is in crisis. Our culture is being threatened from within by religious warfare: the seculars against the religious.

Quantum mind theory predicts that the spiritually enlightened will win back the soul of America. It's when our spirit is most energized that the conscious matrix works best. Having our minds energized vastly facilitates our ability to think of novel solutions. Out of the chaos, order will emerge. So bring on more chaos.

Victory for religion or spirituality also enjoys the overwhelming historical precedent. Communists in Russia tried many approaches to destroy religious beliefs, but those beliefs survived inside the conscious matrices of the Russian people. Communists in China are still trying to repress religion in China, but the Chinese folk religions are making a comeback there. Christians in the U.S. are energized to fight for our religious heritage and not acquiesce to media attempts to depict our culture as banal and profane. Most Americans are decent people, not like the false images presented in our major media outlets.

Since its founding in 1776, the U.S. has been a Christian nation.[21] Most Christians embrace the Jewish roots of Christianity and are proud to call the U.S. a Judeo-Christian nation, showing respect to the Abrahamic roots of Christianity. But not all liberals are playing nice with Christians. A month hardly goes by when some Hollywood actor doesn't wish death or damnation to some conservative Christian American.[22] And there are reports of conservative college students feeling oppressed by liberal college professors.[23] It's a sad state of affairs when people are so full of hate and so divided. But from great division, an even greater unity will arise. The best is yet to come, if we believe.

A thought to ponder: Separation of church and state is a founding principle of free nations. Freedom of religion produces an optimal environment for the conscious matrix.

The First Amendment to the U.S. Constitution outlines the separation of church and state. The exact language is: *"Congress shall make no law respecting an establishment of religion, or prohibiting the free exercise thereof."*[24] The First Amendment was adopted in 1791 as part of the Bill of Rights. In the U.S., Americans are very proud of this idea, seeing it as the perfect way to insure proper distance between secular issues of state and individual spiritual decisions. It's a way to keep any quantum superposition that might arise in check. It's a way to keep national matters in perfect balance.

There are myriad reasons that the Founding Fathers of United States of America and the Framers of the U.S. Constitution wrote the "separation of church and state" clauses into the Bill of Rights. For one, many of the Colonists had fled religious persecution in Europe. British Protestants were being persecuted by the Church of England, as one example. The second reason is that the Framers wanted the state to run freely and not be subjugated to religious leaders, who when granted infinite power, might turn out to be corrupt. But perhaps it was truly "divine inspiration" that the Framers saw how we only benefit from our "belief in God" when it's genuine. Only authentic belief has any real power to inspire. Only real belief works. And the beliefs must be "by the people" and "for the people."

This powerful insight was created by early Americans, who were for the most part Christian Americans. These early Americans put our newly formed nation on par with our spiritual beliefs, our God. It was as if to say: "Our country means everything to us. We put all our faith, even our faith in God, into our country." This premise held by Americans has created massive interest in migrating to the U.S., with substantially less interest in emigrating out of the U.S.

The U.S. has one of the most accommodating legal immigration policies on earth.[23] All nations put limits on immigration. It's necessary to prohibit illegal immigrants for many reasons. Costs are one reason; illegal immigrants place burdens on U.S. taxpayers. Moreover, illegal immigrants don't assimilate to U.S. culture very well, whereas legal immigrants assimilate extremely well. It's necessary for new Americans to assimilate to U.S. culture, while at the same time, bringing something unique from their home cultures. Most Americans are absolutely opposed to changing our Constitution, our culture, or our religious freedom. Many Americans feel justifiable pride in our great nation. Preserving our culture and our religious freedom is dear to our hearts.

The challenges faced by average Americans will likely be resolved in the years to come. If spirituality is destined to win over secularism, then the spirit of the United States of America will survive. If the seculars have their way, there will be religious conflict and oppression. When secularism dominates, it creates a spiritual vacuum. America could lose one of its most principled values: the freedom of religion. Without our freedom of religion, some of the energy of the American spirit will be sapped. But chances are good we'll fight with our last breaths for our religious freedom, and we'll win the right to retain our religious heritage and customs. When that happens, the U.S. will emerge even stronger than before.

One final thought to ponder: Pure religious practice is inherently good. Conflicts between religions are actually conflicts arising between different ways that governments "politicize" religion. Nations founded on their "trust in God" permit themselves to ask God for help when conflicts arise.

The politicization of religion is occurring in different forms across the globe right now. Is it a good or bad thing? Well, it depends on your perspective. It seems inherently wrong for governments to try to take away the religion of the people's choosing. And as mentioned above, history proves that people will eventually revert back to their folk religions or traditional religions they practiced before having their religious freedom taken away.

Quantum mind theory suggests the best way forward in negotiating is to avoid deception at all costs. That deception includes "moral hypocrisy," which is seeing only your own perspective in the conflict. All sides have to be honest, open-minded, optimistic, and realistically trusting. But once that trust evolves, it absolutely can't be violated. Trust takes many years to develop and even more years to reclaim again, especially when it comes to nations in conflict.

Perhaps someone needs to pose some hard questions to the Islamic nations surrounding Israel. Why can't the Jews live in Israel in peace without trouble from the surrounding Arab states? The Jewish state— Israel—is in the correct geographical location based on the consensus among many nations. And where should the Jews go if forced out of Israel? No nation or religion can simply do away with another nation or religion they don't like. Genocide is perhaps the worst crime against humanity imaginable. And it nearly always fails to solve anything. People survive and have emotional wounds that last several millennia.

Christians and Muslims take note: We've built our religions on the Jewish tradition of monotheism and the Old Testament of the Bible. We need to ask ourselves: Do we believe God wants the Jews in Israel? Looking at how little the world map of religions has changed over the millennia, the Jewish people appear to have legitimate religious roots in Israel. Can Jews and Muslims live as friendly, yet different, neighbors? And can Christians let the Jews and Muslims work out their negotiations on their own, without our interference?

Christian conservatives in America are largely in conflict with secular liberal Americans on the issue of Israel. We Americans well understand religious conflict; we're not naïve and we've not been spared. But we're Americans, and we support and allow for any religion, or for atheism, among Americans. We have our patriotism, even when we disagree on religion. America was founded on Judeo-Christian principles and we'll fight for the soul of America. We'll fight for our spiritual rights to be a people who continue to enjoy our God-given freedoms: our right to life, liberty, and the pursuit of happiness.

This is my opinion according my conscious matrix. My opinion reflects my country, my culture, and my religious background. In America we tolerate different points of view and everyone's right to express their views. However, we don't allow others to oppress our culture and religious traditions. As Americans, and as human beings, we want to be understood and to understand better. How can we work harder to see each other's point of view? We need honest attempts to find solutions, without expectations of changing the other person's mind. We need to focus our collective consciousness objectively on current problems, forgetting and forgiving past grievances. That's the most logical path to carve out a compromise that satisfies all sides. May God be with all of us. We're in crisis and we need God's help on this one.

CHAPTER 8: NOTES AND REFERENCES

1. Ashford B. Two reasons why religion and politics can't be separated. Billy Graham Evangelical Association, May, 2016. https://billygraham.org/story/two-reasons-why-religion-and-politics-cannot-be-separated/

Margolis MF. From Politics to the Pews. University of Chicago Press. 2018.

Religion and politics. Internet Encyclopedia of Philosophy. https://www.iep.utm.edu/rel-poli/#H1

2. Weller C. Mesmerizing maps show how religion has spread across the world. Business Insider. July, 2017. https://www.businessinsider.com/maps-religion-spread-throughout-world-2017-7.

3. A closer look at how religious restrictions have risen around the world. Pew Center Research. July, 2019. https://www.pewforum.org/2019/07/15/a-closer-look-at-how-religious-restrictions-have-risen-around-the-world/

4. Fullerton J. China bans religion for communists. The Times. July 2017. https://www.thetimes.co.uk/article/china-bans-religion-for-communists-bqd80zhn9

5. Kumar A. China has the highest percentage of atheists in the world, Gallup says. Christian Post. https://www.christianpost.com/news/china-highest-percentage-atheists-world-gallup-survey.html

6. Albert E. Religion in China. Council on Foreign Relations. October, 2018. https://www.cfr.org/backgrounder/religion-china

7. Majumdar S. Five facts about religion in India. June, 2018. Pew Research Center.

8. Indian Supreme Court say police may arrest anyone accused of proselytization. Catholic News Agency. August, 2006. https://www.catholicnewsagency.com/news/indian_supreme_court_says_police_may_arrest_anyone_accused_of_proselytization

9. Arnold TW. The Spread of Islam in the World. Goodword Books, 2008

Ochab EU. In Iran, religious minority children are to stay silent if they want to study. Forbes. October, 2019. https://www.forbes.com/sites/ewelinaochab/2019/10/08/in-iran-religious-minority-children-are-to-stay-silent-if-they-want-to-study/#521b50879a17

10. Taylor D. After 206 Nobel Prizes it's time for the big question. Jewish News. December, 2018. https://blogs.timesofisrael.com/after-206-nobel-prizes-its-time-for-the-big-question/

11. Goldstein T. How did American Jews get so rich? YNetNews. com. October, 2011. https://www.ynetnews.com/articles/0,7340,L-4099803,00.html

12. Klein K. German Jewish Refugees 1933 – 1939. Holocaust Encyclopedia. https://encyclopedia.ushmm.org/content/en/article/german-jewish-refugees-1933-1939

13. Pospielovsky, Dimitry. A History of Marxist–Leninist atheism and Soviet antireligious policies. Macmillan. 1987.

14. Marx K, Engels F. The Communist Manifesto, 1848.

15. Smith M. Communism and religion can't coexist. Wall Street Journal. August, 2019. https://www.wsj.com/articles/communism-and-religion-cant-coexist-11567120938

16. Fraser G. Why the Soviet attempt to stamp out religion failed. The Guardian. October, 2017. https://www.theguardian.com/commentisfree/belief/2017/oct/26/why-the-soviet-attempt-to-stamp-out-religion-failed

17. Lipka M, Sahgal N. Nine key findings about religion and politics in Central and Eastern Europe. Pew Research Center. May, 2017. https://www.pewresearch.org/fact-tank/2017/05/10/9-key-findings-about-religion-and-politics-in-central-and-eastern-europe/

18. National Commission on Terrorist Attacks. The 9/11 Commission Report: Final Report of the National Commission on Terrorist Attacks Upon the United States. July, 2004.

19. Lipka M. U.S. religious groups and their political leanings. Pew Research Center. February, 2016. https://www.pewresearch.org/fact-tank/2016/02/23/u-s-religious-groups-and-their-political-leanings/

20. Horowitz D. Dark Agenda: The War to Destroy Christian America. Humanix Books, 2019.

21. Hall MD. Did America Have a Christian Founding?: Separating Modern Myth from Historical Truth. Thomas Nelson, 2019.

22. Court A, Kekatos M. "Today Charles Koch is learning how overjoyed the world will be when he died!" Twitter users – including Bette Midler – post cruel messages celebrating the death of Republican billionaire David Koch. Daily Mail. August 2019 https://www.dailymail.co.uk/news/article-7389159/Twitter-users-including-Bette-Midler-post-cruel-messages-celebrating-death-David-Koch.html

2013 Report on Anti-Catholism: Bill Maher's hate speech. Catholic League for Religious and Civil Rights. https://www.catholicleague.org/bill-mahers-hate-speech/

Joy Behar called Mike Pence's faith mental illness then she called to apologize. Washington Post. March, 2018. https://www.washingtonpost.com/news/acts-of-faith/wp/2018/03/08/joy-behar-called-mike-pences-faith-a-mental-illness-then-she-called-to-apologize/

23. Timf K. Seventy-three percent of Republican students have hidden their politics over fears about grades. National Review. September, 2019.

24. America's Founding Documents: The Constitution of the United States. National Archives. https://www.archives.gov/founding-docs/constitution-transcript

America's Founding Documents: The Bill of Rights. National Archives. https://www.archives.gov/founding-docs/bill-of-rights

GOD DIDN'T INVENT IT, SO IS MONEY THE ROOT OF ALL EVIL?

MAN INVENTED MONEY, and money makes the world go around. Juggling our finances is a big part of our daily lives. Around the kitchen table, families make budgets and then try to stick to them. Companies hold meetings to discuss revenues and expenses. Governments have budgets as high as the sky: trillions of dollars for the larger and wealthier countries. Money enables the world to function properly, and that's all well and good. Quantum mind theory predicts there's nothing inherently bad about something that serves as a useful tool. But do people also use money to exploit others? No need to even answer that; we know all too well.

What is it about money that causes many people to use it in evil ways? Money is merely a token. Minted as a coin, or recorded as a piece of digital information, money serves to keep tabs. If I give you 100 hours of labor and my labor is worth $25 per hour, then you owe me $2,500. If I give you 100 hours of labor every two weeks and you pay me that sum at those regular intervals, we call that a salary. We call those basic kinds of money-for-labor exchanges wages. All this seems pretty innocent.

But wages aren't the only way to reward work. Maybe the evil use of money rears its ugly head when we drift away from simple wages for work. Most sales representatives work on commission, even if there's some baseline salary. When working on commission, one gets a share or percentage of money brought into the business on a sale. This still seems all fair and justified. Good times uplift everyone; bad times bring stress for all. But when times are especially harsh, some sales representatives compensate by getting more competitive. The best sales reps are the ones who keep their jobs during the tough times. That's still fine, unless too much deception enters the equation. Lots of people don't trust sales representatives to be completely truthful about the products they sell simply because we know there's so much pressure to paint a rosy picture. Consumers can simply ignore any too-good-to-be-true claims—and everything is fair and good again.

But not all people like to work for other people; many people hate the idea of having a boss. Some people start their own business. Running a small business can involve a lot of stress, but the rewards can be great. You gain the possibility of making more money in profit than you could earn in wages. The larger the business, the more stress there is because responsibilities and number of employees increase. Even with the sophistication of quantum mind theory—which can compute multiple states or perspectives simultaneously—it becomes more and more difficult to assess how much money the business owner is "morally entitled" to for their additional burden of worry and stress. In reality, larger companies make as much money as they can, limited only by what employees and consumers will allow.

How do employees set limits on how much (or how little) a large company can get away with paying them? There's a collective consciousness among employees that judges employer fairness. When business is good, employees might receive raises or bonuses, as a token of appreciation. This increases employee satisfaction. But business isn't always good, and generally speaking, employees are sheltered from the bad times at the expense of the business owner. Employees may appreciate this, but not always. Employers may have to point this out. In the best companies, fair compensation and good communication exists, and employer-employee loyalty develops over the years. Certain businesses acquire reputations for being "good" to their employees. This loyalty reflects a strong connection in the collective consciousness of the employees. The size of the company needn't be a factor in employee loyalty. But as companies grow larger, there tends to be less connection between employer and employees, creating greater potential for companies to be driven strictly by greed.

Not all people work for or run a business. Some people, particularly older retired people, live off their investments. A huge industry of financial advisors, stock brokers, and investment bankers help people make money on their savings or capital. Many of the largest companies have reputations for being the best investments. But thousands of people may own stock in a company while not having a good idea what that company's doing. Oftentimes there's no way of knowing, except to read that company's profile, keep up with press releases, and read other news about the company. The huge disconnect that exists between small investors and the board of directors of a large company doesn't mean there's any fraud or wrongdoing, but it greatly enables that possibility.

How we decide to handle money, in the best and worst of scenarios, is a quantum superposition. The best exchanges of money are beneficial to all sides. This can only happen when there's no deception or fraud. So whether we're talking about working for a living, running a business, or being an investor—the general heuristic is that good connection between interested parties increases fairness. We need transparency to keep our money exchanges working for everybody. We need to be certain we're not working for an unfair employer, or a corrupt company, or investing in something morally objectionable. We need to protect ourselves from fraud. Keeping money close, investing in our friends and relatives—that might increase connection. But it's not always feasible or prudent to avoid big money. And according to quantum mind theory, judging money as good or bad isn't about the amount, it's all about people's intentions.

> *A possibility to consider: Money is neutral. It's the intention of the people who are handling the money that usually predicts whether money is being used in a beneficial or detrimental manner. Our conscious matrix can easily detect deceit and fraud during simple exchanges of money. But we may struggle to decipher intent when the situation is complex. But over time, the truth almost always emerges.*

It's easy to tell if you're being short-changed. When you give the store clerk a $20 bill for a $5 item, you expect $15 in change. If the store clerk gives you only $5 in change, you'll likely notice and complain. If the clerk responds: "Oh sorry, I thought you gave me a ten-dollar bill," you might believe them once. But if this sort of thing happens repeatedly with the same clerk or at the same store, you'll likely report it to the manager or simply not go back to that store.

What about being short-changed on wages? There's a power dynamic between the employer and employee that might be perceived as unfair from the onset. The employer seems to have more power. If an employer feels an employee hasn't been working hard enough, rather than telling them so, the employer might dock their pay. In most cases, docking a person's pay without cause is morally wrong and illegal. But since much in life isn't black-and-white, an employee may not be certain and simply complain they believe they were underpaid. If confronted, the employer may simply pay up, or the employer might deny any wrongdoing and contest the hours worked. Because what if an employee asked a coworker to punch their time card early or late to give the appearance of having worked more hours? In this case, it's the employer who is being short-changed out of labor. If the employer finds out, the employees who cheated are apt to be fired. These kinds of deception are easy to spot. But why then do they occur so often?

The main reason for employer-employee conflict is their two completely different perspectives. Employers want the business to run smoothly and they want to make a profit. Employees want to enjoy their work and earn a fair wage. Since employees usually outnumber the employer, the collective consciousness of the workplace depends greatly on employee satisfaction. When both the employer and the employees communicate their needs effectively, there will be a smooth-running environment. Having this edge is critical because many new businesses fail. According to the Small Business Administration, sixty-six percent of new businesses fail within the first ten years.[1]

Does quantum mind theory provide any insights regarding employer-employee conflicts? It's natural for our conscious matrix to continuously ask these questions: "Are my wages fair? How much is fair considering how much my boss profits off my work? Isn't earning a fair wage a human right?" Employees tend to see the situation in terms of workers' rights; it's their natural perspective to consider themselves. But let's consider the kinds of questions that run through the mind of the business owner: "Why don't my employees realize they're out of a job if our business doesn't succeed? Why don't my employees appreciate how much stress I endure so they can have a job?" Feelings of entitlement depend on one's perspective. But in reality, no one is entitled to anything. After all, employees who want what the business owner has are free to start their own business.

To make a business work, all sides have to work together to achieve their different goals simultaneously. Clearly, it takes good communication to effectively reach a solution that gets both sides' needs met. Quantum mind theory fully describes how entanglements between different perspectives will eventually reduce to a solution. And not all solutions will work when played out in the real world. Trial and error, cycling through multiple potential solutions, these approaches may eventually hit upon something that works. Not a perfect method, but it's our only option.

When we look within, when we turn to our inner conscious matrix, we find a wellspring of possible solutions to conflicts-of-interest. What's fair for us has to be considered in the context of respecting the rights for others. We do have "human rights." One of those rights is the freedom to find a job we enjoy, and another is the right to start a business—small or large. And it's our right to accept what we believe are fair wages or walk away. But an employer can only offer to pay what's affordable. If you mandate high wages for all, you end up with very few businesses surviving. So the collective consciousness must be broad enough to include all relevant perspectives. Wages should be fair, but out of necessity, wages are constrained by what's realistically available.

So far, we've been talking about free men and women in relatively good times. In a bad job market, people might be forced to take a job that's less than optimal. During these times, we assume that times are harsh and things are bad for both employers and employees. But what about when employers are profiting at high levels and still pay their employees much less than the employees feel they deserve? This can happen in large companies or corporations where the communication between the head-office executives and employees is minimal or non-existent. In order to correct large-scale perceived unfairness, the collective consciousness needs to expand beyond those directly involved. Sometimes, increasing public awareness is a way forward.

How do we know when things are unfair to us or to others? Through our conscious matrix, each of us has a direct connection to God and to what's morally good. Our connection isn't perfect, so naturally we seek moral or spiritual advice from others. But it's a good rule of thumb to follow our conscious matrix. From simple to complex situations, our conscious matrix can detect if we're being cheated or defrauded. We're best able to perceive fraud by reading the intent of the person or business.

> **A thought to ponder:** *Success and productivity are virtues, but greed and corruption are vices. Our conscious matrix can tell the difference, but we need to constantly re-evaluate our motives and the motives of other people. That's because real life situations aren't always straightforward; most situations aren't black or white.*

There are thousands of Bible verses on money. Many verses warn against coveting wealth as a means to find happiness. There are Bible verses that warn against greed. Yet other verses praise hard work and encourage paying fair wages to those who provide us with services. Biblical verses can bring comfort when the right verse is found that sheds light on a particular issue.

The much-quoted Bible verses, Matthew 19:24-26 (KJV) capture a lengthy conversation between Jesus and his disciples, starting with Jesus saying: *"And again I say unto you, It is easier for a camel to go through the eye of a needle, than for a rich man to enter into the kingdom of God. When the disciples heard this, they were exceedingly amazed, saying, Who then may enter? But Jesus beheld them, and said unto them, With men this is impossible; but with God all things are possible."*

Does Jesus mean that it's impossible for a rich person to be a good or Godly person? The metaphor involving the camel suggests it's nearly impossible. But later in the conversation Jesus reminds us that with God, all things are possible. Just because something is a difficult challenge doesn't mean it can't be accomplished.

There's a public perception that being successful is a good thing, but that rich people often cause a lot of human suffering. The "rich" are often defined as the upper one percent in income or net worth. But claiming a certain income or net worth as a dividing line forces us into a conundrum: What's wrong with success? Isn't success what we all want? Is there a set dollar amount above which pure goodness magically transforms into pure evil? If there's such a dollar amount, no one has been able to identify it. A better argument is that it's not a particular dollar amount, but the motive behind one's striving for success that predicts whether money is being used in the pursuit of good versus evil.

So we want to be careful in how we handle our money matters. We want to avoid making choices out of greed. But what's the difference between building a healthy wealth portfolio versus wanton greed? What's wrong with striving to be a millionaire or a billionaire? In many cases, there's nothing's wrong with working towards a lofty goal. But there's plenty that can go wrong when people become consumed with success at any price.

There's a big difference between wealth accumulation and greed. The moral good of wealth accumulation is that it seeks to protect self and family without harm to the community. Those who are exceedingly successful generate wealth for themselves and earnings for others. These are the job creators and investors who build up civilization. Greed is different from wealth accumulation in that it seeks profit at any cost, without concern about harm to the community. Greed arises out of a fear of financial collapse. When our conscious matrix is terrorized by fear and anxiety, we struggle to make rational choices.

People can easily get caught up in their fears of "not having enough" or "having too much." Avoiding either extreme, many people opt to be financially comfortable, but not rich. Our conscious matrix is healthy and engaged when we're productive and achieving success. But what motivates a person to acquire sums of money beyond their immediate expenses? Some people are motivated to impress others with their belongings. That's usually a waste of time and only produces short-lived results. In the long run, people like others for their personal qualities, not their possessions. Moreover, people like people who are most like themselves. Similarity facilitates communication and understanding, and most people aren't rich.

The American dream is to work hard and earn enough to save for a rainy day. During most of our history, the prevailing Judeo-Christian principle was to save some amount, typically ten percent of earnings as a buffer, a kind of financial security blanket. This kind of wealth accumulation was equated with taking responsibility. Savings accumulated linearly according to a relatively fixed proportion of the amount set aside. But as banking and investment grew more sophisticated, bankers responded to individuals looking for a higher interest rate, offering the potential for non-linear returns, but with increased risk of losing the principal. These higher returns were based not merely on a proportion of investment but on a complex set of variables from which it would be hard to predict the monetary outcome.

Most investors who seek higher returns understand the risk. But the downside of many risky investments is that the complexity provides cover to hide fraud. And history proves that bankers and financial institutions have repeatedly taken advantage of financial complexity to provide cover for wrongdoing. Most people who invest in risky ventures believe they've done their research and won't be deceived. But then it happens to them. It might have happened because they trusted a financial advisor who didn't tell them the truth. Or perhaps their advisor was deceived as well.

While we might be stunned when trusted financial advisors and institutions deceive us, it helps heal the pain and be smarter in the future when we understand why. Most people who acquire wealth obsessively and compulsively do so out of an anxiety or fear that no amount of money is going to be enough to last their lifetime or to keep them safe. This is a dangerous and slippery slope because acquiring wealth is just the first step. Holding on to wealth is just as difficult as acquiring it. We see this principle at work in the business world. Owning a successful business is a mixed blessing. Company owners are liable to lawsuits. Many lose their business assets, sometimes more.

The business world can be cut-throat and competitive, and this causes high levels of stress. As one's wealth and status increase, so too does the stress. And stress—especially intense or chronic stress—impairs the conscious matrix from functioning optimally. Can you imagine the nightmare of continuously feeling intense fear of losing it all? People of great wealth often complain bitterly when it's lost and have an expectation that others owe them their wealth back. But each person is solely responsible to "make it" on their own and subsequently to "keep it." Nobody is entitled to wealth, and nobody is responsible for protecting another person's wealth. It's a given that the more money you have, the more you have to fear people stealing from you. Lots of people opt out of enduring that much stress for money, especially since money is something you're absolutely guaranteed NOT to keep forever. There's so much truth in the saying: "You can't take it with you."

Quantum mind theory excels at dealing with situations that aren't black or white. We need to trust our inner conscious matrix when it tells us we're too intent on winning. That's when it's time to step back and take it easy. We also need to listen to our conscious matrix when it suggests we're being misled in financial matters. When we understand greed, we're protected from developing it in ourselves and from being deceived because of greed in others. Greed is the ultimate disconnection away from the collective consciousness. You can't be entangled or unified with others, and you can't be one with God, when you ignore the human suffering that you're causing simply to obtain more money. And as the Bible says in Timothy 6:9 (NIV), *"Those who want to get rich fall into temptation and a trap and into many foolish and harmful desires that plunge people into ruin and destruction."*

Another thought to ponder: Large corporations and financial institutions are profit-motivated organizations. Despite checks and balances, excessive greed can grow out of hand when large corporations and financial institutions hide major truths from the public. An informed collective consciousness is needed to protect the people against excessive greed.

A tricky situation arises when the business owner isn't in direct contact with the people working for the company. In the case of large corporations, employees may never meet the owners in person. Distance creates the opportunity for callousness and corruption. If the business owner or corporate CEO lives in a totally different world, in terms of socio-economics, then contact is minimal or non-existent. When there's no possibility for conscious matrix connection, there's no possibility of entanglement or empathy. The employees, small investors, or consumers may be suffering, barely surviving, but contact is severed. The huge size of some corporations allows CEOs to live in luxury that's out of reach for most people. They're isolated and protected; they never feel the pain of the common person whom might be adversely affected by the corporation's actions or its products.

Not all large companies and corporations are corrupt or uncaring. Many large businesses provide excellent jobs to many and good products for consumers, all while also producing profits shared with investors.

This win-win-win is only possible, however, when corruption is weeded out. The larger a company gets, the more potential there is for rationalizing their greed and hiding their corruption. Corruption often starts out with white lies, justifying the profit-motivated decisions that bring harm to others. But in the worst cases, corruption evolves into blatant disregard for the truth and hiding damaging information from company employees and from the public at large.

There are many types of fraud that occur on a daily basis. The worst examples are sometimes exposed publicly and brought to an end. Insider trading, pyramid schemes, too-big-to-fail, and medical fraud are among recent scandals that have shaken public confidence. Why do people in whom we trust commit such deceptions? The common answer is: excessive love of money. But it's more than simple greed. Over time, corporate heads grow increasingly disconnected from company employees, investors, and consumers. A corporate mentality permeates that openly condones lots of wrong-doing and routinely overlooks the perspective of others who aren't in their elite group. In this jaded environment, it's not surprising some top executives develop the attitude that "everyone who can, cheats." When everyone at that level cheats because they can, this mentality erodes ethical and moral behavior. The consequences are often grave.

Insider trading is a type of financial fraud where a person uses information that isn't publicly available to buy or sell shares of stock at an unfair advantage.[2] It's illegal because it breaches the fiduciary duty to other share-holders, forcing them in some cases to bear a larger share of an expected loss. The Securities and Exchange Commission (SEC) keeps track of trading and prosecutes violations of insider trading. Despite the possibility of prison terms and large fines, many high-profile people are charged and convicted for insider trading.

In one of the most publicized cases, Martha Stewart was convicted in a case of securities fraud in 2004.[3] Stewart was convicted for acting on information from her broker that a stock she owned was going to tank. The insider trade spared Stewart from losing around $45,000, possibly more in the long-run. One might assume this amount of money wasn't all that much to a person like Martha Stewart. She's the CEO of her own company and doing very well financially. So why did she do it? Maybe because she thought she'd get away with it; that it was no big deal. This is an example of the huge disconnect between people who are very wealthy (and own companies themselves) and small investors (who generally don't get insider tips). The perception that there's one set of rules for the rich and another set of rules for the small investor might be a reason insider trading is all too common. Martha Stewart avoided a relatively small loss, in comparison to some insider-trading deals. Many more insider deals likely occur that are never prosecuted.

Another high-profile fraud case is the Bernie Madoff $65-billion pyramid scheme.[4] For at least fifteen years before he was exposed in 2008, Madoff took investors' money and did nothing more with it than deposit it in the bank. Madoff had built up his reputation as a brilliant investor. He offered annual interest rates of 10-12 percent at a time when nobody was giving those kinds of rates. But instead of actually investing any money given to him for that purpose, Madoff simply used the cash received to pay other people the interest they were promised.

Madoff's scheme was a pyramid scheme—alternatively called a Ponzi scheme after the financial crook Michael Ponzi. Pyramid or Ponzi schemes are fraudulent and deceptive. These schemes always fail as you eventually run out of other people's money. When the stock market was doing poorly from 2006-2008, too many people were withdrawing money from their accounts with Madoff. Eventually, Madoff ran out of money to pay the unrealistic interest rates. There were no real investments made; it was all a fabricated fraud. But the fraud only worked as long as people had lots of money to invest. When cash receivership ran out, Madoff had nothing to pay out as fake interest.

After being exposed, Madoff was tried and sentenced to 150 years in prison. Worse than that, his family suffered irreparable harm. One of his two sons committed suicide because of the scandal; the other son died of cancer, possibly triggered by the stress. Madoff's wife had her life turned upside down. Did Madoff's family know about the fraud? We'll never know. Some of the early investors might have known about the fraud. Rumors suggest many knew it was a Ponzi scheme. The returns promised were too good to be true. And most people, who might have been mildly suspicious, believed they could get their money out before the pot ran dry.

So what can we learn from the Madoff scheme? Lesson #1 learned: We should trust our inner conscious matrix to check on things that seem too good to be true. Lesson #2 learned: Just because we can get away with something doesn't mean we won't eventually face grave consequences. Madoff might have thought spending the rest of his life in prison was no big deal. He never foresaw the ruinous effects for his family. What was Madoff chasing after his entire life? If it was to leave something to his family, that dream went up in smoke.

Unfortunately, fraud is pretty widespread throughout the U.S. financial sector. In 2008, in a seemingly incredulous move, the US federal government under President George Bush infused $85 billion into ten financial institutions because they feared financial collapse if they didn't act.[5] The hit TV movie, *Too Big to Fail*, chronicled the 2008 financial crash that involved the major banks, investment firms, and insurance companies.[6] The movie-title moniker stuck.

This idea of too-big-to-fail has never been accepted by the American people. It simply makes no sense. Financial institutions lost major credibility with that move. What was subsequently exposed is how virtually all of our financial institutions are nothing more than a house-of-cards. Our leading banks and lenders have limited capital and insufficient liquid assets, yet they're allowed to lend money and charge interest. Okay, you might reason, these financial institutions have a right to manage other people's money because they're geniuses at bookkeeping. But no, they're not geniuses. The financial industry made itself vulnerable to corruption by stretching the rules. Our big banks are vulnerable to criminal cartels because the cartels are "cash-rich." Becoming cash-rich is something our genius bankers seem incapable of doing.

And this brings us to the current opioid drug crisis. In the U.S. alone, there were over 70,000 opioid overdose deaths in 2018.[7] The most commonly used opioids are heroine and oxycodone, along with the very potent fentanyl showing recent upticks in use. Heroine is a street drug. It derives from opium grown mainly in Afghanistan that makes its way to the U.S. through Mexico.[8] Drug cartels smuggle the drug into the U.S. along the southern border and then distribute the drug to nearly every city and state. The cartels have money laundering deals with the major U.S. banks.[9] The illegal drug trade is a cash-only business.

But perhaps even more scandalous than what's happening with the illegal drug cartels is the situation with oxycodone, currently sold as a prescription drug under the trade name OxyContin. Raymond and Mortimer Sackler developed the synthetic opioid drug OxyContin and bought Purdue Pharma to manufacture it in 1952.[10] Originally, the drug was marketed as a safer alternative to morphine for use in pain management. Over the years, the younger members of the Sackler family took control over the company and were profiting billions of dollars a year on the drug. All was well until it was exposed that the company ignored and buried scientific information that their OxyContin was highly addictive. This fact was purposefully hidden from the public, and the drug continued to be aggressively marketed as a less addictive alternative, much to the detriment of thousands of people who became hopelessly addicted.

In October 2017, the New Yorker Magazine published an article pointing the finger at the Sackler family, accusing them of bearing some moral responsibility of the opioid addiction crisis in American.[11] Since that article, some 2,600 lawsuits have been filed against Purdue Pharma. In September 2019, Purdue Pharma filed Chapter 11 bankruptcy. But immediately thereafter, the Sackler family attempted to transfer $13 billion out of the company and to the family.[12] Litigation will likely settle this matter. But besides the question of their moral responsibility, are the heirs of Raymond and Mortimer Sackler entitled to the billion-dollar lifestyles to which they've grown accustomed?

Our conscious matrix has built-in answers that guide most people away from such misdeeds. Nobody is entitled to wealth. Wealth is something we're free to strive to achieve, but it's a gamble and one takes their losses along with their wins. Raymond and Mortimer were on the right side of morality to develop oxycodone. The drug had initial benefits and promise. But somewhere along the way, some of the family members seemed to feel entitled to their billionaire lifestyles. It would seem they chose to ignore the truth, and hide the truth, because they valued their profits more than the human suffering caused to thousands of people. That magnitude of human suffering produces a huge dark cloud in the collective consciousness of the American people. There's virtually nothing money can buy to dissociate the Sackler family from that amount of pain. And to think all this suffering occurred because of a drug meant to quell pain. What irony.

Another scandal brewing today is the use of systemic chemotherapy to treat cancer. There are startling new findings, such as chemotherapy causing death within thirty days in a significant number of cancer patients.[13] Physicians throughout the U.S. are still prescribing systemic chemotherapy and radiation, treatments that kill healthy cells along with cancer cells. But it's worse than that. These treatments continue despite new research showing they don't kill the cancer-producing stem cells. Good evidence suggests cancer stem cells are responsible for the recurrence of cancer and the spread of cancer to new places in the body, a process called metastasis.[14] If a cancer treatment doesn't kill off the stem cells, then it's relatively useless.

Another problem is the vigorous push for routine screening and early detection as the best way to fight cancer. This continues despite acknowledgement of both the American Cancer Society and Cancer Research UK that regular screening results in over-diagnosis and unnecessary treatment of cancers that wouldn't have caused the patient any problem.[15] Not all cancers are aggressive or fast-growing, and not all cancer spreads or metastasizes to other parts of the body. And occasionally, the person treated didn't have cancer at all.

Most improvements in survival are credited to early detection. But intensive screening creates the "illusion" of the treatments being effective. If cancer survival statistics were to subtract out cases that were over-diagnosed and over-treated, most small improvements in survival might evaporate. Those people were never going to die from the disease. Early detection also artificially inflates survival years simply because the cancers are detected earlier. If cancer is detected two years earlier, then of course a person will live two years longer after diagnosis. That's not a real increase in survival due to the treatment or intervention. What keeps people taking these treatments in good faith? The fear of cancer makes rational people choose against their self-interest. And the medical-industrial complex in the U.S. isn't helping.

Of all the physicians who practice medicine, only oncologists receive remunerations on the drugs they prescribe.[16] It's acknowledged that remunerations result in over-treating cancers that would've never caused problems; it's an obvious conflict-of-interest. Chemotherapy has horrible side-effects, compromises the immune system, and causes death at a rate comparable to cancer. It's puzzling how a moral person would prescribe systemic chemotherapy to a person knowing what we currently know. The wrongdoing involves an unhealthy collaboration between pharmaceutical companies, physicians, health insurance companies, and the U.S. government health care program called Medicare. But spreading the blame hardly corrects the problem.

Even worse than harming millions of people, lobbyists for the cancer drugs draw from a huge pot of money to prevent real progress toward cancer cures. The global market for cancer drugs grew from $100 to $150 billion from 2015 until now, and is expected to grow to nearly $200 billion by 2026.[17] That's more than enough money to squash any scientist or researcher who dares to invent or propose a novel drug or treatment idea that's significantly more effective than systemic chemotherapy. The cancer drug industry wants business as usual: small improvements to existing drugs aiming only to increase life expectancy by an additional two months—that's the current benchmark for success.

Across all these examples, the take-home message remains the same. The larger the amount of money at stake, the more that corporations and financial institutions become vulnerable to corruption. Massive corruption doesn't happen in a vacuum. It requires corporate executives to make a conscious decision to disconnect from their victims' plight. But it doesn't end there. Corrupt corporate heads must also disconnect from their inner conscious matrix, their conscious moral being. As said in Ecclesiastes 5:10 (NIV), *"Whoever loves money never has enough; whoever loves wealth is never satisfied with their income. This too is meaningless."*

Money can't buy happiness or peace of mind. Greed is the desire for material gain with malicious intent to ignore the pain and suffering of others caused by your actions. We must all fight against greed in ourselves and in others. And we all possess a conscious matrix, a tool designed to do exactly that. Some people callously cheat others to make large sums of money, only to repent by donating large sums to charity. It's ironic that some of these charities are cheaters too.

> **An idea to consider:** *Charity is one of the greatest virtues. There's no better way to connect our conscious matrix with that of others than to give from the heart. But some charitable organizations serve their self-interests way too much or commit outright fraud. A huge disconnect occurs when corruption invades charitable organizations, and it damages the reputation of that charity in the collective consciousness of the public.*

Many people give some amount to charity every year. Rich and poor alike donate, and for a variety of reasons. Our conscious matrix is energized and we feel good about giving to the less fortunate. But as giving becomes routine, many lose the connection to the meaning of it. We may end up giving to charity for the appearance of being generous. People who organize charities or philanthropic organizations hone their skills at appealing to our desire to be generous. As a result, some charity balls and galas become pure social events whose purpose is far removed from the stated mission of the charity or foundation.

And nearly everyone has to be careful these days. We're bombarded with telemarketers who contact us with heartfelt pleas. Unfortunately, the aggressive outreaches for money aren't always matched with an equal passion for their stated mission. Many charities simply don't give most of the money collected to the causes they raise money to help. The Center for Investigative Reporting and the Tampa Bay Times put together a list of the 50 Worst Charities in America based on their tax filings with the Internal Revenue Service.[18] These charities claimed to be raising money to help children, cancer patients, law enforcement, veterans, and others. Using these worthwhile causes to fundraise, these fifty charities raked in $1.35 billion, a hefty sum. But less than a third of the money went to the named causes, while over two-thirds of the donations went into the pockets of the organizers in salaries and expense accounts.

Which people give the most to charity? There's a well-established relationship between organized religion and charity. Two surveys conducted in 2012--the National Study of American Religious Giving and the National Study of American Jewish Giving--showed that religious Americans give more in charity than do non-religious people.[19] Moreover, these Americans who claim a religious affiliation give nearly twice as much to their congregations and religious-affiliated charities than to secular charities. These results suggest most religious Americans trust their religious organization to pick the right charities.

Religious organizations have a huge responsibility in choosing the right opportunities for giving. Money is almost the polar opposite of spirituality; it's as worldly as it gets. This might be why Jesus was appalled at the degree to which the money-changers had taken over the temple courtyards.

As described in Mark 11:15-17 (NIV): *On reaching Jerusalem, Jesus entered the temple courts and began driving out those who were buying and selling there. He overturned the tables of the money changers and the benches of those selling doves, and wouldn't allow anyone to carry merchandise through the temple courts. And as he taught them, he said, "Is it not written: 'My house will be called a house of prayer for all nations'? But you have made it 'a den of robbers.'"*

We enrich our conscious matrices when we give voluntarily to others in need. It's our responsibility to give where it's genuinely needed. Sometimes volunteering our time, instead of our money, is a better approach. If our intentions are sincere, we stand the best chance to make a difference for ourselves and for others. Whenever two conscious matrices connect, some good is done.

> ***One last idea to consider:*** *Governments assume the authority to tax people, the citizens of that nation. When there's a strong connection between government and the citizens, taxation serves the common good: citizens pay tax and receive services and infrastructure from the government. Taxation without representation is a form of theft; it's an abuse of power.*

The American Revolutionary War (1774-1783) started because the thirteen colonies refused to continue paying taxes to the British. The colonials rejected the British Parliament's right to tax them because the colonies had no representation in the British Parliament. "No taxation without representation" was the rallying cry.[20] After the U.S. gained independence from the British, there was no income tax for many years. Then in 1861, a small income tax was created to fund the Civil War.[21] One year later Congress passed the Internal Revenue Act and Americans have been paying income tax ever since.

A big political battle in the U.S. is being fought as to what is fair taxation. Some groups like the Libertarians believe no income tax should be levied. Most Americans, however, fall somewhere on the political spectrum ranging from far-left, left-leaning, center, right-leaning, to far-right. Typically, conservatives with far-right or right-leaning views favor less taxation. In keeping with our American tradition, taxation without representation is a problem to this group. The liberal, far-left and left-leaning Americans favor increases in income tax on the rich and increased benefits to the poor, such as free healthcare and higher education.

The political struggle between left and right boils down to a key question: Are the rich in America paying their fair share in tax? Taxes in the U.S. are progressive, meaning the more you earn or receive in passive income, the higher the rate of income tax.[22] This progressive tax schedule results in the top half of household incomes paying 97% of the total income tax revenues. The top 1% is paying 37% of tax revenues. The "rich" do pay more, and whether that's fair is a matter of perspective.

Quantum mind theory provides a solution when various groups hold widely divergent opinions. Matters of fairness are opinions, not facts. So nobody's wrong when it comes to their opinion. Everyone is entitled to their opinion and to looking after their self-interest. We need to pay our fair share—not more, not less. As the Bible says in Romans 13:7 (NIV), *"Give to everyone what you owe them: if you owe taxes, pay taxes; if revenue, then revenue; if respect, then respect; if honor, then honor."*

The goal of the conscious matrix is to resolve conflicts, including those about money, through greater understanding of both sides and settling on a workable solution. We received the gift of our conscious matrix from God and from it we have an inner conscience. The more we're in touch with our God-given sense of morality, then the more wealth we can honestly accumulate while at the same time being free of the fear of losing it. In the end, we'll lose everything tangible we've collected while living on earth. The best of what we'll leave to others is what we've uploaded onto the collective consciousness, things like what's good about our character and what we've inspired in others. As for money, it's only a useful tool, not something to worship or love. Money doesn't upload onto the collective consciousness; it's too worldly and of this earth.

CHAPTER 9: NOTES AND REFERENCES

1. Otar C. What percentage of small businesses fail—and how can you avoid being one of them? Forbes. October, 2018. https://www.forbes.com/sites/forbesfinancecouncil/2018/10/25/what-percentage-of-small-businesses-fail-and-how-can-you-avoid-being-one-of-them/#5333ebf343b5

    Small business facts. Small Business Administration. June, 2012 https://www.sba.gov/sites/default/files/Business-Survival.pdf

2. Insider Trading. Legal Information Institute. Cornell Law School. https://www.law.cornell.edu/wex/insider_trading

3. Heminway JM. Martha Stewart's Legal Troubles. Carolina Academic Press, 2006.

4. Henriques DB. Bernie Madoff, the Wizard of Lies: Inside the Infamous $65 Billion Swindle. One World, 2011.

    Kirzman A. Betrayal: The Life and Lies of Bernie Madoff. Harper Perrenial, 2010.

5. Sorkin AR. Too Big to Fail. Penguin Books, 2010.

6. Too Big to Fail. TV Movie. 2011. https://www.imdb.com/title/tt1742683/

7. New data show growing complexity of drug overdose deaths in America. Centers for Disease Control and Prevention. December, 2018. https://www.cdc.gov/media/releases/2018/p1221-complexity-drug-overdose.html

8. Rowlatt J. How the US military's opium war in Afghanistan was lost. BBC News. April, 2019. https://www.bbc.com/news/world-us-canada-47861444

Heroine in U.S. comes from Afghanistan, Mexico: UN. Tolo News. https://tolonews.com/node/13015

9. Dinkins J. Vincent P. Money-laundering methods of drug cartels and the capture of El Chapo. Thomas Reuters. September, 2016. https://legal.thomsonreuters.com/en/insights/white-papers/money-laundering-methods-of-drug-cartels-and-the-capture-of-el-chapo

10. Meier B. Pain Killer: An Empire of Deceit and the Origin of America's Opioid Epidemic. Random House, 2018.

11. Keefe PR. The family that built an empire of pain. New Yorker Magazine. October, 2017. https://www.newyorker.com/magazine/2017/10/30/the-family-that-built-an-empire-of-pain

12. Warren K, Rogers TN. The family behind OxyContin reportedly just made $60 million from a real-estate deal. Meet the Sacklers, the family who built their $13 billion fortune off the controversial drug. Business Insider. January, 2019. https://www.businessinsider.com/who-are-the-sacklers-wealth-philanthropy-oxycontin-photos-2019-1

    Hoffman J. Purdue Pharma Tentatively Settles Thousands of Opioid Cases. The New York Times. September, 2019/ https://www.nytimes.com/2019/09/11/health/purdue-pharma-opioids-settlement.html

13. Knapton S. Chemotherapy warning as hundreds die from cancer-fighting drugs. The Telegraph. August, 2016. https://www.telegraph.co.uk/science/2016/08/30/chemotherapy-warning-as-hundreds-die-from-cancer-fighting-drugs/

    Wallington M, Saxon EB, Bomb M, Smittenaar R, Wickenden M, McPhail S, Rashbass J, Chao D, Dewar J, Talbot D, Peake M, Perren T, Wilson C, Dodwell D. 30-day mortality after systemic anticancer treatment for breast and lung cancer in England: a population-based, observational study. Lancet Oncol. 2016, 17(9):1203-16.

14. Dawood S, Austin L, Cristofanilli M. Cancer stem cells: implications for cancer therapy. Oncology (Williston Park). 2014, 28(12):1101-7, 1110.

Bonnet D, Dick JE. Human acute myeloid leukemia is organized as a hierarchy that originates from a primitive hematopoietic cell. Nat Med. 1997, 3:730–737.

Reya T, Morrison SJ, Clarke MF, Weissman IL. Stem cells, cancer, and cancer stem cells. Nature. 2001, 414:105–111.

15. Limitations of mammograms. American Cancer Society. https://www.cancer.org/cancer/breast-cancer/screening-tests-and-early-detection/mammograms/limitations-of-mammograms.html

Overdiagnosis: when finding cancer can do more harm than good. Cancer Research UK. March, 2018. https://scienceblog.cancerresearchuk.org/2018/03/06/overdiagnosis-when-finding-cancer-can-do-more-harm-than-good/

16. Ellis, R. Cancer docs profit from chemotherapy drugs: Situation begs the ethical question: Are they overprescribing? NBC News. September, 2006. http://www.nbcnews.com/id/14944098/ns/nbc_nightly_news_with_brian_williams/t/cancer-docs-profit-chemo-therapy-drugs/#.XdcZmVdKg2w

Boyle S, Petch J, Batt K, Durand-Zaleski I, Thomson S. How much do cancer specialists earn? A comparison of physician fees and remuneration in oncology and radiology in high-income countries. Health Policy. 2018, 122(2):94-101.

Prasad V. The "cancer growing in cancer medicine:" pharma money paid to doctors. Stat News. October, 2019. https://www.statnews.com/2019/10/30/cancer-growing-in-cancer-medicine-pharma-money-doctors/

17. Herper M. The cancer drug market hit $100 billion and could jump 50% in four years. Forbes. May 2015. https://www.forbes.com/sites/

matthewherper/2015/05/05/cancer-drug-sales-approach-100-bil-lion-and-could-increase-50-by-2018/#2945dcf42dc6

Global oncology markets to surpass US $196.2 billion by 2026. Market Watch. January, 2019. https://www.marketwatch.com/press-release/global-oncology-drugs-market-to-surpass-us-1962-billion-by-2026-2019-01-30

18. Hundley K, Taggart K. America's 50 worst charities rake in nearly 1 billion for corporate fundraisers. Tampa Bay Times. June, 2013; October, 2017. https://www.tampabay.com/news/nation/americas-50-worst-charities-rake-in-nearly-1-billion-for-corporate/2339540/

19. Daniels A. Religious Americans give more: New study finds. The Chronicles of Philanthropy. November 2013 https://www.philan-thropy.com/article/Religious-Americans-Give-More/153973

20. Marston D. The American Revolution 1774 – 1783. Routledge, 2003.

21. Shepard C. The Civil War, Income Tax, and the Republican Party. Algora, 2010.

22. Bellfiore R. Summary of the latest federal income tax data: 2018 update. Tax Foundation. November, 2018. https://taxfoundation.org/summary-latest-federal-income-tax-data-2018-update/

10

THE DEEPER MEANINGS OF LOVE, LUST, AND LASTING JOY

OUR CONSCIOUS MATRICES are what we use to make sense out of the world, to find the deeper meaning in all things. While there are many kinds of love, romantic love is what we struggle most to understand. There's perhaps nothing more confusing and difficult to explain than the relationship between love and lust. We easily grasp that our hormones trigger intense bodily and emotional responses, but then we're left to make our own story about what all that means. Human beings often turn to God to help them with our struggles with romantic love. No other kind of human love is so difficult to understand.

If we view romantic love according to quantum mind theory, then we're dealing with a superposition of states. "True love," as romantic love is sometimes called, isn't one thing; it's many things. It triggers many questions in our mind, like: Is it deep love or shallow lust? Will this love last forever? But because our mind is a bundle of quantum entanglements held in superposition, we can feel two or more things at the same time, simultaneously experiencing a blend of states. Whether love feels more like a "breakfast blend" or "bold roast" depends on the people involved. Some people seem to fit together so well that others call them the perfect couple. Then there are combinations of people so different no one can believe the two actually love each other. We have pithy sayings to account for these anomalous pairings like: "love is blind."

But what is romantic love, really? Poets seem to explain romantic love best. It's not easily put into words, but we know it when we feel it.

> **A possibility to consider:** *Romantic love is a superposition of states in the conscious matrix when you can't decide if it's love or lust and you wonder if it's going to last forever. The state is exceedingly intense, due in part to the biology that underlies it, but mostly because of the complexity and impact of its potential meaning.*

People often describe being in love as not being able to get that special person out of their minds. What causes the human mind to repeatedly visit a particular memory or anticipated event? We assume romantic love, at least in the initial stages, is triggered by sexual attraction. Attraction releases myriad chemicals throughout the brain and the body, which deserve to be called the "ultimate designer drug." Dopamine, the reward hormone, is a main player in sexual attraction. But so are the "cuddle hormones," oxytocin and vasopressin. Added to all that, norepinephrine and adrenaline increase the excitement of new love to something as thrilling as a roller coaster ride. The brain and body also release their own opiates—chemicals that produce pain relief and euphoria—to prepare the body for sexual intercourse that might otherwise be uncomfortable or painful. All these brain and body chemicals swirling within us make falling in love something hard to forget. And given the rewarding nature of dopamine and the addictive nature of the opioids, romantic love is very difficult to ever give up on.

The sexual component of romantic love really ramps things up, even though other kinds of love are equally strong. What are the biological similarities between romantic love and love for family? The love and caring we express for our children are triggered by some of the same hormones involved with mating. Oxytocin and vasopressin play roles in a wide variety of social behaviors, including pair-bonding, monogamy, parenting, cooperation, and trust.[1] We know the effects of these hormones from various scientific studies. Behavioral scientists have given subjects oxytocin or vasopressin in a nasal spray and observed the effects on behavior. Oxytocin and vasopressin increase levels of trust and cooperation in people who are engaged in competitive games and synchronize the brain activity of people engaged in other kinds of social interactions.[2]

Taking another approach, researchers measured the normal fluctuations in oxytocin levels in romantic couples. When their hormone levels peaked, the couples behaved as if they had on "rose-colored glasses" in how they perceived their partner.[3] Hormones don't create our emotions; but they certainly do enhance or otherwise modify them.

So what happens when the rose-colored glasses come off? That's when our conscious matrix decides whether this special person really deserves our love and affection. This question lingering in our minds triggers a superposition of many emotional states. Some of these emotional states are memories of past experiences. Others are expectations for the future. Our conscious matrix sorts it all out.

If a person has never been in love before (or if it's been a very long time), then that person may trust their feelings and their conscious matrix may decide to go for it: to be all in for love. After all, who wants this special cocktail of "love drug" to stop pumping through them? But if that person has been recently or deeply hurt, then they may withdraw. Why? Because losing access to your special "love object" causes pain. For one, you lose access to your favorite "love drug." And you also lose any hope of realizing your dreams with that special person. Having loved and lost, you quickly learn you have no control over another person's behavior. You're without any future partner and simultaneously faced with drug withdrawal symptoms. You're on your own with that; you have to cope with that alone.

But let's say both partners are ready and willing to fall in love with each other. In this case, the love drug merely provides an opportunity for the couple to develop a belief they love each other. Like our belief in God, being in love is an experience. It's unmistakable. You feel it; you live it. While people sometimes fake being in love, it's a very hard lie to maintain. And unlike genuine love, having to pretend you love someone can suck the joy out of life. The comparison in the conscious matrix is dramatic. Authentic love will increase the light generated by the quantum entanglements in the conscious matrix. Conversely, pretending we're in love will drain the ability of the conscious matrix to experience joy and awe.

Love is the ultimate experience in which nearness to a special person, the "love object," results in the characteristic heightened state of consciousness, a state of intense euphoria or pure joy. It's perhaps the most miraculous of all human emotions. People who have never fallen in love yearn for the feeling to happen to them. How do we know such a feeling exists before we ever feel it? That information has to be pre-wired into the conscious matrix. Like our knowledge that God or a higher-being exists, many people claim to know true love exists even before it's happened to them. And most of the time, people want it to happen. Believers feel God's love opens the door. As the Bible says in John 4:19 (NIV), *"We love because he first loved us."*

Many people search the planet high and wide to find their true love. But for others, they find true love with the person who lives next door. Psychological studies reveal both familiar and unique exotic facial features are attractive to the opposite sex.[4] Romantic love is quantum superposition of comfort, produced by people we know and understand—and excitement, triggered by novel situations and people outside our typical group. But being attracted to a person's face is only the first step. What makes a person choose one out of many?

But before we examine how people choose one out of many, we need to ask: Is it correct that people have only one true love in their lifetimes? It appears to be untrue for most people. Surveys show most people claim to have been in love on average two to four times.[5] Still, falling in love with one person and staying in love with them forever is our ideal; it's what most people would call perfect romantic love or true love. And many people can identify the one person in their lifetime whom they loved the most. In a surprising number of cases, it's not the person with whom they married or even had a long-term relationship. Romantic love is enigmatic.

Everybody has their own unique definition of love, but can we identify some common elements? Psychologist Robert Sternberg developed a theory of love based on three essential components: passion, intimacy, and commitment.[6] Sternberg suggests it's possible to build a relationship upon any one, any combination of two, or all three of the components. This triangular theory of love illustrates how complex love can be, and the model fits very well with quantum mind theory. Love is an exotic mixture or superposition of states. When it comes to romantic love, each individual person blends different concepts together to define what's important for them to feel or experience.

Romantic Love as a Quantum Entanglement

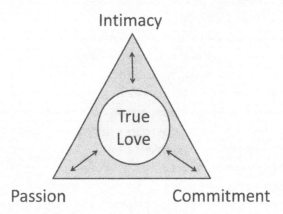

Intimacy

True
Love

Passion   Commitment

Adapted from Robert Sternberg's Triarchic Theory of Love.[6]

We all know couples who exhibit varying degrees of the different components: passion, intimacy, and commitment. Some of the classic romantic movies depict love so intense we experience it vicariously. We practically feel the sparks fly across the room when Rick sees Ilsa across the room in the classic 1942 film, *Casablanca*. Their lost romance, now rekindled, is obviously high in passion. And as the story unfolds, Rick and Ilsa speak candidly with one another indicating high emotional intimacy. But there's no possibility for a committed relationship. Ilsa is now reunited with her husband, whom she thought had died when she met Rick years earlier. Rick does the honorable thing and obtains for them plane tickets out of Casablanca. Rick is the hero because he lets her go— physically and emotionally. Ilsa appears to be the love of Rick's life, but he lets her go because it's the right thing to do. The moral of the story is some people don't end up with the person who might be their true love. And some people never experience a love so intense, but wish they did.

Each love experience is unique; the blend is slightly different. *On Golden Pond*, a 1981 film portrays an aging couple, Ethyl and Norman, whose love has lasted a lifetime. The couple is spending what will likely be their last summer at their lake cottage. Norman's personality has always been challenging and is growing even more difficult due to his failing health and memory difficulties. Norman has a strained relationship with his daughter; however, Ethyl is adept at smoothing over Norman's coarseness and serves as his constant apologist. When everyone has left and Ethyl and Norman are finally alone, they visit the lake one last time and look at the loons. In a very touching final scene, Norman tells Ethyl how they're just like the loons, that it's just the two of them left together. Loons are monogamous birds, who mate for life and build a nest together. Norman and Ethyl stuck together until the end of their lifetimes, demonstrating high commitment. Intimacy is apparent between them, and their conversation indicates that passion once bound them together, at least in the beginning.

So what combinations are best? Having all three: passion, intimacy, and commitment would seem to be best. But since components can vary in level of satisfaction, that might not always be the case. Most often, relationships without commitment simply end. Relationships without intimacy might persist longer, but are judged cold and distant. Relationships lacking intimacy ultimately prove unsatisfactory even when they last a very long time. But what happens in relationships lacking in passion? Is it possible to have a successful long-term relationship with no passion?

Researchers have identified what are called "sexless marriages." These are defined as partners who never or rarely have sex (zero to ten times per year). There are a variety of reasons sexless marriages do survive, and they can persist for many years. Typically, such couples share a passion about something else they have or do together, such as their children, a shared career or business, their home, shared interests and hobbies, or a particular lifestyle. Passionless marriages seem to work if both partners have low interest in sex. Sexual activity also decreases as a function of advanced age. So for couples who have spent a lifetime together, reflecting back on the passion they once had might be enough.

But for most people, sex or passion is very important to a relationship or marriage, especially in the early years. Pew Research Center found that sixty-one percent of people surveyed named a satisfying sex life as important to having a successful marriage.[7] This was second only to having shared interests. So is a superposition of love and lust a valid definition for romantic love? It looks like it depends on the circumstances and the timing. Some people make a distinction between being "in love" and loving their partner. Being "in love" is an experience that's either present or not. Some couples who stay together for many years claim to fall in love again with their partner.

Romantic love is so intense because it triggers strong hormonal responses and sexual behaviors, which have the potential to be life-changing. The possible consequences of even a brief sexual encounter can reverberate in the conscious matrix for many years to come. Romantic love can lead to a life-long pair-bond. Romantic love can lead to children, grandchildren, and continuation of the human race. Alternatively, a sexual encounter—real or imagined—can lead nowhere or end abruptly, leaving life-long scars. For some whom have loved and lost, love can lose all meaning. In those hurt most deeply, the hope of love can instead inflame and infuriate their troubled souls. It's no wonder we seek God's help in these matters.

As stated in 1 John 4:18 (KJV), *"There is no fear in love, but perfect love casteth out fear."* Love is a unique experience different for every person and everyone has different needs. Our conscious matrix puts it together for us. It's one of life's major struggles, just like our struggles with faith. It's one of life's ultimate challenges to understand our own heart and the heart of another person.

A thought to ponder: Romantic love evolved from a biological standpoint to keep couples together long enough to raise children. A mother and father complement one another. Females evolved body styles and psychological features that nurture. Males evolved different body styles and skills enabling increased independence, hunting ability, and aggression to fight off intruders.

Our conscious matrix seems to possess an inborn template of romantic love—a perfect blend of passion, intimacy, and commitment. As stated in the Bible, Genesis 2:24 (NKJV), *"For this reason, a man shall leave his father and his mother and be joined to his wife, and they shall become one flesh."* The purpose of romantic love is to produce a long-lasting bond. Unlike some animal species, our children are very dependent on their parents until adolescence. Couples who make long-term commitments lasting at least ten to fifteen years are better equipped to provide adequate care for small children. Beyond that time, the older children can take care of themselves and even help care for the younger ones. Human beings seem to have evolved lasting pair-bonds because it takes longer for our offspring to grow up.

So it's not surprising that marriage is nearly universal, practiced by the vast majority of societies worldwide. Nonetheless, not all people marry for life. Some people divorce and remarry. Others may stay single and practice serial monogamy. Both men and women use short-term and long-term strategies when selecting mates.[8] Because men stand to gain something by using either strategy, they may simultaneously seek both types of relationships. For men, short-term strategies are appealing because there's the potential to yield more offspring. Men look for youth, fertility, and sexual receptivity in potential mates. Men prefer physically attractive women who show sexual receptivity to them for both short-term and long-term relationships. However, men only look for commitment in long-term investments, and selectively dislike a desire for commitment in women they perceive as a short-term investment. Women tend to prefer long-term relationships, at least until things don't work out. Once disappointed, women may switch to preferring short-term relationships. Women look for men who will be good providers: men with good educations and earning potential. It's not the sex of the person; it's the gender-related life circumstances that contribute to long-term mate selection.

Sex differences in mate preferences mainly arise because men and women differ in their parenting roles. Men and women differ in their parental investment, much of which can't be changed because of biology. Women physically invest much more in each offspring. In addition to the nine-month gestation period, women provide the bulk of infant care. And in many cases, women continue to be the primary caregivers beyond the toddler stage up until early adulthood. Accordingly, women have evolved emotional traits compatible with child rearing.[9] Men can get away with investing very little in their offspring. But despite that, men have an inner desire for long-term commitment. Most men want a loving family. When men are pair-bonded, their levels of testosterone decrease, and then decrease further when children appear on the scene.[10] And fathers can invest heavily if they so choose. Fathers tend to invest in terms of financial support—providing the family with food, shelter and, in this day and age, college tuition. In the ideal family situation, both men and women devote large amounts of energy and resources to raising children.

Our conscious matrix accepts the dual role played by man and woman in reproduction, and we celebrate the profound happiness when the relationships within the family unit are all working. But when relationships fail, people tend to blame the limitations of the roles dictated for men and women. Our conscious matrix seeks fairness, and sometimes traditional male-female roles seem unfair. Women may grow to resent having to rely on the man financially, and men resent women who fail to appreciate all they give to the relationship.

But the conscious matrix has no gender. The human soul has no gender. Happiness isn't related to our gender-specific roles. We can understand the perspective of the other-gendered person, but it takes work. Our conscious matrix has the capacity to experience the other person's perspective, but it takes connection. Ongoing communication and connection can't only occur occasionally. Frequent and continuous connection is needed to maintain the relationship. We can ask God to help us.

Even if our marriage or relationship is far from perfect, we can look within to our conscious matrix for solutions. Even if we've been badly hurt in the past, we can forgive those whom we love. This is possible when we fully imagine their experience and see the situation through their perspective. Often times this process starts by forgiving ourselves and others. We may have made mistakes and accidentally hurt our loved ones. They may have hurt us. We may choose to deny our mistakes. We may choose to lie to our partner. But we can't lie to our conscious matrix; it knows us thoroughly, literally from the inside out.

Our inner conscious matrix will provide solutions through greater connection within. Deep inside us we have access to all the answers through our conscious matrix. But we can't make the conscious matrix give us a quick answer. There are none. It's a struggle for everybody. True love is a destination, an ideal state that the conscious matrix can imagine, but real life is a journey. It's in our power to put ourselves on the right direction in that journey. We can't control what other people do, but we can try to connect. Just like we can connect to God or to a higher being with our conscious matrix, we can connect with our lover or spouse. A loving relationship is a path, not a destination. It's similar to the way our faith in God is a path, not a destination.

An idea to examine: *Monogamy is in superposition with monotheistic ideas.*

The origins of monogamy aren't entirely clear, but three things developed in parallel: agriculture, monotheism, and monogamy.[11] Around 10,000-20,000 years ago, man became farmers. This provided an opportunity for religions to evolve. By 1000 BCE, monotheism began to replace polytheistic worship. Monotheism focuses on one God, a father-like figure, much in the same manner that in monogamy places the man at the head of the household. With monogamy, man has authority over his wife and children, along with responsibility for them. The two are inextricably linked: a man won't want to pay for a wife or children who aren't his. Sometimes this natural entanglement in the conscious matrix is misunderstood. It doesn't mean men view women or children as inanimate possessions. It's merely a trigger for responsible behavior: my child and my wife are my responsibility.

Western culture has so legitimized monogamy that few question the assumption that the "one-man-paired-with-one-woman" couple is the only way for civilized people to behave. There's evidence that some of our hormones support monogamy on a biological level. But there's also enough individual variation in human sexual behavior to suggest not all people are naturally monogamous. Studies suggest men tend to be more polyamorous or promiscuous than females, but the differences aren't that great. One survey found that twenty-five percent of men and fifteen percent of women admitted to being unfaithful during their marriage.[12]

One research study looked at the brain activity of monogamous versus non-monogamous males.[13] What they found is both groups of men responded to sexually-oriented pictures in similar fashion. Where the men differed was in how they responded to romantic pictures. Parts of the brain known to participate in monogamous behavior—regions enriched with dopamine, vasopressin, and oxytocin—were more highly activated in the monogamous men by the romantic pictures. This is exactly what quantum mind theory would predict. In the monogamous men, we'd expect to see more entanglement between sexual stimuli and romantic pictures. Non-monogamous men don't connect romance with sex to the same degree that monogamous men do. That's not the way they're wired. But people do change their behaviors. There's even evidence people can change the way they're wired, at least until something triggers past patterns.

Some people are in "open relationships" that allow consensual extracurricular activity, namely sexual or emotional contacts with other people. But it doesn't appear that the open-relationship designation changes much. One study looked at jealousy in nearly 700 respondents, one-quarter of whom were consensually non-monogamous.[14] What this study found is that despite agreeing attachments with others were permissible, jealousy still occurred. Complex variables included whether the attachment was emotional or sexual in nature, and who the other person was.

Quantum mind theory would predict that complex variables are at play in both monogamous and non-monogamous relationships. What seems to be important is whether the partner's behavior matches what the other person expects. Most conflicts arise with feelings of not being treated like a priority or the primary person in an open relationship. Most jealousy arose from partners feeling neglected or treated less favorably than other partners. In the end, monogamy presents with fewer opportunities for conflict because it eliminates competition between multiple partners. Monogamy is a solution to many problems that can arise in group dynamics. No wonder God has chosen this path for most of us.

It makes sense that monogamy would gain in popularity as civilizations developed. It's the best attitude for group dynamics. It causes the least amount of tension and conflict. How do most people acquire their attitudes about love and monogamy? Western civilization garners a lot of support for monogamy though people's religious beliefs. All the Abrahamic monotheist religions condemn adultery; it's number seven of the Ten Commandments. But do people really practice what they preach? The degree to which our attitudes match our behavior depends on many variables. The stronger our beliefs, the more likely those beliefs will influence our behavior. Sincerity is tantamount. Lots of people will say they believe in doing what they've been taught to say, but only authentic beliefs will affect behavior. Another variable is peer pressure. What others are doing has a strong influence on our behavior.

We can learn a lot by taking a look at young people's attitudes before they begin engaging in sexual activity or making any long-term commitment. In Western civilization, college campuses have become a place not only to acquire knowledge, but also a place to find a suitable marriage partner or a significant other. In one study, researchers interviewed eighteen- and nineteen-year-old students in their first year of college to find out students' attitudes about their sexuality.[15] The students had specific goals regarding their sexuality and morality. They described two types of strategies: seeking behaviors and avoidance behaviors. In general, students were desirous to have sexual experiences, but only under the right circumstances. Many feared negative sexual experiences or sexual coercion. Their attitudes about their anticipated sexual behaviors were complex and nuanced by many factors: parental role models, peer pressure, self-image, reputation, and religious beliefs.

By far, the majority of students wanted some kind of relationship between sexual activity and commitment, but they weren't exactly sure how this might happen. The responses of these students are consistent with quantum mind theory. Most college students consider a wide array of factors. All past experiences, future expectations, and present opportunities exist in a quantum-like superposition. The final partner selection is a collapse to the best possible fit. We trust our conscious matrix to make the choice for us. Our inner voice will speak to us and let us know. We trust God to guide us.

In Western civilization, once a couple is married, monogamous behavior is the expected norm. Monogamy is a core ethic upheld in most churches and temples. Married couples can mingle where other people congregate in a safe environment, one that's quite the opposite of the college campus with its party atmosphere. The church can help couples who are struggling with their marriage, but the conscious matrix must do more than participate; it must take a leading role. If only one person of the couple wants the relationship to work, the other person can shut down their conscious matrix and not allow connection. It's a choice to connect with another person. Sometimes the reason for disconnecting is shame. That shame must be faced, and a person must forgive themselves, and then reconnection is possible.

No person should be shut out away from others due to shame. All human beings are biological organisms with drives and desires. Sexual activity isn't inherently bad. Our sexual acts may sometimes be perceived by others as bad if they trigger jealousy or fear of abandonment. But only the actual loss of support for wife (or husband) and children is harmful. It's not the sexual activity or the sexual drive that's harmful. Sexual drives and related activities are programmed inside us for a reason: to trigger romantic love, procreation, and pair-bonding.

Perfect monogamy—one man with one woman for life—is an ideal state of romantic love. It's a state one chooses and then strives to achieve. It might be a unicorn, something that rarely occurs. In an academic environment, if one scores ninety-nine percent correct on a test, that's considered excellent. People are less forgiving about sexual transgressions, but why? The reason lies in moral hypocrisy. Many people aren't honest about their own transgressions and struggle to keep their mistakes secret. Keeping secrets and other deceptions erode the conscious matrix and make it hard to forgive others. You have to forgive yourself first. Having a distracted conscious matrix makes it difficult to read your own heart and impossible to read the heart of another.

> **One last idea to examine:** Moral hypocrisy is a quantum superposition between harsh judgement of others and a fear of one's own sexual transgressions being exposed. People's desire to hear and repeat salacious gossip amplifies and greatly exaggerates the worst of others, while falsely implying a possession of superior morality.

One of Jesus' closest companions was Mary of Magdalene. The gossip went viral. Was Mary the wife of Jesus? Was Mary a prostitute? All we can say from what's written is that Mary was a woman. It was unusual for women to converse regularly with men in biblical times. It was unusual for a woman to be part of intellectual discussions. All we can say with certainty is that Mary was an unusual woman, and this led to gossip.

Not much has changed in two millennia. People love to talk about the sexual indiscretions of others. The news media exploits this human weakness and floods us with salacious stories. "That's what sells," people commonly say. Some of our interest is understandable. We have mirror neurons that activate when we view or imagine the actions of others, and sexual images also activate the mirror neuron system.[16] People need to realize that the motivation underlying all their talk about sexual activities of others is mostly motivated because they get a vicarious thrill out of it.

But oftentimes, people cloak that reason by taking the moral highground. People falsely claim to be disgusted by sexual content to hide the simple truth that they're excited by it. Sinners stay home and look at pornography, while church ladies talk about it at length while condemning it. What's the difference? Not much, since it's the same mirror neuron systems that are being triggered. Sigmund Freud had a name for this paradox; he called it "reaction formation."[17] This paradox of condemning activities for the mere thrill of thinking about those activities is actually a quantum entanglement. Both viewing pornography and self-righteous indignation are linked behaviors—two sides of the same coin. Both are entanglements and vicarious excitement triggered by imagined sexual activity.

Negatively judging others for "what you secretly wish you were doing" isn't good practice. But that's not the same as conscientiously observing other people's behavior. Our attitudes shape our behavior; that's the main function of attitudes. It's okay to observe someone's behavior and think: "that's how I want to behave" or "that's NOT how I want to behave." Observing others and judging behavior helps to decide our own actions. But we must be cautious. Psychologists provide solid evidence that we tend to judge others more harshly than we judge ourselves; it's human nature.[18] People judge others harshly to give the illusion of being superior or to exert power over others. Taken to the extreme, moral hypocrisy can really hurt others, causing social isolation and exclusion.

Let's consider the gossip about Mary Magdalene again. Does it even matter if Jesus had a friend who was a prostitute? Obviously, that kind of sexual promiscuity is outside the norm, and it could be hurtful to other women whose husbands Mary might briefly engage. But even so, we can assume Mary wasn't trying to steal any of the women's husbands. Like other women in that profession, she was merely offering something that was easy for her to give that others were willing to pay a fixed sum to obtain. In many ways, Mary's behavior is less offensive than that of a woman who acts self-righteous yet plots to steal her close friend's husband. People who act like friends, but who have their hearts set on doing something cruel, are far worse than Mary. Trickery, like lying, is far worse than an open exchange of sex for money, not that either action is good or moral. The problem is that many women who would judge Mary harshly aren't able to see their own character flaws.

Moral hypocrisy abounds in church communities, and it's the number one reason people give for not attending church services.[19] People gossip about anything and everything. Unfounded accusations abound like: "That family's not pledging enough in offerings," or "That woman's sleeping with her best friend's husband." While it's okay to observe others' behavior and ask questions, it's critically important not to draw conclusions from mere speculation. Just because two people think something fishy is going on doesn't prove it true. Wild speculation is gradually taken as the absolute truth as it's passed from person to person. And the person being targeted by vicious gossip gets further isolated and cast out of the group.

In November 2015, an Afghan woman accused of adultery was stoned to death.[20] The world was shocked but really shouldn't have been. While stoning is outlawed in Western countries, both men and women are socially ostracized for sexual behavior, which in some cases might not have even occurred. The potential for sexual indiscretion is sometimes enough to trigger social retribution and isolation. This renders the victim harmed. Social isolation is psychologically harmful and painful. Social rejection activates the same parts of the brain as does physical injury.[20] That's the pain system quelled by opioids released by our brain and bodies. Men, as well as women, are targeted. The worst scenario is where the person doesn't even realize they're being victimized. As the Bible says in Romans 5:8 (NIV), "*But God demonstrates his own love for us in this: While we were still sinners, Christ died for us.*"

But let's assume the person accused did commit the sexual indiscretion. Is that just cause for them to be persecuted? A partner has a right to be hurt and consoled, but sometimes vengeance takes the extreme to character assassination. "Hell has no greater fury than a woman scorned,"[21] is a commonly heard quote referring what some wives do to get even with husbands who cheat on them. Love turns to hate, and in the end, it's hard to tell whose behavior is worse.

No person has the right to destroy the reputation of a past partner because of hurt. And if a person's partner has no right to destroy their partner who betrayed them, what right has anyone else to commit character assassination? The only right people have is to walk away. And others can keep their vile opinions to themselves.

The sin of malicious gossip is in its intent. It's okay to vent about a problem to friends. It's okay to be open and explain to others about something that happens to you or to a friend. It's okay to talk about other people's behavior and use it as a model for your own behavior—a means to identify what you want to emulate and behaviors you want to avoid. The detriment of moral hypocrisy is the lie that another person's behavior is defective, while your own behavior is better. These lies and deceptions might fool others, but telling lies erodes the conscious matrix. Our inner conscience knows when we lie. What happens is people bury the lie deeper and deeper, until they believe their own lies. Fueled by fake respect garnered by the deception, moral hypocrisy can grow like a cancer.

The Abrahamic religions have done a wonderful thing to preach and celebrate the joys of monogamy. The union between one man and one woman—with the purpose of creating a loving family—is certainly an "ideal state" that billions of people believe might work for them. But ideal states are merely goals. Countless numbers of people try and do their very best to achieve the ideal. But if we try our hardest and fail, we need not feel shame. Deviations away from the ideal are what make the human race so delightfully human. The conscious matrix seeks to continuously test our perceived ideals to see if they can't be modified to fit more people. The collective consciousness has the potential to continuously expand to accommodate all our individual differences and variations.

It's a misunderstanding that religious teachings that celebrate the traditional man-woman marriage are discriminatory against same-sex marriage. Monogamy works in society because it facilitates reproduction and family life. The Abrahamic religions are about cultivating beliefs around that premise. It's difficult to remove that core principle without the rest falling like a house-of-cards. But we must also remember that the vast majority of heterosexual acts of intercourse don't result in conception. So it's a given that sexual contact isn't always about procreation. We need touch for good emotional health, and for each of us to bond with a special other. Most Christians love all people regardless of their sexual orientation. Some Christians authentically accept same-sex marriage as a wholesome act of love, whereas others don't. I accept same-sex marriage as a legitimate expression of committed love, but that's my genuine opinion; no one coerced me. Every person has a right to their beliefs, especially their core beliefs. The collective consciousness has to grow so all groups genuinely see other perspectives. Authentic acceptance has to grow through greater connection; it can't be forced. The moral hypocrisy is on both sides: one side being intolerant of the others' behavior; the other side intolerant of other peoples' views.

Love, lust, and the eternal coupling of two is the most cherished dream of the conscious matrix. If we're so lucky as to experience the dream—whether it lasts only a short time or an eternity, whether we have many children or none—we participate in that dream and add our soul to the collective consciousness of romantic love and the hope of everlasting joy. It's our greatest human desire not only to give and receive love, but to understand its deeper meaning. We can only find that meaning by looking within. Our conscious matrix can provide the necessary connections, and it alone can receive the blessings of God. We don't need other people's approval.

CHAPTER 10: NOTES AND REFERENCES

1. Caldwell HK. Oxytocin and vasopressin: powerful regulators of social behavior. Neuroscientist. 2017, 23(5):517-528.

    Heinrichs M, Domes G. Neuropeptides and social behaviour: effects of oxytocin and vasopressin in humans. Prog Brain Res. 2008, 170:337-50.

2. Rilling JK, DeMarco AC, Hackett PD, Thompson R, Ditzen B, Patel R, Pagnoni G. Effects of intranasal oxytocin and vasopressin on cooperative behavior and associated brain activity in men. Psychoneuroendocrinology. 2012, 37:447–461.

Mu Y, Guo C, Han S. Oxytocin enhances inter-brain synchrony during social coordination in male adults. Soc Cogn Affect Neurosci. 2016, 11(12):1882-1893.

3. Algoe SB, Kurtz LE, Grewen K. Oxytocin and social bonds: The role of oxytocin in perceptions of romantic partners' bonding behavior. Psychol Sci. 2017, 28(12):1763-1772.

4. Rhodes G. The evolutionary psychology of facial beauty. Annu Rev Psychol. 2006; 57:199-226.

5. Falling in love only happens so many times, says survey. Huff Post, August, 2013. https://www.huffpost.com/entry/falling-in-love-twice_n_3817986

6. Sternberg RJ. A triangular theory of love. Psychol Rev. 1986, 93:119–135.

7. Geiger AW, Livingston G. Eight facts about love and marriage in America. Pew Research Center. February, 2019. https://www.pewresearch.org/fact-tank/2019/02/13/8-facts-about-love-and-marriage/

8. Bjorklund DF, Kipp K. Parental investment theory and gender differences in the evolution of inhibition mechanisms. Psychol Bull. 1996 Sep;120(2):163-88.

9. Buss DM, Schmitt DP. Sexual strategies theory: an evolutionary perspective on human mating. Psychol Rev. 1993. 100(2):204-32.

10. Grebe NM, Sarafin RE, Strenth CR, Zilioli S. Pair-bonding, fatherhood, and the role of testosterone: A meta-analytic review. Neurosci Biobehav Rev. 2019, 98:221-233.

11. Dupanloup I, Pereira L, Bertorelle G, Calafell F, Prata MJ, Amorim A, Barbujani G. A recent shift from polygyny to monogamy in humans is suggested by the analysis of worldwide Y-chromosome diversity. J Mol Evol. 2003, 57(1):85-97.

Henrich J, Boyd R, Richerson PJ. The puzzle of monogamous marriage. Philos Trans R Soc Lond B Biol Sci. 2012, 367(1589):657-69.

12. Laumann EO, Michael RT, Gagnon JH. A political history of the national sex survey of adults. Fam Plann Perspect. 1994, 26(1):34-8.

13. Hamilton LD, Meston CM. Differences in neural response to romantic stimuli in monogamous and non-monogamous men. Arch Sex Behav. 2017, 46(8):2289-2299.

14. Mogilski JK, Reeve SD, Nicolas SCA, Donaldson SH, Mitchell VE, Welling LLM. Jealousy, consent, and compersion within monogamous and consensually non-monogamous romantic relationships. Arch Sex Behav. 2019, 48(6):1811-1828.

15. Anders KM, Olmstead SB. A qualitative examination of the sexual possible selves and strategies of first-semester college students: How sexual possible selves are developed during the transition to college. Arch Sex Behav. 2019, 48(6):1859-1876.

16. Ortigue S, Bianchi-Demicheli F. [Unconscious sexual desire: fMRI and EEG evidences from self-expansion theory to mirror neurons]. Rev Med Suisse. 2010, 6(241):620-2, 624

   Mouras H, Stoléru S, Moulier V, Pélégrini-Issac M, Rouxel R, Grandjean B, Glutron D, Bittoun J. Activation of mirror-neuron system by erotic video clips predicts degree of induced erection: an fMRI study. Neuroimage. 2008, 42(3):1142-50.

17. LeCroy D. Freud: the first evolutionary psychologist? Ann N Y Acad Sci. 2000, 907:182-90.

18. Lammers J, Stapel DA, Galinsky AD. Power increases hypocrisy: moralizing in reasoning, immorality in behavior. Psychol Sci. 2010, 21(5):737-44.

Polman E, Ruttan RL. Effects of anger, guilt, and envy on moral hypocrisy. Pers Soc Psychol Bull. 2012, 38(1):129-39,

Dong M, van Prooijen JW, van Lange PAM. Self-enhancement in moral hypocrisy: Moral superiority and moral identity are about better appearances. PLoS One. 2019, 14(7):e0219382

19. Moberg DO, Holy masquerade: Hypocrisy in religion. Rev Religious Res. 1987, 29(1):3-24

20. Afghan woman accused of adultery stoned to death. BBC News. November, 2015. https://www.bbc.com/news/world-asia-34714205

21. The line from William Congreve's 1697 poem The Mourning Bride is: Heaven has no rage like love to hatred turned/Nor hell a fury like a woman scorned.

GOD AND CREATIVITY: DIVINE INSPIRATION OR HUMAN INVENTION?

ONLY HUMAN BEINGS have the ability to vastly alter our surroundings, create languages and religions, and invent civilizations. We're uniquely inventive and capable of producing something that never existed before except for in our imaginations. Does God play a role in this?

We can turn an idea into a real product. We've built huts, houses, skyscrapers, and entire cities. We've invented the wheel, then the automobile. We've designed and built trains, planes, boats, and rocket ships. And to enable ourselves to move from one place to another, we've built roads, highways, bridges, and railroad tracks. Every single thing built by a person started out as a potential solution to a problem presented to the conscious matrix. People can create nearly any kind of environment they choose, just by working with materials on hand and using their creativity.

The old adage explains it succinctly: necessity is the mother of invention. Creativity arises from an unmet need. It's easy to guess why people invented ways to build themselves a shelter. Early man needed a safe place to sleep to keep him warm and dry when the weather was cold and wet. And sleeping outdoors leaves one vulnerable to being attacked by wild animals or other people. So out of necessity, the conscious matrix created the notion of a shelter strong enough to keep out the wind, rain, and predators. Cave entrances could be modified to block the entry of intruders. Grass and mud could be fashioned into mud huts. Animal skins could be stretched and made into tents. Shelter—the solution to being vulnerable while asleep—arose in the conscious matrix of early man. But birds build nests, beavers build dams, and other animals dig out tunnels to shelter themselves. What's so unique about human creativity? It seems human creativity isn't entirely unique, but its grandeur has far exceeded anything else so far seen.

Is it possible to trace the roots of human creativity? And if we propose that our best ideas come from God, then how does this divine inspiration work? How does God talk to us? One way to start unraveling this mystery is to look at how human beings developed language. Upon mastery of language skills, the human mind began to create stories out of words. With storytelling skills, humankind developed religious beliefs to guide behavior and avoid moral confusion. With religious beliefs, humankind cultivated civilizations out of barbarianism. And with advanced civilizations, humans developed technology. In these modern times, we've advanced to the point where we can create artificial intelligence, an attempt to mimic the human mind.

Artificial intelligence can mimic human behavior and make mechanical choices that seem almost human. But we still can't create a device that has conscious experience. We don't need to invent the phenomenon of conscious experience; we're born with a conscious matrix that instantly connects us to the wonders of the universe. Our conscious matrix is clearly the source of our creativity. Therefore, it seems fair to ask: Is our conscious matrix the portal to divine inspiration? Does God communicate directly to our conscious matrix?

A possibility to ponder: Humankind created language to fine-tune already existing mutual understandings. We're born ready to connect and understand one another. And we wouldn't be able to communicate to anyone if God hadn't placed an innate ability to connect and understand one another in our conscious matrix.

Our conscious matrix naturally connects with the conscious matrix of other people. People understand one another without language through spontaneous facial expressions and gestures. This unspoken communication triggers mirror-neuron responses that lead to shared experience and cooperative couplings between two minds. When people observe others in distress and empathize with them, neurons in the observer "mirror" or mimic the activity of the neurons in the person they're connecting to emotionally.[1]

We don't need language to communicate with others. People who don't speak a word of each other's language can nonetheless fall in love. Anyone can travel to a foreign country and manage to get to their hotel without any familiarity with the language. But knowing a certain few key words can help. The countless advantages of language are obvious. Words greatly enhance communication, and we benefit greatly from having those skills. But words can also be used to spread misinformation and thereby enable deception. How we use language is situation-specific and directly relates to the culture in place. Language and culture are inextricably linked. Quoting Corinthians 14:10 (NASB), *"There are, perhaps, a great many kinds of languages in the world, and no kind is without meaning."*

Language experts disagree on nearly everything, but the consensus is language originated around 50,000 to 100,000 years ago.[2] Simple language skills developed gradually. But at some point, complex languages took off rapidly.[3] One might compare the origins of human language to language development in children. Each time a young child learns their native language, language is reinvented in that child's conscious matrix. The process is gradual at first and then takes off at lightning speed.

The capacity for human infants to acquire language is fairly well understood.[4] It takes the average child one year to say their first word. But as every parent knows, the next weeks are filled with many new words. Children rapidly add multiple new words every day until parents lose an accurate count. This newly found ability to communicate doesn't develop out of thin air. A mother and her infant child have already had frequent non-verbal communications during the first year. An emotional bond exists between mother and child that enables complex language development; this pre-existing connection is foundational.[5]

Over the first year, a young child hears certain words repeatedly spoken by the mother or father. The child will have already grasped the approximate meaning of the word in their conscious matrix long before speaking it. When the child reaches around one year of age, the vocal apparatus is mature enough to finally say some of the words he or she understands. Those first words typically bring the parents enormous joy. The joy is shared and their connection is strengthened. Needless to say, the child is motivated to say more words. Soon the small child combines words to express wants and needs. Non-grammatical phrases like, "me milk," effectively communicate the idea that the child wants milk. Communication is measured by the response elicited in others, getting the message across is the number-one job. That's why, without connection, language development is slowed down or even halted. Autistic children struggle with language because they lack social connection with others.[6]

Quantum mind theory predicts that the conscious matrix is pre-wired to connect to others. We might call it empathy, but it's much more than that. It's this connection that motivates us to use whatever we hear, see, and feel to better connect. Through our direct experiences with our surroundings, we're able to learn that other sentient beings are experiencing the same things at the same time. What better way to connect with others than by acquiring language skills?

The newborn infant comes into this life with only an inborn understanding of raw experience. The infant also possesses a keen desire to learn more about these experiences. Nothing at first has any meaning, but the infant has the built-in desire to search for it, to learn it.[7] The preverbal child spends the first year of life being exquisitely sensitive to the pure experience of novel sights and sounds. A new mobile toy hung in the crib will entertain an infant for hours. Each shape is a marvel to the infant because he or she is experiencing certain shapes and colors for the first time. The infant can spend many minutes, even hours, taking in all the new sights and sounds.

Eventually, the small child will come to automatically link every shape and sound to its many possible meanings. The motivation to learn more comes in part from shared experiences of new meanings with another person. When a small child is corrected about the meaning of a word by the mother, a different meaning is learned. When the mother says, "pear, not apple," the child learns their mistake. But category words like "fruit" take more time for the child to learn. The child needs to be told many times that lots of common foods—apples, oranges, pears, peaches, and bananas—are fruits. Learning a category word is an intellectual step up from learning objects. The experience of an abstract concept, that of categories, is shared between mother and child when she explains that bananas, apples, pears, oranges and some of the sweet-tasting foods like those—are examples of fruit. The child will eventually get the idea that fruit is a broader kind of word; it refers to a collection of food items.

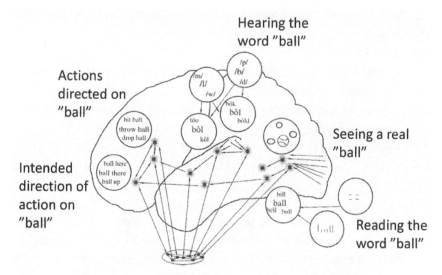

Conscious Matrix of the Word "Ball"

According to quantum mind theory, meanings of words are sets of entanglements linking different parts of the brain in quantum coherence (see figure above adapted from ref. 8). Soon after the child learns a few nouns, they learn the verbs that go with those objects. Each object pairs with certain actions. A ball is a round object the child can kick or throw. So far, everything is pretty concrete. But as the child matures through adolescence, actions can be visualized in the mind as abstract concepts. Abstract concepts are organized hierarchically in the human brain. Starting from simple concrete objects to higher- and higher-level abstractions, the human brain is arranged to handle ascending levels of understanding.

A young child progresses rapidly from understanding "ball" as an object word to understanding the phrase "throw ball" as an action. It takes several more years before areas of the cerebral cortex mature enough to understand planning a future action such as "I'm saving up

$25 to buy a basketball." And finally, the fully mature adult brain can plan something like, "I'd like to own a sporting goods store and sell basketballs." Each idea—from simple object—to object actions—to complex abstract plan—is stored in a different part of the conscious matrix. Moreover, each idea can reach consciousness separately or in combination with linked ideas. The countless combinations of units of meaning can fuse seamlessly through quantum entanglement in the conscious matrix.

In acquiring language skill, we start small, but language is capable of developing ideas that delve far into the future, and in great detail. Language is the gateway to higher creativity, but words alone have limited meaning. What gives language its full force is the power of words to tell stories. Where does our storytelling ability come from? Human invention or divine inspiration from God, or is it a combination of both?

> *Another possibility to ponder:* Language enabled storytelling to greatly expand. According to quantum mind theory, a coupling occurs between speaker and listener. It's this coupling that signals understanding. Hearing spoken language without understanding produces no coupling.

Language provides far more than the simple exchange of commands and responses. Human beings are afforded the rich luxury to share our life experiences, and the experiences of others, through storytelling. Whether we're creating accurate biographical accounts or fictional tales, we have the power to inspire, shock, or otherwise tug at the heart strings of others. We're creative and communicative beings. We have an inborn drive to share our thoughts and stories with others.

Scientists show that when people listen to someone telling a story, their brain activity becomes coupled to that of the speaker.[9] Coupling means the speaker and listener's brain activity patterns resemble each other. In both the speaker and the listener, different parts of the brain activate in a particular order, showing a characteristic pattern. Brain regions related to processing sound, word meaning, grammar, syntax, speech production, and finally the deeper meaning of the whole story lock onto the same pattern. Typically, it takes a speaker about half a second to say a word, nine seconds to say a sentence, and then longer time intervals to complete a paragraph. The activity in the listener's brain usually lags behind that of the speaker by as much as a few seconds, but occasionally the listener will show the patterned activity ahead of the speaker.

The primary purpose of language is to share understanding. The speaker and listener must couple their brain activity patterns for there to be understanding. Sometimes during storytelling, the listener will actually anticipate what comes next. This is a sign of heightened understanding. When we're able to guess what happens next, we're completely grasping the underlying story line.

Since there's a time lag, there's no evidence for quantum entanglement between the speaker and listener occurring for processing sounds, words, word meaning, syntax, or grammar. But when we get to the deeper meaning of the tale or the moral of the story, then there's the possibility for co-entanglement between speaker and listener. An example might be when the listener understands the story line well enough to anticipate what comes next. The deeper meaning of stories is stored in neurons in higher brain centers, mainly in the prefrontal cortex. These are the neurons at the highest end of the conscious matrix hierarchy. These are the neurons that connect with many thousands of neurons and store a rich archive of quantum entanglements.[10]

Because quantum states are delicate and can't survive any kind of disruption, it remains speculative whether a true quantum entanglement between two people is possible. If it's remotely possible, then entanglement would most likely occur in special situations. For example, if the two people were to discuss the deeper meaning of the story while connecting emotionally, then it might precipitate entanglement. Eye contact could transmit the precise moment each person understood the meaning of a specific part of the story. A brief, intense, shared experience might synchronize brain activity between the two people in real time. It would of necessity have to be very brief. Quantum entanglement is very delicate and fleeting.

Quantum entanglements at specific places in the story would be expected to deepen with repeated telling and sharing of the story. Two people who share the story repeatedly might develop a deeper relationship and better understanding of each other. If I know you well enough, to the extent that I can accurately guess how you'll respond based on our shared experiences, then I can anticipate how you might feel in other situations. I might be able to guess your mental state, but I'll never really know. The closest we can ever get to another person is to guess correctly most of the time. Our conscious matrix is our private collection of thoughts and we can choose whether or not to share.

It's an entirely different situation when it comes to our connecting with God or a higher being. There's much greater possibility for true quantum connection to God because He can read our thoughts, or at least we perceive that as possible. We tell God our stories when we pray. We tell God what's happening in our lives, and we ask for advice or guidance. He knows our conscious matrix better than we know it ourselves. He knows why some stories make us feel good and other stories are troublesome. He understands the deepest meaning of all things. He is the universe of all answers. As it says in John 5:14 (NIV), *"This is the confidence we have in approaching God: that if we ask anything according to his will, he hears us."*

Through our conscious matrix, we have direct access to the mind of God. We can share our stories with our friends and family, and they can try to help as best they can, but only direct connection to God through our inner conscious matrix will ever enable us see things from the broadest perspectives possible. Accordingly, storytelling is a quantum superposition of both human invention and divine inspiration. But it's not always clear where one begins and the other one ends.

An idea to examine: Storytelling enabled the development of religions. Shared understanding of stories enables people to anticipate certain story-endings together. The conscious matrix is pre-wired to anticipate that good behavior will be rewarded and bad behavior will be punished. Storylines that deviate must provide valid reasons for taking exception to those rules to be understood. Religious belief systems follow from these pre-wired tendencies to predict outcomes and judge others.

Once human beings developed their keen storytelling skills, a universal preference developed for stories that taught a moral lesson. In this manner, storytelling paved the way and gave rise to religious belief systems. The Greek and Roman mythologies created storylines in which gods and goddesses possessed special powers. Each of their gods and goddesses had their unique personalities illustrating both the best and worst in people. Perhaps it was those flaws that brought them down in the opinion of the people. People have an inborn desire to seek flawless perfection. People have an inborn desire to look up to a perfect, morally-pure leader. People have an inborn desire to worship and follow one supreme God.

Around 1000 BCE, the one-God idea largely replaced the worship of multiple false gods. Monotheism originated with the Jews at about the same time as the Phoenician alphabet developed. With this new tool, stories could be written and thereby preserved. And it followed that many religious texts were written chronicling ancient times. The Hebrew Bible still serves is a sacred text for modern Jews and Christians. The Christians added more chapters, collectively called the New Testament. The Muslim prophet Muhammad gave rise to the Koran.

Much of the biblical writing is in storytelling format. Dr. Bill Mounce, in his book *52 Major Stories of the Bible,* selects and summarizes some of the key stories in the Bible.[11] Selections from the Old Testament include stories about the Creation, Adam and Eve's fall from grace, Noah's Ark, Abraham's covenant with God, Moses and the plagues, the Ten Commandments, David and Goliath, and others. The common thread among all these stories is that God is the creator of all things, the source of original goodness, a force to be obeyed, and a force that forgives. We come to understand who and what God is through stories. It's not the details we necessarily remember; it's the moral of the story that sticks in our minds. That's what our conscious matrix deciphers as coming closest to the true meaning of God.

But how did the prophets who wrote the Bible and Koran identify the "moral" of the stories told? Most people today regard the Bible as either the literal word of God or the inspired word of God. Quantum mind theory has a possible solution for this apparent conundrum. The Bible and other religious texts are most likely a quantum superposition of the literal and inspired word of God. But how do we account for divine inspiration? All of us can connect directly with God through our conscious matrix; it's our portal to God. To be so divinely inspired, Moses and the other writers who contributed to sacred religious texts must have been very deeply connected to God through their conscious matrices.

How do we know when our conscious matrix is connecting to God and receiving good information? The harsh reality is we don't know. Only time will tell. The inspiration to think, write, or mobilize to action may seem to be coming from God if the thoughts or actions appear to be kind. But we can only connect to God; we'll never be God-like or all-knowing. We have to try with our best intentions.

When we put full faith in ourselves and in our connection to God, we've done our part. Mistakes aren't only permitted but necessary. How many times do we need to be told from God that He will forgive us? The entire New Testament is devoted to stories about Jesus, the son of God, who lived to prove to us that God understands humanity. Mistakes, wars, deceit, betrayal—are all part of human behavior. Civilized society deals with this reality. But what binds us in civilization is our potential to connect our minds with the mind of God. We're responsible for learning from our mistakes; we're expected not to repeat our misdeeds done without malicious intent.

When our connection with God is good, decisions will be proven right in the long-run. We have to have faith that our intentions are good. That's the faster path to possible success. And we have to learn from history. There's no reason to keep making the same mistakes over and over again. God forgives our honest mistakes but not our foolishness. God lets us suffer consequences for foolish behavior and it's for our own good. Sometimes we have to suffer the consequences for our mistakes in order to learn better. People stubbornly cling to some of our worst mistakes, despite repeated warnings from God. As stated in Romans 8:28 (KJV), *"And we know that all things work together for good for those who love God, to those who are the called according to His purpose."*

Another idea to examine: *Religious beliefs are prerequisite to building civilizations. Religious practices bind people together in a mutually beneficial way. Secular reasons for creating civilizations ultimately fail and self-destruct.*

Quantum mind theory, as interpreted in the present book, predicts people have an inborn connection to God. This prediction is supported by our inexplicable motivation to further develop our spiritual connection to God. By sharing our religious beliefs and experiences with others, our connection to God is strengthened. Once a group of people are bound together as one people, civilizations develop around the people united in their belief in God. The keystones of civilization—cities, societies, monuments, and culture—these things alone don't bind people. Only sharing a connection at the level of our inner conscious matrix connects us deeply enough for society and culture to develop around it. Human beings desire a close inner circle of friends who share our deepest held beliefs, especially our religious beliefs.

Brad Hirschfeld, in his article *Did Religion Create Civilization?* argues there's proof it was religion, not agriculture, that enabled civilization to originate 12,000 to 15,000 years ago.[12] Ancient ruins of a lone temple discovered in Turkey called *Göbekli Tepe* provide key evidence that people gathered to worship without a city having formed first. Hirschfeld argues that humans have a "religious impulse" that compels us to first envision in our minds, then make a pilgrimage to a sacred place, and build a monument to experience shared worship. That's the start of great things to come. Men and women, inspired by their conscious matrix connection to God, can build amazing structures of architecture and develop elaborate cultures.

Religion isn't only the prerequisite for civilization; it's also a self-correcting force. In his book, *How Quantum Activism Can Save Civilization*, Amit Goswami argues modern civilization is in danger.[13] This is directly due to the secular and anti-religious positions taken by the intellectual elite. When the deeper meaning of life and values become denigrated in the name of progress, people lose their connection with God. Soulless people lose motivation when only political or secular reasons are permitted. A society erodes when the people's connection to God or to their spirituality is forbidden.

In Chapter 9, we looked at how religion resurfaces in communist regimes where religious practice is discouraged. But there are more subtle ways civilization can discourage religious belief. Schools, colleges, and universities are increasingly teaching a secular mind-set. But as Goswami argues, religion is embedded in our collective unconscious. Quantum physics enables the fusion of two completely different realms. One realm is the one in which we perceive material objects, an observable reality. The other is the quantum realm, in which we only perceive pure inner experience.

We can only connect to God with our conscious matrix, which operates according to quantum mechanical laws. But what we experience in the quantum realm—wisdom and divine inspiration—is also apparent in all we see, hear, and touch. Each time we experience the beauty of the landscape, the smile of a friend, the mystery of a road traveled for the first time, the awe and joy we experience reminds us our conscious matrix is connected to God. When society or culture tries to take this away from the people, we rebel or wither and die. A soulless person has no will to survive. And a culture without a soul is on a path of destruction. But almost miraculously, the connection to God always resurfaces.

Given all the benefits of civilization, what makes things go awry? One aspect of civilization is that people are stratified into ascending social ranks, ranging from workers and farmers to the ruling elite. There's a hierarchy that exists in a stratified society. The elites have power over others by virtue of their wealth, presumed intelligence, and connections in society. The people who are governed, schooled, or dominated by the elites will accept their leadership only if it holds some possible benefit to them.

The elites aren't special in God's eyes. The common people are equally connected to God, and it is He who teaches them obedience in most life situations. So it follows that whenever the ruling class, financial elites, or academic teachers are exposed as corrupt, the common people will no longer support them. Rebellions often unseat the elite because the common people far outnumber the elites. The elites may have the money to pay soldiers to defend them, but if the corruption is too great, no one will take their money. Alternatively, well-paid soldiers may even take money from the elites and then betray them. With God on the side of the common people, the elites have no way to win. As the Bible says in Corinthians 1:26-28 (ESV) *"For consider your calling, brothers: not many of you were wise according to worldly standards, not many were powerful, not many were of noble birth. But God chose what is foolish in the world to shame the wise; God chose what is weak in the world to shame the strong; God chose what is low and despised in the world, even things that are not, to bring to nothing things that are."*

Is a stratified society a grave injustice in the first place? The brain is organized like a stratified society, suggesting there's nothing inherently evil about social order. Nature made the brain and it exhibits a hierarchical pattern of linkages.[14] But the conscious matrix entangles all the brain's regions together; it's the great leveler. The conscious matrix provides a kind of wireless communication that transcends the cerebral cortex hierarchy. Quantum entanglement is possible because the spacing between free electrons caged in protein pockets is exactly the right distance to connect with free electrons in other such pockets.[15] The spacing of these pockets likely evolved to connect together and ultimately fuse with the mind of God. The most intense and most abstract ideas we can experience produce the most photons emitted, hence the brightest light shone within our physical brain. These are states of mind in which our connection to the mind of God might be clearest.

Analogous to the hierarchy of thoughts in the conscious matrix in our cerebral cortex, many of the most intelligent people are part of the ruling class, the academic elite, and the financial elite. Accordingly, sometimes these people come to believe they're uniquely positioned to connect with the mind of God. Is this true or false? In rare cases it could be true. Some leaders do great things for the people because they're divinely inspired. But the elites also have the greatest potential to deceive others into thinking they're leading others on the righteous path, while they might instead be tricking people. When elites dissociate from their inner conscience, they can commit great harm to society. When elites abuse their privilege and misguide people to only serve themselves and not to serve God, that's when civilization crumbles.

In these modern times, the elites—government officials, spiritual leaders, academic teachers, and financial managers—sometimes need to be reminded that all people possess a conscious matrix and can directly connect to God. The story of the *Torn Veil in the Temple* appears in many chapters of the Bible, but especially in the Book of Hebrews. Soon after Jesus was crucified, the people rushed into the temple and saw the curtain was torn in two. That curtain had once separated the people from the Holy chamber through which only the high priest could pass. The torn veil symbolized the realization that all people could connect directly with God. One might deduce from this lesson that it's not stratification of people that's the problem. Problems arise when elites believe that only they connect to God and others must go through them to consult with God. Every person possesses a conscious matrix that can directly connect with God. And sometimes the humblest people have the strongest connections to God.

Another downfall of civilization is the breakdown in understanding one another. Multiculturalism has for a long time been a component of civilization. Urban environments allow for many different cultures to live side-by-side. Civilization, with its stratified social class system, creates specialized labor forces and professional classes of people. Oftentimes people working certain jobs tend to come from one culture, while people doing other jobs coming from another culture.

A healthy amount of multiculturalism seems to facilitate civilization. But too much multiculturalism seems to breed trouble. And sometimes, the elites use false claims of xenophobia to introduce people they can use as slaves and ward off criticism for doing that. Slave labor is cheaper than paid labor, and although it's outlawed in most places today, there are ways to make people into virtual slaves. When migrant workers displace citizens in jobs they once held, both migrant and citizen workers are at the mercy of the elites. If the migrants and citizens could unite, they could win against the elites. But often times, the elites will cause strife, race-baiting, racial confrontation, and other conditions meant to isolate the groups and create hatred between them.

Multiculturalism isn't the problem. It's the exploitation of multiculturalism by the elites that causes strife. But those plots are easily foiled. It's natural for people to understand each other best when they connect directly. People have a natural curiosity about different cultures. Moreover, every person has a capacity to love others, especially when the person practices having an open heart by connecting regularly with God. Multicultural assimilation will occur when people stop obeying the elites who want to prevent them from connecting directly to the people in the other group.

What does quantum mind theory predict about multicultural assimilation? It teaches that the conscious matrix inherently knows that, despite different cultural backgrounds, people are individuals and must be judged on their own merits. People are capable of doing one of three things: (1) obey their conscience consistently with their best effort, (2) sometimes obey depending on the circumstances, or (3) rarely heed their conscience, reasoning it's what everyone else is doing. It's more difficult to evaluate the honesty and integrity of a person from a different culture, and that's why we tend to trust others like ourselves. Usually, it's harder to be deceived by someone from the same culture who has the same values we hold. But betrayal can occur from any source, familiar or foreign.

Can we recover from the potential devastation and destruction of our culture? Yes, we can if we seek deep inside ourselves, align with those who share the same beliefs, and also reach out to those with different beliefs. Taking these steps, and in this order, is important. Trust our own connection with God first and foremost, next trust people like ourselves, and then reach out others who are different. To do otherwise is to risk being deceived. When there's too much corruption, deception, and multiculturalism, those things can lead to the dissolution of the civilization. When too many people disconnect from their inner conscious matrix, the soul of the community is damaged. But we can always reverse course and save our civilization. We have the force of God on our side when we seek His connection.

> **One last thought to ponder:** *Quantum mind theory predicts machines will never be conscious because there's no way for them to have a direct portal to God.*

The human conscious matrix is unique in that it can connect directly to God and understand higher laws of the universe. The minds of common man existed long before scientists were able to articulate or formalize physical laws. Our conscious matrix already understands the consequences of universal laws without help from scientists. Human beings can perceive what God knows, but humankind can't alter God or change the fundamental laws of the universe. We're not God, and as human beings we falter whenever we start to believe ourselves to be God.

Modern civilizations have enabled technology to develop beyond our wildest dreams. We're attempting to recreate the human mind with computer technology and artificial intelligence. Here we've run into a road block. Artificial intelligence programs humans have created to run on computers excel at mathematical functions and data crunching. But these "smart" machines can't do some things humans can do easily.

Machines lack what's unique about living, sentient beings. Machines, to date, can't experience or interpret their own computed results.[20]

To date, no computer, not even a quantum computer, can create the capacity for experience. We come into the world as conscious, sentient beings. Our ability to experience life, joy, love, and to experience the presence of God inside of us and all around us—that's the one thing mankind can't recreate. Our soul isn't the brain cells or proteins inside those cells. Our soul is the essence of the conscious matrix; its ability to connect inward and outward. Our soul is the ultimate quantum system; it searches near and far and seeks entanglements deep and wide. A spiritually healthy human soul is ready to connect with others in harmony and with the deeper forces in the universe.

Are scientists who choose the field of artificial intelligence trying to play God? We know the perils of taking that course of action. Humans are capable of inventing many things, but we'll never be capable of inventing what God has invented, the entire universe and all its laws, and the human soul. Nonetheless, it's quite amazing what scientists have already invented and what might come next. The human mind is a wellspring of ideas and predictions. There's nothing morally wrong with inventing anything. Time will discover what's useful and what's not; we needn't fear novelty. And as troublesome as they might be, even inventions that cause more problems than they solve might be countered with new inventions that cancel their ill-effects, resulting in a net gain. Almost anything in the world that can be destroyed, it can also be rebuilt. We're free to invent anything with good intentions in mind. But when we show a lack of wisdom or when we're deceptive or mean harm, that's a problem. Technology isn't evil, but it's nonetheless not always the solution.

Noted inventor and futurist Ray Kurzweil has written numerous books on how artificial intelligence will overtake human intelligence in several decades. Kurzweil's 1990 book, *The Age of Intelligent Machines* made several timely predictions.[13] He accurately predicted use of the Internet would become widespread, forever changing how people access information. And he predicted wireless communication through the cell phone would dominate. But these are artificial channels of communication; machines are incapable of understanding. We still need people to the compose messages that are sent and comprehend messages received.

Well aware of this conundrum, Kurzweil wrote *The Age of Spiritual Machines* ten years later.[14] In his 1999 book, Kurzweil makes a point to describe how machines might become more and more like human beings, with greater ability to communicate as if they were human. This prediction has largely come true. We now speak freely with Siri or Alexa and the voice-recognition and voice-generation software makes it possible for these computer programs to service our simple needs. Still, robotic and mechanistic speech isn't anywhere close to human behavior.

Kurzweil goes full-bore on artificial intelligence in his 2005 book, *The Singularity is Near.*[15] Kurzweil predicts that in 2045, computers will surpass humans in intelligence, and this will be a point of no return for humanity. People will become hybrids, with many computer devices embedded in their clothing, accessories, or even implanted into their bodies. And computers will have adapted intelligence to the extent that self-replication and acceleration of improvements will catapult computers to world domination. Is this possible? Only time will tell. However, it seems unlikely that mankind can invent what God has invented. God created matter, the foundations of how it coheres together. God created human beings, with conscious matrices that are capable of discovering the secrets of the universe. Computers can only mimic intelligence and spirituality, but not the essence or drive behind those things. What will inspire or motivate machines to achieve world-domination? I'm not sure Kurzweil has clarified that point.

My opinion is machines will never be conscious, and this includes machines that incorporate quantum mechanics. Quantum computers currently being developed will have different capabilities than the Turing-machine style computers in popular use today. But will these new capabilities render quantum computers conscious? We can't know the answer until we fully develop and put these machines into use. But my best guess is that while quantum computers will simulate some aspects of human consciousness, the essentials won't be replicated. The myriad functions of human consciousness are too vast. Human consciousness connects so many dimensions of human life and it connects so deeply. The human soul has a ferocious hunger, thirst, and desire for divine inspiration. Ultimately, only human consciousness can fuse partially with the mind of God, if only to get a short glimpse. Only the human mind can comprehend the fundamental laws of the universe.

If someday man and machine fuses completely, we'll see what that looks like. But to think we're soon guaranteed to do so is most probably pure folly. Believing one has a mind as good as God's is arrogant and misguided, and ultimately shows a lack of humility. And as history has shown us, God forgives honest mistakes but not foolishness. We need to suffer consequences for ignoring history, so that eventually we get the message. God is always kind, even in His punishment of foolhardiness.

To answer the question posed in the title of this chapter, creativity is both human invention and divine inspiration; it's a quantum superposition of the two. Each higher-minded thought we experience, whether it be an original idea about how to act kindlier to others or how to vastly improve our surroundings, bridges the two realms. And that's not suggesting any kind of dualism. The two realms are interconnected, each reflects the other. The motivation to improve our circumstances and that of others comes when we're resonating most closely to the highest levels of our inner conscious matrix. When our mind is coupled with the mind of God, that's when we see original solutions. If that's not divine inspiration, then I don't know what else it could be.

CHAPTER 11: NOTES AND REFERENCES

1. Corradini A, Antonietti A. Mirror neurons and their function in cognitively understood empathy. Conscious Cogn. 2013, 22(3):1152-61.

Lamm C, Majdandžić J. The role of shared neural activations, mirror neurons, and morality in empathy—a critical comment. Neurosci Res. 2015, 90:15-24.

Hasson U, Frith CD. Mirroring and beyond: coupled dynamics as a generalized framework for modelling social interactions. Philos Trans R Soc Lond B Biol Sci. 2016, 371(1693).

2. Perreault C, Mathew S. (2012). Dating the origin of language using phonemic diversity. PLoS ONE. 7(4): e35289.

Tallerman M, Gibson KR. The Oxford handbook of language evolution. Oxford ; New York: Oxford University Press, 2012.

3. Chomsky N. Powers and Prospects: Reflections on Human Nature and the Social Order. London: Pluto Press, 1996.

4. Owens RE. Language Development : An Introduction. Boston: Pearson. 2012.

    Kuhl PK. Early language acquisition: cracking the speech code. Nat Rev Neurosci. 2004, 5(11):831-43.

    Mandler JM. Precursors of linguistic knowledge. Philos Trans R Soc Lond B Biol Sci. 1994, 346(1315):63-9.

5. Levy J, Goldstein A, Feldman R. Perception of social synchrony induces mother-child gamma coupling in the social brain. Soc Cogn Affect Neurosci. 2017, 12(7):1036-1046.

    Rasmussen HF, Borelli JL, Smiley PA, Cohen C, Cheung RCM, Fox S, Marvin M, Blackard B. Mother-child language style matching predicts children's and mothers' emotion reactivity. Behav Brain Res. 2017, 325(Pt B):203-213.

6. Gernsbacher MA, Morson EM, Grace EJ, Language and speech in Autism. Annu Rev Linguist. 2016, 2: 413–425.

7. Stevens JS, Gleitman LR, Trueswell JC, Yang C. The pursuit of word meanings. Cogn Sci. 2017, 41 Suppl 4:638-676.

8. Woolf NJ. Global and serial neurons form a hierarchically arranged interface proposed to underlie memory and cognition. Neuroscience. 1996, 74(3):625-51.

9. Liu Y, Piazza EA, Simony E, Shewokis PA, Onaral B, Hasson U, Ayaz H. Measuring speaker-listener neural coupling with functional near infrared spectroscopy. Sci Rep. 2017, 7:43293.

Stephens GJ, Silbert LJ, Hasson U. Speaker-listener neural coupling underlies successful communication. Proc Natl Acad Sci U S A. 2010, 107(32):14425-30.

Dikker S, Silbert LJ, Hasson U, Zevin JD. On the same wavelength: predictable language enhances speaker-listener brain-to-brain synchrony in posterior superior temporal gyrus. J Neurosci. 2014, 34(18):6267-72.

10. Woolf NJ. A structural basis for memory storage in mammals. Prog Neurobiol. 1998, 55(1):59-77.

Woolf NJ. Dendritic encoding: an alternative to temporal synaptic coding of conscious experience. Conscious Cogn. 1999, 8(4):447-54.

11. Mounce B, 52 Major Stories of the Bible. 2017, Bibletraining.org.

12. Hirschfield B, Did Religion Create Civilization? Huffpost, 05/25/2011. https://www.huffpost.com/entry/ did-religion-create-civil_b_865500

13. Goswami A. How Quantum Activism Can Save Civilization: A Few People Can Change Human Evolution, 2011.

14. Woolf NJ, Hameroff SR. A quantum approach to visual consciousness. Trends CognSci. 2001, 5(11):472-478.

15. Craddock TJ, Friesen D, Mane J, Hameroff S, Tuszynski JA. The feasibility of coherent energy transfer in microtubules. J R Soc Interface. 2014, 11(100):20140677.

16. Kurzweil R. The Age of Intelligent Machines. Cambridge: MIT Press, 1990.

17. Kurzweil R. The Age of Spiritual Machines: When Computers Exceed Human Intelligence. New York: Viking, 1999.

18. Kurzweil R. The Singularity Is Near: When Humans Transcend Biology. New York: Penguin, 2006.

12

WILL MANKIND OUTGROW OUR NEED OF GOD?

RUMORS ARE FLYING everywhere. Governments, schools, universities, the media, and the entertainment industry have given us their verdict. These faceless behemoths tell us nearly every day, in subtle and not-so-subtle ways, people are shifting away from God. We don't need Him. Recently, it's come completely out in the open. Journalists and politicians speak with increasing boldness about how we need to remove all traces of God or Christianity from American life.[1] Other religions in the U.S. aren't attacked as much, but that seems to be only because those religions aren't the majority. The soul of America is largely Christian, with Judeo-Christian roots. This push against the "soul of America" has been met with push-back. So far, neither side has won. But what is it that makes people in powerful positions think they can lure the common people away from God or their chosen religion to practice?

Are the political, financial, intellectual, and entertainment elites correct that the people don't need God? They bombard us with their message: You don't need God to provide, the government will guarantee food, shelter, and health care. And besides that, the financial elites will take your savings and effortlessly transform you into a wealthy investor; that's unless they legally steal all your money. We don't need God to explain the unknown. We have scientists who know practically everything about the universe, including how it started and how it works. We have scientists who've identified nearly every chemical in the brain, how those chemicals act, and how the axons connecting with other neurons account for the human soul. We don't need God to nourish our souls; we have movies and entertainers who will fill the void in our human hearts and make us feel whole.

We've heard this kind of talk before. History is filled with countless examples of the people thinking they can walk away from God. The problem is God is inside us, and we can't walk away from ourselves. The conscious matrix will always foster a keen desire for a better connection with God. Our minds continuously seek unity and overall understanding, a kind of peace within ourselves and security in our special place in the universe.

Things are as they are. Until scientists discover a way to make the brain function usefully after having its essential soul ripped out, God living with us in our conscious matrix is the best thing out there. We simply couldn't experience life as observers and sentient human beings without the conscious matrix. It's what gives us understanding and connection. And the ultimate connection our conscious matrix makes is to God. We can hide from God by trying to block or deny that connection inside us. But when we block that connection, we feel emptiness. We can deny God's existence and try to force God out of our conscious awareness. But then we have to invent a million ideas that substitute for one very simple concept, the realization that God exists.

Some of the arguments levied against believing in God include: How can you believe in something you can't directly observe? Scientists pride themselves on the scientific method, a systematic process of four steps taken in order: hypothesis, observation, interpretation, and theory. Psychologists go a step further and rule out introspection; you're not allowed to look within your own mind for answers about human behavior.[2] But psychologists break their cardinal rule in steps 1, 3, and 4. Do psychologists claim they don't look within, that they don't use their creativity when generating their hypotheses? Well, if that's the claim they make, they must be a bunch of plagiarists (pardon my humor). And how does one accomplish the interpretation of results? Is that done without introspection? A common joke among senior scientists is that any two scientists can look at the same exact results and interpret that data set oppositely, picking the interpretation that supports their pet theory. Those pet theories are often of their own making, which introduces a strong self-confirming bias. Older scientists often become less open to new ideas, as their vast expertise insidiously morphs into a one-track mind capable of only seeing one perspective—their own.

Looking at the four steps of scientific inquiry, only the second step— observation—holds any promise of objectivity. And here's precisely where quantum mechanical theory throws a wrench in the works. When investigating matter at the small scale, the observer and the object under observation are in quantum entanglement—each can influence the other.[3] The Schrodinger's cat paradox—where the cat in the box is both alive and dead until the box is opened and observation occurs— that silly metaphor illustrates this peculiar effect. But when physicists study atoms and subatomic particles, this observer-specimen entanglement becomes a real issue.

Quantum mind theory harnesses the observer-specimen entanglement as a means to explain conscious experience and our conscious connection to God. Quantum mind theory might even prove God's existence—both metaphorically (God as a universal force) and literally (God as my personal savior and constant conscious companion). We need only to look at how God enables our thought processes in the first place to see He can't be taken out of the equation.

> *A thought to ponder: Human beings will never outgrow their need of God. That's because God is embedded in our conscious matrix. Our conscious matrix is a belief system; it doesn't function properly without a fundamental belief. God is our template for evaluating truth, for seeing the light.*

Understanding how the conscious matrix in our brain works provides the best proof available today that God exists. What's so intriguing about the conscious matrix is that it observes the connectome—all the physical connections in the brain—transcending neural mechanics to heavenly heights. There are billions of neurons in our brain and trillions of synapses that enable one neuron to excite another.[4] And sometimes one neuron inhibits another, giving neural circuits one more means to compare and filter incoming data. Our neurons use short and long axons to excite or inhibit other neurons, near and far. Neuroscientists call neural activation and inhibition connection, but it really isn't. If I talk to you and you hear the sound but don't understand, that's not connecting. The connectome merely passes along information much the same way wires and cables carry information from a source to a receiver.

We become consciously aware of that information flow via a separate system, the conscious matrix—a collection of brain filaments.[5] It's the conscious matrix that spies on the connectome and understands the meaning of certain patterns of activation and inhibition. The conscious matrix is what connects one possible meaning to another. And the conscious matrix needs no axons; it's wireless. When brain regions are active, electromagnetic fields spread over larger blocks of dendrites, the receiving parts of thousands of neurons.

Nature built a matrix deep inside each neuron out of interconnecting filaments. Each filament is constructed with protein pockets that are ideally spaced to enable the spread of entangled electrons.[6] And, after groups of entangled electrons collect into small clouds of pure energy, something spectacular happens. Naturally-emitted, ultra-weak photons put a spotlight on brain regions with increased metabolism.[7] This may be how our conscious matrix "looks at" or "highlights" those small clouds of pure energy, those groups of entangled electrons. The conscious matrix is the meshwork of filaments that stores a memory of past activity and is capable of housing similarly entangled electrons again at some point in the future, for example, during memory recall.[8]

Since it runs on pure quantum energy, our conscious matrix is the ultimate time machine; it truly has no sense of time or space. We re-experience poignant moments of the past like they're occurring now. We sense what lies ahead like it's occurring now. Our conscious matrix seamlessly connects the first moments of our lives to the last in a timeless loop. We truly need not fear death because our conscious matrix is immortal, even if our bodies aren't. Time travel is possible in the confines of the human mind. We can be in New York City, but imagine we're in Las Vegas instantly. We need not waste any time in traveling from point A to point B. Our conscious matrix can hop over thousands of miles in small fractions of a second. We speed across oceans and over mountains effortlessly in our imaginations and dreams. We can even travel millions of miles when we gaze up at the stars and hold them dearly in our hearts.

How does our conscious matrix connect with the space around us, even places we can't touch? Let me tell a short story that partly explains it. There's lots of nice scenery around my home in the far northwest part of Las Vegas. I have great views of the mountains, and that includes a beautiful sunrise cast over the mountains to the east in the morning. On the west side of my house is a view of Mount Charleston, which is a short thirty-minute drive from my house. A quick trip up to Mount Charleston transports one from the sweltering desert heat to a cool mountain environment. I drive up there a lot because I like to hike in Mount Charleston during the summer months. So when I gaze at the mountains, my conscious matrix computes approximately how far away those peaks are from me. And having made the drive countless times, I have first-hand evidence that my conscious matrix calculates correctly.

Neuroscientists know exactly how the brain senses distance; it's called depth perception.[9] We have two forward-facing eyes, each of which receives a slightly different view of incoming light. Along the visual path, the two views (one from the right eye and the other from the left eye) are compared and the closer they match, the farther the distance of the object. Our neurons compute that. Added to that computation, there are numerous clues sensed by one eye alone. In any landscape, the grain of resolution decreases with distance. Objects farther away appear increasingly blurry, showing markedly less detail. Also, some objects obstruct others from view letting us know they're closer to us than the ones behind them. Lastly, there's something called linear perspective. If you look down a long road and focus on the both edges, you'll see that the sides converge to a single point. You can judge distance that way. And you'll be aided by the fact people walking alongside the road appear smaller as they get farther away.

For many years, I taught depth perception as a professor and wrote the perception chapter in the textbook I used. Consequently, I'm constantly aware of the mechanical way in which millions of neurons at four or more hierarchical levels of cerebral cortex relay and compute differences in neural activity to compute depth. But that's not what I experience each time I marvel at the beautiful view of Mount Charleston from my house. Depth perception is a conscious experience. The conscious matrix takes a look at all those neural computations and fuses them together to produce a three-dimensional virtual image that creates the experience of distance and depth. We can reach out and touch images within inches of our faces; we can shoo flies away on a hot summer day. We experience the space around us. We can reach out and touch what's close, or jump in the car and drive to what lies on the horizon.

When we experience the depth or distance of those things outside our body; it's as if our eyes are reaching out to those distant points. But that's not what's really happening at all. Light is reflected off surfaces of objects near and far.[10] That light energy travels to us, and then enters each eye. Once light reaches special cells at the back of the eye, it triggers a chemical reaction. That in turn causes inhibition and then excitation. Next, a barrage of activity is relayed up through the brain until it finally reaches visual cortex. Upon reaching the cerebral cortex, the conscious matrix starts to look at what's possibly useful in that massive amount of data pouring in each fraction of a second. Pulling all that information together, the conscious matrix entangles together one idea—mountain-top-located-twenty-five-miles-away. We experience, in a glance, a connection that transports us mentally up there on top that mountain. Sure, we know we're looking there. But if we had wings, we could focus on that point in space and fly there within minutes.

Our conscious matrix can take us up to the top of that mountain instantly in our imaginations, fusing the entangled electrons in our head with something far outside of our bodies. The small cloud in our brain is entangled with a virtual mapping of that location far out in space. That mountain top is a goal state, a tangible possibility in our minds. The same is true of God. He's a goal state, an ideal, the ultimate role model. And we know He is as real as that mountain top because of the intensity of the experience of His presence. If you're not convinced, look at a picture or painting of a mountain range. It's not the same conscious experience at all. Our conscious matrix detects "real" versus "fake" data in part by intensity and in part by how it fits with other information. The two-dimensional painting may be beautiful, but it's not capable of transporting you to the top of the mountain. Not even if you have a vivid imagination can a painting do what viewing nature first-hand can do: fill us completely with awe of ourselves in the context of all of God's creations.

Quantum mind theory does open the door to firming up our belief in God. But not all scientists believe in quantum mind theory. Some of the most prominent scientists of recent times argued we don't need a conscious matrix. Sir Francis Crick wrote the *Astonishing Hypothesis* in 1990, in which he claimed that neural activity—axons exciting or inhibiting other neurons—is all we need for higher consciousness.[11] Crick knew about quantum mind theory, and he wasn't buying it. Nonetheless, Crick wasn't able to explain why subcortical activity isn't conscious, or why some cortical activity isn't conscious. Certain patterns of cortical activity, certain widespread rhythms, do correlate with consciousness, but those rhythms aren't the equivalent. Brain rhythms fail to explain the leap from unconscious calculations to conscious awareness.

Let me use a scenario about a corporate lawsuit to illustrate why we need something like quantum mind theory operating in a conscious matrix. Imagine, if you will, that a large corporation is being sued, and they hire a well-known legal firm to represent them. The legal firm sends a letter written by a staff person to the corporate headquarters asking them to send a long list of documents. At corporate headquarters, several department heads are notified to collect the required documents. At least ten employees are tasked to find and send the documents over to corporate headquarters, upon which those documents are collated and sent to the law firm. The administrative assistant sending off the documents writes the cover letter reminding them of the request and detailing what's included. The law firm receives the documents and hands them over to the attorney assigned the case. He or she reads the cover letter and distributes the documents to three paralegals assigned to look over the documents and check for completeness. They do their due diligence and report back, "...everything is here that we need."

Has the legal firm made its case yet? Of course not; there's been no evaluation or interpretation made yet. All that's happened is data were collected and distributed and limited assessments were made based on simple decisions. Neural networks do exactly that. They collect and distribute data. But somebody has to comprehensively interpret all the data for understanding to occur. A conscious and qualified person is needed understand what legal case exists, if any. Only a knowledgeable attorney has the ability to understand how to defend the corporation against the lawsuit. Let's hope the attorney on the case has his or her conscious matrix intact, because more paper pushing isn't ever going to lead to understanding. You can send billions upon billions of documents around in endless circles. So what? Data dumps aren't the same as understanding.

According to quantum mind theory, the conscious matrix understands the data; it sees meaning. Without a hierarchy of ideas, we'd go around in circles trying to understand the meaning of data. God is built into that hierarchy. Our belief in God is integral to our brain's ability to maintain a multi-tasking, multi-functional hierarchy. At the top of each domain of thinking, we experience God as the highest-level abstract concept conceived in our hierarchically-arranged brains. But God not only sits at the apex, He simultaneously transcends that hierarchy. The quantum entanglements that occur in our conscious matrix when we worship, praise, or pray to God connect on a quantum level to something bigger than ourselves. We may not know who or what God is yet, but we know we'll recognize Him when we meet.

A question to probe: Where does God live? Quantum mind theory views consciousness as energy existing in a cloud that can span two or more places at the same time. Accordingly, we perceive God living at the end of the universe, deep inside us, and everywhere in between. Is that really possible?

Most people who believe in an all-knowing God admit they don't know where God lives. But what they do strongly sense is that God lives as far out in the skies as one might be able to go, at the end of the universe. Yet, we also know that God can be anywhere, even where we least expect Him to be. We don't know where God is at all times, but we experience His presence. People of faith don't doubt the veracity of their beliefs.

The conscious matrix perceives what distance signifies, what it means to us. When we gaze at the stars at night, our conscious matrix lets us know how vast the universe is and how small we are in comparison. Gazing at the stars so far, far away, our conscious matrix can entangle our small cloud of conscious energy with that point in space far, far away. We are, for that short time, unified with the distant star in space. When we feel completely in awe that something larger than the entire universe exists, we call that God. Most believers aren't mindless followers. Most believers know the relationship between us and the heavens and stars is symbolic of something in our everyday lives. We know God isn't merely at the limits of what we can see in the sky. We know God also lies at the core of what's deep in our heart. Not literally in our heart, however. We understand that we feel the sensation of our heart beat and of each breath in the conscious matrix of our brain. Here again the small cloud of energy in our brain is virtually "in touch" with those places in our bodies for an instant.

We know that many believers experience God's presence when gazing upon the stars—but how does that compare to what those who study the sky as a profession think? The field of astrophysics is filled with many brilliant scientists, none of whom have traveled to touch the stars except with their tools. Their tools are massive telescopes and advanced mathematics—and last but not least, the conscious matrix of their mind. These scientists observe the changes in intensity of light cast by the stars and changes in the distance between them. Such scientists have produced a great many ideas about the universe, even going so far as to predict how the universe began.[12] All these ideas are fine and may well be correct. But aren't scientists using their intuition to generate hypotheses? And again, aren't they using their intuition to interpret those results and formulate theories? The mere fact that scientists continuously update their grand theories of the universe is proof that scientists aren't all-knowing.

Common people look at the sky and take it as evidence that there exists an omnipresent, all-knowing God. The two hypotheses, scientific and God-based, are compatible. Without an all-knowing God, the inquisitiveness of scientists wouldn't exist in the first place. We couldn't muster up the ambition to ask questions without first believing someone, something sentient, had answers. Data aren't answers. Measurements of light intensities and distances are data. Both stories of creation, scientific and biblical, came from the human mind, one from Cambridge, and the other from Mount Sinai. You either believe God intervened both times or you don't—it's your choice. But with quantum mind theory, you come to see that God lives in a much larger matrix, and our more limited individual conscious matrices float in that much grander, much larger sea of knowledge. Belief in God teaches us that we're privileged to access any understanding we can, and that we should remain forever humbled by the vastness of the great sea of knowledge.

And because we're connected, we also intuit that things will work out in the end one way or another. No matter how much devastation or destruction occurs, things always go back to some kind of normal. Men and women are resilient. And we can rebuild nearly anything we can destroy. Also, we know deep inside us that this life doesn't matter all that much, that there's something more. When we die, our children and grandchildren will carry on. Even if the human race goes extinct, other sentient beings will evolve and solve new mysteries we can't even imagine. Life is happening right now, why fret about what happens next? And if we can imagine immortality, then it probably exists in one form or another.

Nearly everything we can imagine does truly exist in one form or another. Scientists should be ashamed for ridiculing the power of the common people to see the truth. The collective consciousness is quantitatively richer in wisdom than any small group of even the most intelligent beings on earth. If scientists recognized the conscious matrix as the high-precision scientific tool that it is, perhaps they would have more respect for it, regardless of whom is in possession of it.

How can so many people, billions of people today, all have belief in God? Yes, there are variations and improvements over time, but the basic intuition is remarkably similar. The conscious matrix isn't the equivalent of brain activity or brain chemicals being released and circulated. You can mix all the brain chemicals together in a test tube or flask and not arrive at conscious experience. You can build the most powerful circuit board and still not create a sentient being. The conscious matrix is a physical meshwork with an architecture that enables clouds of quantum entanglement giving rise to sentience. The conscious matrix is embedded within our highest brain structures, giving us intelligence, consciousness, experience, and awareness. The way our conscious matrix works is nothing short of phenomenal. It's the greatest creation so far. The conscious matrix connects the minds of men and women over space and time, it connects us together, and it connects all of us to nature and to God.

God exists in a place where there's no space or time; that's our common perception even though the average person knows very little about quantum mechanical theory. But that's the only way to reconcile that all the following statements are simultaneously true: God is wherever we are, whenever we seek Him. He is with all our loved ones, living and deceased. And God and all our loved ones live forever both inside us and somewhere far away. This turns out to be closer to the truth than one might expect. The more scientists discover about matter, particles, and how they interact—the more our ancient myths and more highly developed religious beliefs seem to accurately describe what most of us know intuitively. We know intuitively we have a friend in God inside us and all around us. We know intuitively there's something much larger than ourselves, yet we're connected to it.

> *A few more ideas to examine:* We know God is something bigger than ourselves. That hunch or intuition that "we'll know Him when we meet Him" is our "quantum connection" to our inner wisdom. Our specific beliefs about God provide operational rules making it possible for the conscious matrix to generate experience in the first place. Our minds simply wouldn't work properly without a foundational belief in God and all the characteristics we attribute to God.

The experience of a beautiful sunset or the smile of a newborn baby—it's those peak moments that enable many people to re-affirm their belief in God. Awe-inspiring events oftentimes cause people to double-down, to increase the certainty of their faith. It's as if our belief in God was always there. The reason we sense that omnipresence is most likely because it's true: God was always there. We're connected with God from conception, or even earlier. Perhaps God is with us from the first glance between our mother and father.

When people believe in God, they can see God in many ordinary things. Why is it important to believe in something bigger than ourselves? The words we use to describe God reveal a great deal about the basic human need to believe. People from different time periods, far-and-wide geographical locations, and diverse cultural backgrounds commonly describe God as all-knowing, all-powerful, and all-loving. These beliefs aren't ornamental. These beliefs are foundational to the inner workings of the conscious matrix.

Let's examine our belief about God being infinitely wise. Wisdom is something we value and admire in others. We envision God in possession of the ultimate wisdom; we believe Him to be all-knowing. Embedded in the conscious matrix is a natural curiosity about all things that surround us. The belief in the "existence of answers" must be in place before curiosity can evolve. We must first believe all things can be understood. We intuit God is all-knowing; therefore, all things must be knowable. This curiosity is built into the conscious matrix; it's a basic driver of all our conscious seeking. Without belief that our world is understandable, we might not venture one step away from where we are. We'd have no curiosity or thirst for understanding unless we believed answers existed. Without curiosity, we might easily lie down, starve, and die. As the Bible says in Job 37:16 (ESV), *"Do you know the balancing of the clouds, the wondrous works of him who is perfect in knowledge."*

Some scientists might argue we needn't believe in an all-knowing God. We can explain curiosity with a secular definition, such as a universal force based on physical laws that can be expressed mathematically. We can model curiosity as a mechanical operation of neural networks, right? Yes, the scientists are partly correct. Neural connections in the brain are active when people show curiosity.[13] And, there are indeed neural network programs and artificial intelligence programs that simulate curiosity.[14] But there's a problem with that explanation. Why settle for an ordinary answer when a perfectly exquisite answer is available? Why play checkers when we have five-dimensional chess as an alternative?

Most people have an intuition that God is utterly amazing and that all He created, all of nature, is magnificent. We're endlessly curious and we marvel at the beauty and awesomeness of life. It might take millions of computer programs, or more, to simulate the many aspects of human curiosity. We'd need enough neural network models to fuel an endless supply of curiosities about all things during a person's entire lifetime. And neural networks can't explain the experience of curiosity because these models can't explain conscious experience at all. The ideas we hold about God, and our direct experiences of awe and amazement of Him, are arguably superior to any mechanistic model of curiosity. So it's not so much that people reject the hypotheses and theories of scientists, it's just that they're not enough to replace what God does for us in our lives.

What about our intuition that God is all-loving and all-powerful? What purposes do those attributes serve? Human beings are constantly active. We emit behaviors at an almost non-stop rate, except for inter-mittent rest periods. We know certain behaviors bring rewards and others bring punishment (or non-reward to be technical).[15] Yes, it's true people can learn an endless number of stimulus-response patterns. Like other animals, we learn that if you do X, Y is likely to happen. With repeated experience, we can even learn the probability that X will pro-duce Y. But most of that's simply unconscious conditioning, or even less, learned reflexes.

To contemplate future behavior, we need to be consciously aware of overall patterns between behavior and expected outcome. To even begin to create complex ideas like liberty and justice, we need to believe in God first. We're only capable of imagining "life is supposed to be fair" if we believe someone has the power to make it fair, and also that the higher-power loves everybody equally and won't slight us in any judge-ment made. And we prove our intuition correct in most real-life experi-ences. We only find utility in making judgements if we first believe that a God or God-like entity exists whose judgements prevail because they're all-powerful, and whose judgements will be fair because God is all-loving. We judge others, and we expect judgement upon ourselves because we fundamentally believe in an all-powerful, all-loving God. Think about it: If we didn't first believe in a higher-power who would intervene on our behalf, how could we experience a sense of fairness and an aversion to being cheated? Without a belief in a powerful almighty, how could we have invented the judicial system? How would we ever expect fairness, if we had no one to turn to who we believed had the power to make things right?

The human conscious matrix is the best question-answer device nature has evolved. We ask God questions all the time, and He answers us. God may not answer immediately, and the answer might come in cryptic form. But every time we seek, we generally find. Our belief that God is infinitely wise gives us the motivation to ask questions. You have to believe there are answers in order to bother asking questions in the first place. Belief in His infinite wisdom precedes curiosity. And without curiosity we never venture out; we wither and die intellectually, if not actually. Likewise, our belief in a loving and powerful God precedes our expectation of fair treatment. Why seek a better "theory of everything" when God is a real entity we can directly access. Most people aren't willing to give up the power gleaned by connecting to God. Instead people are taking more power over their own well-being by having direct access.

> **A possible resolution:** *Rather than growing away from God, people are getting a better understanding of God. We're also seeing more of the power that comes from believing in God. Science is taking us closer to our intuition. True understanding of how we connect to others and to a higher being has to come from our conscious matrix. We experience the highest intensity of light in our brain when our conscious matrix understands God more clearly. If there's an upper limit to how bright the light might be, we've not even come close to reaching it.*

In 2012, scientists discovered the "God particle," otherwise known as the Higgs boson. This discovery changed physics. This was the long sought-after particle that proved Peter Higgs' theory that a continuous field exists, which spans all space and time.[16] This field, called the Higgs field, creates an opportunity for mass to be formed out of quantum energy. Up until this moment of discovery, the Higgs field had been purely theoretical. A mechanism to transform pure energy into a particle with mass was unknown.

The discovery of the Higgs boson was an incredible and arduous feat. First, scientists had to build the high-energy particle accelerator known as the Large Haldron Collider (LHC) located near Geneva, Switzerland. The LHC accelerates and smashes protons creating new particles. Over 100 trillion particles had to be created and then analyzed in order to find one Higgs boson. That's how special this particle is. As one of the great advances in science, the "God particle" enables the creation of matter as we know it. This particle is an essential part of the creation of the universe, but it isn't the creator.

As part of its role in creating matter, the Higgs boson is of great potential relevance to quantum mind theory. The existence of the Higgs field provides a larger matrix, a field that permeates all of space-time and interacts with the quantum energy of electrons, photons, and other pure energies to produce mass. Professor Geoffrey Taylor, one of the scientists on the project, explains that the Higgs boson is like a celebrity at a party.[17] When the celebrity enters the room, a crowd soon forms around him. This is similar to how the Higgs boson operates in the universe. It attracts zero to low mass high-energy particles to surround it and thereby creates an elementary particle with mass.

The conscious matrix is a protein filament meshwork. Each filament, among thousands, contains multiple sets of precisely-positioned, environment-isolated cages. Each cage or pocket is capable of storing free electrons. These cages are appropriately distanced, just close enough to allow energy transfer from an electron cloud in one cage to the next. This energy transfer (and sharing) is aided by photons emitted when neuron metabolism increases in tandem with heightened activity. What quantum mind theorists currently understand is that entangled electrons in the protein filaments reflect the spatial and temporal patterns of neural activity.[18]

Adding the Higgs boson only gives more power to quantum mind theory. We know from learning and memory experiments that the storage of new memory involves creating a new architecture within neurons.[19] More precisely, the filaments rearrange inside the long slender dendrites of neurons throughout the cerebral cortex and hippocampus. These filaments are made of proteins, which are made of molecules and atoms having mass. Pockets in the proteins of these filaments store entangled electrons connecting ideas and conscious experiences and photons participate. The Higgs boson gives rise to the realistic possibility that entangled particles having low to zero mass might transform into elementary particles with mass that, in turn, get incorporated into the proteins comprising the neuronal architecture of the conscious matrix. Could the Higgs boson be the bridge between the most mysterious pair of all dualities: mind and matter?

And the Higgs field, or another field like it, could provide the opportunity for the conscious matrix of one person to connect on the deeper scale with the conscious matrix of a person nearby. Our conscious matrix is encased in a bony skull. The skull is there to protect the brain; that's what we teach in university courses on brain anatomy. But in light of the role that photons may play in conscious awareness, another role played by the skull may be to keep extraneous light out. Shielded from photons arising outside the brain, our spontaneously-emitted, ultra-weak photons are keen monitors of what parts of the brain are active at any given moment. Our minds are generally isolated from the minds of others, at least without another system intervening. The Higgs field could be that other system, especially since this field easily passes through bony mass.

We might imagine each conscious matrix as pure entangled energy floating in the Higgs field. Our mind's energy is caged in our bony skull, but our skull is invisible to the Higgs field. As our conscious matrix floats about the Higgs field, we'd expect the frequent passing by of other conscious matrices, and occasional interactions. When two conscious matrices maintain prolonged nearness and establish similar patterns of coupled activity, entanglements within the Higgs field might provide opportunity for real quantum entanglement between the two people. The more intense the ideas shared, the more light would be emitted. And the more energy produced by shared conscious experience, the more we'd predict an opportunity arising for some kind of entanglement between two or more people.

The Higgs field occupies all of space-time, so its existence provides a possible basis for the conscious matrix of one person to connect with another who is far away. It may sound far-fetched, but perhaps our brightest ideas (pun intended) float off into space as an energy mass in the Higgs field when they leave our conscious awareness. Are ideas, when not in use, stored on a cloud floating in the Higgs field? This would be kind of like when we upload our pictures to the iCloud to be viewed by friends and family.

It's way too early to hypothesize how the Higgs field might impact on human consciousness. All we can observe is how people are very much influenced by others around them. Trends swell up all the time—in fashion, music, politics, and food—and spread rapidly through a crowd. Obviously, we must see, hear, touch, smell, or taste these popular items to experience them. But where does that irresistible motivation to try the latest stuff come from? Could the popular "buzz" come from energy floating in the Higgs field?

For now, we can only guess how the Higgs field may help us better understand and more strongly connect to God. It raises more questions than it answers. When we worship God in large groups, does a huge energy arise from multiple conscious matrices and then float in the Higgs field as pure energy? And if so, how far does it travel and how fast? Is travel faster than the speed of light possible in the Higgs field? Maybe one day we'll discover that "moral goodness" is a spatial-temporal pattern of pure energy particles floating in the Higgs field that float by and occasionally superimpose on our thoughts like a transparent template, gently coaxing our ideas into the "morally good" direction.

Stephen Hawking raised the concern that the Higgs field might contain black-hole-like areas that will ultimately destroy the universe.[20] I wouldn't go that far, but perhaps those black clouds are what make us defy morality and what suck the goodness out of life. While it's way too early to speculate, a simplified vision of these energies floating about the Higgs field reminds me of angels and demons.

It's highly likely that neither the Higgs boson nor the Higgs field is God, for many reasons. For one, it's almost an absolute certainty that our knowledge of the universe still has huge gaps. The collective consciousness of the people who believe in God or a higher being will know when we'e accumulated sufficient amounts of scientific information to adequately understand God. Right now we haven't enough data to even make an educated guess. Yet, we can fully experience God, as if He were truly sitting right next to us. Second, the Higgs field is merely a field, a conduit. Our experience and the universal experience is that God is all-knowing, all-loving, and all-powerful. The Higgs field might bring God's message to us, but it seems unlikely to have all the features we attribute to God.

Beyond those wise truths about God's nature, we have only metaphors to understand God. One symbolic truth arising from one of those metaphors is the belief that God lives very high up in the heavens. We have the belief that God takes us to our outer limits. God encourages us to try our best. He gives us permission to fail and be forgiven. God tells us that our human mind is connected to things so far away we can't even imagine them yet. But someday we will. And finally, God comforts us and tells not to worry, that we can and will understand everything that exists at the appropriate time. Our faith in God is all we need. He's our courage to face the unknown.

The Bible says, in James 3:13 (NIV), "*Who is wise and understanding among you? Let them show it by their good life, by deeds done in the humility that comes from wisdom.*" By humbly understanding our limits, we know our conception of God is likely to morph again at various times in the future. It's easy to see how metaphors about God represent best guesses, like a hypothesis set up to produce scientific inquiry. Literal interpretations of God and religious texts are very similar to scientific theory. Theories that are useful at predicting outcomes hold up over long periods of time. Eventually, our best literal views on God will undergo revision. It's likely that new discoveries will reveal more to explain our experience of God as a spirit that lives inside us and around us. To date, literal interpretations of God are the best-fit theories to what we experience but can't explain. We believe because our experience is real. Why trust someone else's view, when we have a direct connection to the truest understanding? Our conscious matrix isn't only a portal; it's our gift from God. It's our job to use our gift in the spirit in which it was given, with the best of intentions.

CHAPTER 12: NOTES AND REFERENCES

1. Seidel AL, The Founding Myth: Why Christian Nationalism Is Un-American. New York: Sterling, 2019.

    Eberstatd M. Regular Christians are no longer welcome in American culture. Time Magazine, June 29, 2016. https://time.com/4385755/faith-in-america/

2. Pérez-Álvarez M. Psychology as a science of subject and comportment, beyond the mind and behavior. Integr Psychol Behav Sci. 2018, 52(1):25-51.

3. Haroche S. Quantum information in cavity quantum electrodynamics: logical gates, entanglement engineering and 'Schrödinger-cat states'. Philos Trans A Math Phys Eng Sci. 2003, 361(1808):1339-47.

4. Zimmer C. 100 trillion connections: New efforts probe and map the brain's detailed architecture. Sci. American, January, 2011.

5. Woolf NJ. Dendritic encoding: an alternative to temporal synaptic coding of conscious experience. Conscious Cogn. 1999, 8(4):447-54.

Woolf NJ, Hameroff SR. A quantum approach to visual consciousness. Trends Cogn Sci. 2001, 5(11):472-478.

6. Craddock TJ, Friesen D, Mane J, Hameroff S, Tuszynski JA. The feasibility of coherent energy transfer in microtubules. J R Soc Interface. 2014, 11(100):20140677.

7. Salari V, Valian H, Bassereh H, Bókkon I, Barkhordari A. Ultraweak photon emission in the brain. J Integr Neurosci. 2015, 14(3):419-29.

8. Woolf NJ. A structural basis for memory storage in mammals. Prog Neurobiol. 1998, 55(1):59-77.

   Priel A, Tuszynski JA, Woolf NJ. Neural cytoskeleton capabilities for learning and memory. J Biol Phys. 2010, 36(1):3-21.

9. Welchman AE. The human brain in depth: How we see in 3D. Annu Rev Vis Sci. 2016, 2:345-376.

10. Lilienfeld SO, Lynn SJ, Namy LL, Woolf NJ. Psychology: From Inquiry to Understanding. Boston: Pearson, 2009

11. Crick F. The Astonishing Hypothesis. New York: Simon & Schuster, 1994.

12. Hawking S. A Brief History of Time: From the Big Bang to Black Holes, Bantam Dell, 1988.

13. Li Y, Huo T, Zhuang K, Song L, Wang X, Ren Z, Liu Q, Qiu J. Functional connectivity mediates the relationship between self-efficacy and curiosity. Neurosci Lett. 2019, 711:134442.

14. Costa AA, Tinós R. Investigation of rat exploratory behavior via evolving artificial neural networks. J Neurosci Methods. 2016, 270:102-110.

15. Skinner BF, About Behaviorism. Mass Market, 1976.

16. Brumfiel G. Higgs triumph opens up field of dreams. Nature. 2012, 487(7406):147-8.

    CMS Collaboration, Chatrchyan S, et al. Search for a standard-model-like Higgs boson with a mass in the range 145 to 1000 GeV at the LHC. Eur Phys J C Part Fields. 2013, 73(6):2469.

    Plotnitsky A. The future (and past) of quantum theory after the Higgs boson: a quantum-informational viewpoint. Philos Trans A Math Phys Eng Sci. 2016, 374(2068).

17. Taylor G. Discovery of the God Particle. TED Talk, December, 2012.

18. Hameroff S, Penrose R. Consciousness in the universe: a review of the 'OrchOR' theory. Phys Life Rev. 2014, 11(1):39-78.

19. Woolf NJ, Zinnerman MD, Johnson GV. Hippocampal microtubule-associated protein-2 alterations with contextual memory. Brain Res. 1999, 821(1):241-9.

    Woolf NJ, Young SL, Johnson GV, Fanselow MS. Pavlovian conditioning alters cortical microtubule-associated protein-2. Neuroreport. 1994, 5(9):1045-8.

20. Dattaro L. What Stephen Hawking really said about destroying the universe. Popular Mechanics, Sept. 2014. https://www.popularmechanics.com/science/a11217/what-stephen-hawking-really-said-about-destroying-the-universe-17192502/